Database Management System

MALAY K. PAKHIRA
Associate Professor
Department of Computer Science and Engineering
Kalyani Government Engineering College
Kalyani, West Bengal

PHI Learning Private Limited
Delhi-110092
2013

₹ 250.00

DATABASE MANAGEMENT SYSTEM
Malay K. Pakhira

ISBN-978-81-203-4674-1

Published by Asoke K. Ghosh, PHI Learning Private Limited, Rimjhim House, 111, Patparganj Industrial Estate, Delhi-110092 and Printed by Mudrak, 30-A, Patparganj, Delhi-110091.

Contents

Preface ... *ix*

1. Database Systems ... 1–13

1.1 Database ... 1
1.2 Database Management System (DBMS) ... 2
1.2.1 Components of a DBMS ... 2
1.2.2 Application Areas of DBMS ... 3
1.3 Classical File Based Systems ... 3
1.3.1 Disadvantages of Classical Technique ... 5
1.4 Modern DBMS Approach ... 6
1.4.1 Three-layer Architecture ... 7
1.4.2 Schema of Different Layers ... 7
1.4.3 Data Independence ... 9
1.4.4 Advantages of DBMS Scheme ... 10
1.4.5 Database Users ... 10
1.4.6 Role of DBA ... 11
1.5 Significance of Database Systems ... 12
Exercises ... 12

2. Modelling a Database ... 14–21

2.1 Representation of Data ... 14
2.2 Data Models ... 15
2.3 Entity-Relationship Model (E-R model) ... 16
2.4 Logical Data Models ... 16
2.4.1 Hierarchical Data Model ... 17
2.4.2 Network Data Model ... 17
2.4.3 Relational Data Model ... 18
2.5 Comparison of Logical Data Models ... 18

2.6 Other Data Models 21
Exercises 21

3. Modelling with E-R Diagram 22–41
3.1 E-R based Modelling 22
3.1.1 Entity and its Characteristics 23
3.1.2 Relationship and its Characteristics 26
3.2 Symbolic Representation of E-R Components 28
3.2.1 Relationship 28
3.3 Mapping between Entities 28
3.3.1 Different Types of Mapping 29
3.4 Use of Entity Sets and Relationship Sets 30
3.5 Modelling with E-R Diagram 31
3.5.1 E-R based Design Process 31
3.5.2 E-R based Design Examples 32
3.6 Advantages and Disadvantages of E-R Model 40
3.6.1 Advantages of E-R Model 40
3.6.2 Disadvantages of E-R Model 41
Exercises 41

4. Principles of Relational Database Management Systems 42–59
4.1 Foundations of Relational Model 42
4.1.1 Relation 42
4.1.2 Relational Schema and Instances 43
4.1.3 Organization of a Relation 44
4.1.4 Data Manipulation 45
4.1.5 Data Independence 45
4.1.6 Integrity Constraints 46
4.2 Application Areas of RDBMS 46
4.3 Advantages of RDBMS 46
4.4 RDBMS Packages and their Developers 47
4.5 CODD's Rules for RDBMS 47
4.6 Relational Operations 48
4.6.1 Relational Algebra 48
4.6.2 Relational Calculus 54
Exercises 57

5. Relational Database Design 60–91
5.1 Designing a Database 60
5.1.1 Properties of a Good Design 60
5.2 Functional Dependency 61
5.2.1 Closure of a Set of Functional Dependencies 63
5.2.2 Armstrong's Inference Rules 66

5.2.3 Equivalence of Sets of Functional Dependencies 66
5.2.4 Minimal or Canonical Cover of Functional Dependencies 67
5.3 Relational Decomposition 72
5.3.1 Attribute Preservation 73
5.3.2 Dependency Preservation 73
5.3.3 Lossless-join Decomposition 74
5.4 Normalization 75
5.4.1 Need for Normalization 76
5.4.2 Mathematical Foundation of Normalization 76
5.4.3 First Normal Form (1NF) 77
5.4.4 Second Normal Form (2NF) 79
5.4.5 Third Normal Form (3NF) 82
5.4.6 Boyce-Codd Normal Form (BCNF) 83
5.4.7 Some Conversion Algorithms 84
5.4.8 Fourth Normal Form (4NF) 85
5.5 Importance of Normalization 89
5.6 Limitations of Normal Forms 90
Exercises 90

6. Structured Query Language 92–109
6.1 SQL—A Query Language 92
6.2 Data Sub Languages 93
6.2.1 Data Definition Language (DDL) 93
6.2.2 Data Control Language (DCL) 99
6.2.3 Data Manipulation Language (DML) 101
6.3 Single Row Functions Used in SQL 103
6.3.1 Arithmetic Operations in SQL 103
6.3.2 Group Operations in SQL 103
6.3.3 String Functions in SQL 103
6.3.4 Date Functions in SQL 104
6.4 SQL*PLUS 105
6.4.1 Features of SQL*PLUS 105
6.4.2 Editing Commands for SQL*PLUS 105
6.4.3 Help System in SQL*PLUS 106
6.5 Data Dictionary 106
6.5.1 Database Users and Data Dictionary 106
6.5.2 SQL Commands to Access DD 108
Exercises 108

7. Information Retrieval and Data Manipulation 110–139
7.1 Features of SQL 110
7.1.1 Query Handling in SQL 110
7.1.2 Query Using Joined Relations 122

7.2 Sub-query Handling 123
7.3 Join Operations 125
7.3.1 Self Join 125
7.3.2 Inner Join 126
7.3.3 Outer Join 127
7.4 Data Consistency and Integrity Constraints 129
7.4.1 INSERT Statement 129
7.4.2 Update Statement 131
7.4.3 Delete Statement 132
7.5 Transaction Control Statements 132
7.6 Views of Tables 133
7.6.1 Types of Views 133
7.7 Embedded SQL 134
7.7.1 How SQL Statements are Embedded? 134
7.7.2 Example of Embedded SQL Program 135
Exercises 137

8. Programming with PL/SQL 140–170

8.1 Basics of PL/SQL Programming 140
8.1.1 PL/SQL Programming Environment 141
8.1.2 PL/SQL Block Structure 141
8.1.3 PL/SQL Programming Features 143
8.1.4 Control Flow Instructions in PL/SQL 150
8.2 PL/SQL Programming 155
8.2.1 Subprograms in PL/SQL 156
8.2.2 Passing Input and Output Parameters between Subprograms 158
8.3 Exception Handling in PL/SQL 159
8.4 SQL Cursor 163
8.5 SQL Trigger 165
8.6 Benefits of PL/SQL 169
Exercises 170

9. Query Processing and Optimization 171–184

9.1 Query Processing 171
9.2 Query Optimization 175
9.2.1 Logical Transformation of Query 176
9.2.2 Heuristic Alternative Generation 176
9.2.3 Evaluation Alternative Plans 178
9.3 Common Rules of Algebraic Manipulation 178
9.4 Algorithms for Relational Algebraic Operations 178
9.4.1 Computing Selection 179
9.4.2 Computing Projection 179
9.4.3 Computing Cartesian Product and Join 179
Exercises 183

10. Concurrent Transaction Processing 185–203

10.1 Transaction and Concurrency Control 185
  10.1.1 Properties of a Transaction 186
10.2 Serial and Concurrent Transaction Schedules 187
  10.2.1 Serializability 187
  10.2.2 Serial Schedule and Serializable Schedule 187
  10.2.3 Concept of Lock and Unlock 189
  10.2.4 Serializability Test Algorithm 190
  10.2.5 Different Types of Locks 191
  10.2.6 Serializability Test Considering Read and Write Locks 192
10.3 Two Phase Lock-Unlock Protocol 197
10.4 Deadlock 198
  10.4.1 Deadlock Handling 199
10.5 Concurrency Control Using Timestamps 200
  10.5.1 Timestamp Ordering 201

Exercises 202

11. Database Recovery 204–213

11.1 Transaction State Diagram 204
11.2 Recovery Strategies 205
  11.2.1 Write-Ahead-Logging 205
  11.2.2 Shadow Paging 210
11.3 Recovery of Non-volatile Storage 212
11.4 Residual Dump Backup Strategy 212
11.5 Other Backup Strategies 212

Exercises 213

12. File Organization, Indexing and Hashing 214–243

12.1 Storage Devices 214
  12.1.1 Storage of Database 214
  12.1.2 Storage of Records 215
12.2 Heap File Structure 215
12.3 Sorted File Structure 216
12.4 Indexed Files 217
  12.4.1 Primary Index 218
  12.4.2 Clustering Index 220
  12.4.3 Secondary Index 220
12.5 Multilevel Indexing 224
12.6 B-Tree Indexing 227
12.7 B^+-Tree Indexing 234
12.8 Hash File Structure 238
  12.8.1 Internal Hashing 238
  12.8.2 External Hashing 240

Exercises 243

13. Data Warehousing and Data Mining 244–253

13.1 Data Warehousing 244

13.1.1 Characteristic of Data Warehouse 245

13.1.2 Need of Data Warehouse 245

13.1.3 Components of Data Warehousing System 246

13.1.4 Functioning of a Data Warehouse 246

13.1.5 Advantages of Data Warehouses 247

13.1.6 Limitations of Data Warehouses 247

13.2 Data Mining 247

13.2.1 Evolution of Data Mining 248

13.2.2 Data Mining Tools 250

13.2.3 Data Mining Algorithms 250

13.2.4 Role of Data Mining and its Applications 251

13.3 Association Rule Mining 252

13.4 Text Data Mining 252

13.5 Web Data Mining 253

Exercises 253

Bibliography* *255

Index* *257–261

Preface

Database Management System is a very important and fundamental subject for students studying a course related to Computer Science and Engineering or Information Technology. It has wide applications in industry as well as in real-life problem-solving. Computer based autonomous systems invariably have a database component in them. Depending on the area of application, databases may be of different categories. While a research database may contain important references, citations, technical contents, reports and resources, a business database may include business data records such as organizations, projects, products, orders, shipments, etc. Banking and Railway Reservation Systems are two very common real-life application areas of database management systems.

In this book, I have tried to cover all the important aspects of database management systems—from theoretical foundations to practical applications. There are many texts on this subject available in the market. A majority of them are very rich in technical contents, with great details of subject matters and other relevant aspects. However, when we look at the need for an entry level student, we must try to simplify matters with ample clarification, illustration, examples and presentation in a compact form. Therefore, I have tried to maintain all of the above features in the present text. Some of the most important features of this book include lucid presentation of material, numerous solved problems, sufficient figures and tables and chapter-end exercise problems.

This book contains thirteen chapters in all. The contents cover almost all the essential materials that may be included in diploma and undergraduate syllabi. The initial five chapters emphasize on building a strong foundation of Relational Database Management Systems. Chapters 6, 7 and 8 deal with query generation, data manipulation, and application programming. Query processing and optimization details are given in Chapter 9. Real-life concurrent Transaction Processing and Database Recovery fundamentals are dealt in Chapters 10 and 11, respectively. Chapter 12 covers aspects of physical database design in detail. Chapter 13 describes some higher level topics and applications of Data Warehousing and Data Mining. All the chapters contain sufficient examples and clear illustrations along with necessary theoretical details.

This text is primarily written for diploma and degree level engineering students. Also, the students of computer applications and management courses will be amply benefited. I believe that students at the undergraduate level will find this book a valuable one.

Malay K. Pakhira

Preface

[illegible]

CHAPTER 1

Database Systems

The present day information explosion forces each and every enterprise or organization to maintain a huge amount of data or information in a secured and efficient manner. This data or information must be well organized and easy to handle. Also, different activities of the concerned enterprise or organization need different chunks of data or information already stored by them. So data must be related to certain specific activity or application. It is, therefore, necessary to maintain different data items in different storage area. Each such storage area, organized in a specific way, is termed a *database*. For the purpose of maintaining security measures, users of data should have limited or restricted control over the database, and a centralized overall control should be imposed. And for efficient handling of data in a database, we require a sophisticated data manager. Such a data manager provides a convenient way to access and manipulate data. Software that performs these tasks is called the Database Management System (DBMS).

1.1 Database

Formally defined, *a database is a collection of interrelated data organized in specific forms in order to suit for specific applications*. A database is maintained by some organization or enterprise for efficiently handling the tasks of their daily activities, called *transactions*. For example, a bank maintains a *banking database* for storing customer data, account data, loan data and many others. Data are stored in several files with minimum amount of redundancy among them. Data must be shared in nature in order to facilitate concurrent access and processing. There must be a overall centralized control of data in order to maintain safety, security and integrity of the database. A database, therefore, can be characterized as follows:

- Repository of a collection of interrelated data records or data files.
- Data in a database are organized for efficient storage, retrieval and processing (in relation to some application).
- Data in a database must be shared in nature in order to facilitate concurrent access and processing.
- Database provides a centralized control of data to its users.
- Database is designed to maintain a large volume of data efficiently and effectively.

1.2 Database Management System (DBMS)

A database is the central item in a system for storing, processing and retrieving data or information. Such a system is called a Database System. The other components of this system can be identified as other software, hardware and users. Since the question of controlling or managing data is very essential in designing and maintaining a database, we can better use the term Data-Base Management System (DBMS). A DBMS is, therefore, a collection of interrelated data and a set of programs that manage or control the use of data. It provides an interface between the database and its users. The primary objective of a DBMS is to provide means to organize data in storage media and also to enable users with easy and efficient access mechanisms. A modern database management system is shown in Figure 1.1. Major roles of a DBMS can be summarized as:

- Defines data structures for data storage.
- Provides suitable mechanism for data access and data manipulation.
- Maintains system integrity.
- Provides safety and security measures for data.
- Provides mechanism for data sharing among users concurrently.

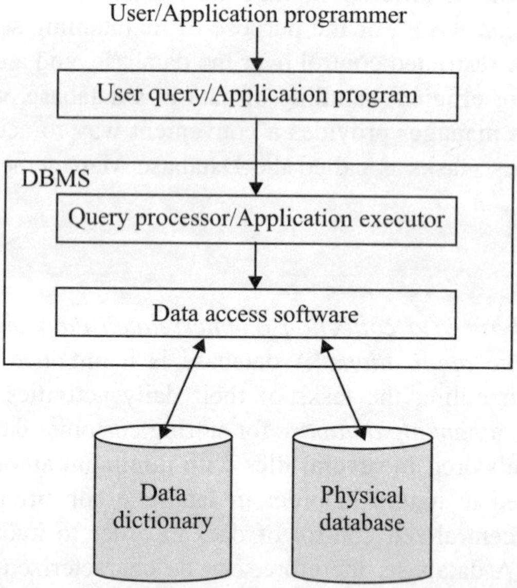

Figure 1.1 Schematic of a database system.

1.2.1 Components of a DBMS

From the above discussion, it is clear that a DBMS is a versatile software package that handles many data related operations of its host enterprise. It allows the users to access and modify data as per requirements. It has the ability to organize the data in suitable forms before presenting it as output. It has a very close relationship with the operating system, system software and hardware of the host machine. The components of a DBMS can be summarized as follows:

- **Database:** It is the storage area in the computer's auxiliary storage where a collection of related data concerning, a certain application is maintained. The data stored in a database may be any arbitrary types including numerical, character, strings, text, images etc.
- **Software:** This component manages or controls the use of data stored in the database. It works in association with system software like the operating system routines of the host machine to solve user queries.
- **Hardware:** DBMS is software and works only on the hardware of the host machine. Database itself may be maintained in auxiliary devices as a back-up.
- **Users:** They are the reasons why a database is maintained. Many different types of users may access the database for various purposes. Technical users, like the Database Administrator (DBA) can use it for technical manipulations, while ordinary users can get answers for their queries.

1.2.2 Application Areas of DBMS

In almost all major real-life business areas we see the use of DBMS. Some of the most important ones include the following:

- **Banking:** Maintaining customer information, loan schemes, account details, daily transactions etc.
- **Railways:** Booking (reservation), train information, passenger information, etc.
- **Airlines:** Booking (reservation), flight information, passenger information, etc.
- **Telecommunications:** Billing, keeping call records, customer information, etc.
- **Finance:** Earn-expenditure records, payments, purchase of financial instruments, etc.
- **Universities:** Students' information, course details, registration, examination, etc.
- **Sales:** Product information, customer records, sales records, etc., and so on.

1.3 Classical File Based Systems

In traditional file based record keeping system, data are stored in *flat files*. These files can be accessed directly under the supervision of the operating system as separate entities. No structural relationship exists between any two such files. A user can get complete access over any of the data files in a non-concurrent fashion.

If a number of users wish to get access to a particular file at the same time, the only way is to have different copies of the concerned file. Every time when a file is copied into another, an amount of data duplication occurs. Hence, it is necessary to unify all the changes in the file made by different users, in order to maintain consistency of data, after the day's transactions are over. However, it is a very difficult task in such a system.

Generally, all the necessary data are not likely to reside in a single file. If all the files do not have uniform organization, it is difficult for application programmers to handle multiple file types. In such a situation, application programs become data dependent (programs depend on organization of data files). This kind of data-application dependency makes the system inflexible, and it becomes necessary to organize and reorganize the data depending on the need of the application.

Characteristic features of a classical file based system can be summarized as follows:

- Data are stored in Flat Files.
- User access is under operating system (OS) control.
- Every user is presented with a single view of stored data.
- Multiple users can work on a particular data file by copy mechanism.
- There was no control over data usage.
- No central supervision of data is present (files may reside in different machines).

In Figures 1.2 and 1.3, classical file based record keeping systems are depicted. In Figure 1.2, the database is consisting of *N* number of flat files *File* 1, *File* 2, ..., *File N*.

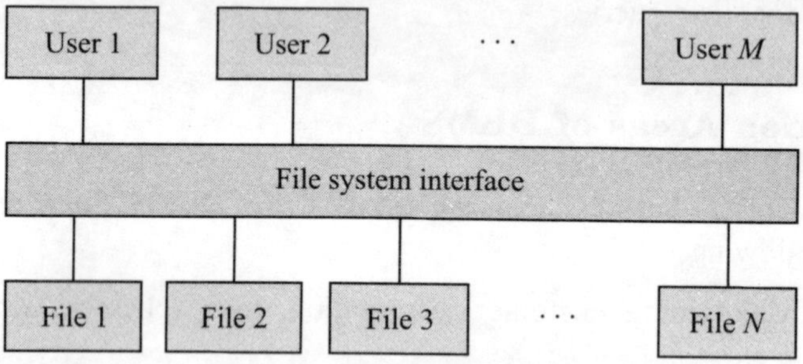

Figure 1.2 Schematic of a classical file based system.

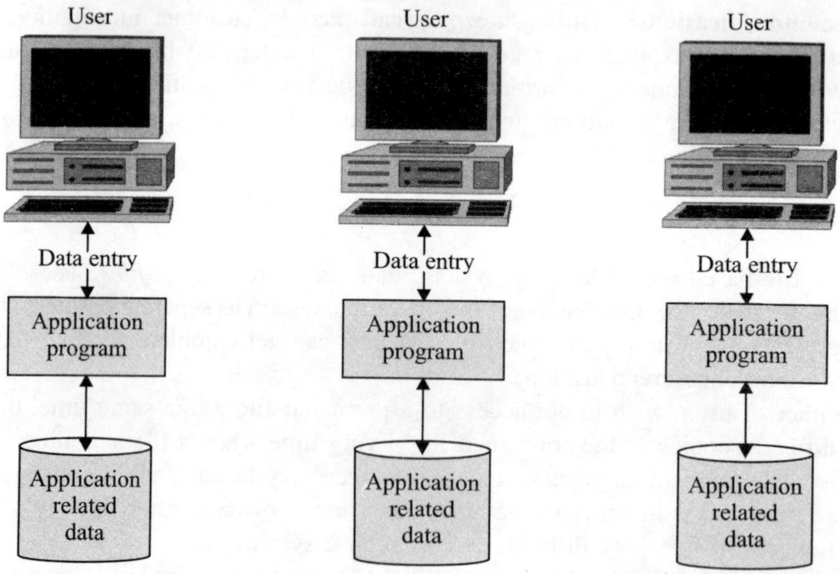

Figure 1.3 A typical example of classical file based system for a database.

Any user may get access to any of the files using a copy mechanism. If we consider a banking system, these files may store the records of accounts, customer information, loan records, deposit and withdrawal records etc., separately. A bank staff may copy and use any (one or more) of the files for his/her job requirements.

That is, a user can copy any of the files in his/her own machine and work on this copy. After his/her work is over, the final version is written back in the original flat file. Note that, a number of users may use the same file (copied version) and eventually, write back, and this is a powerful source of data inconsistency. Each user is using a separate machine having a separate operating system. Therefore, accesses to data files may be heterogeneous in nature. Also, each user may be using different programming languages for manipulating data; causing a data-application dependency.

1.3.1 Disadvantages of Classical Technique

In file based systems, data are stored in flat files which are easily accessible to any of the users as per their requirement, and hence they are *not secure*. For example, in the case of a banking application, whenever a customer desires to get information about his balance, he may get access to relevant information of other customers also. This is because all records are stored in a file which is opened by the customer in question.

In many cases, the same data or information is duplicated in multiple files. This type of *duplication of data* or *redundancy* leads to consumption of more storage than required, and also causes many kinds of access anomalies. If the data is modified in one file, but not in the other, the file system becomes *inconsistent* (containing different values for the same data in different files or instances). The above might occur as there is no way to ensure *propagation of updation* to all related files.

Sometimes, all related data records may not be stored in a single file, rather they are scattered in different files using different formats. It then becomes difficult for application programmer to write a single unified code to access data from all related files. This problem is called *data isolation*. Due to the above reason, the programmer has to write codes which are dependent on the data storage structure (in files). This problem is called *data dependency*. This means that applications become dependent on data structures. It is difficult to reorganize data in different structures according to the requirements of new applications. Thus, data organization is *inflexible*.

When multiple users attempt to access the same file concurrently, each of them may be allowed to get a copy of their own. After operations are over, there is no provision for a unified updation from all copied files. This, results in data *inconsistency*.

From the above discussion, we can arrive at the following drawbacks of a file based system:

- Data is not secured (access anomaly).
- Data may be redundant (data duplication).
- Data may be inconsistent (isolated updation anomaly).
- Data file organization may be suitable for only specific applications (data dependency).
- Running a new application may require reorganization of data files (inflexible).

1.4 Modern DBMS Approach

In modern database systems, data are centrally controlled under the supervision of a DBMS software. Here, only a single copy of a file is maintained thereby duplication or redundancy of data is avoided. Users trying to access a file or data simultaneously, can be allowed on a request-grant basis. So data can be shared concurrently without any chance of inconsistency. Necessary user authentication and integrity restrictions can be imposed by the DBMS. Data back-up and recovery mechanisms can be applied easily. The overall performance of the DBMS is also controlled by a human expert called the database administrator (DBA). Important characteristic features of a DBMS are enlisted as:

- Data are organized depending on application needs.
- Data access is via the DBMS.
- Different users get different views of data.
- DBMS maintains centralized control.
- Concurrent access by users.
- Data consistency is maintained by DBMS.
- Database is under the control of DBA.

The software components of DBMS can be layered as shown in Figure 1.4. The database containing data records is at the bottom of the system. Any access request from the user must pass from the application layer through the DBMS and OS (Operating System) layers. Operating system routines access bare data (raw data) from the database, the DBMS layer converts data into suitable view as requested by the application program.

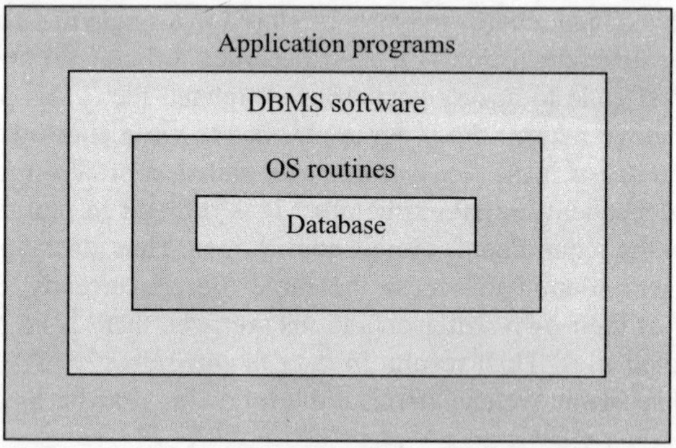

Figure 1.4 Different layers of a DBMS.

In practice, for ease of description, we commonly consider the DBMS and OS layers by merging them into a single layer called the DBMS layer. This is shown in Figure 1.4. Different software layers of a database system are shown in Figure 1.5.

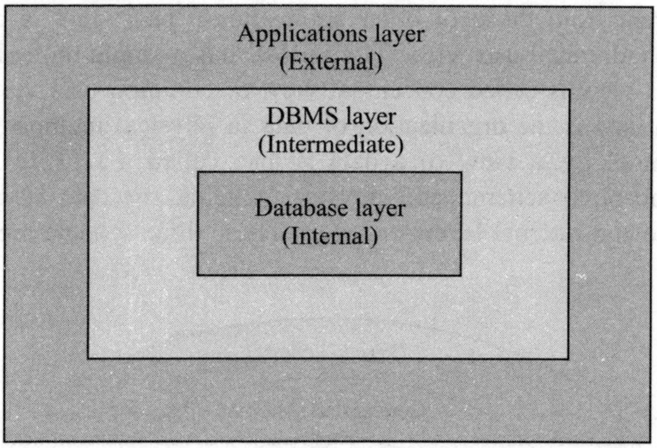

Figure 1.5 Three important (major) software layers of a DBMS.

1.4.1 Three-layer Architecture

Based on the concept of layers of data and software routines, a commercial DBMS package is supposed to maintain a three-layer architecture. This architectural model has been standardized by ANSI/SPARC (American National Standards Institute/Standard Planning and Requirements Committee).

In Figure 1.6, three different levels of a three-layer architecture is depicted. These three levels are external, conceptual and internal levels. The external level is associated with the user applications and user views of data. The conceptual level involves the DBMS software and a combined common view of all data in the database. The internal level deals with physical representation and organization of data. A three-layer architecture of database system is shown in Figure 1.6.

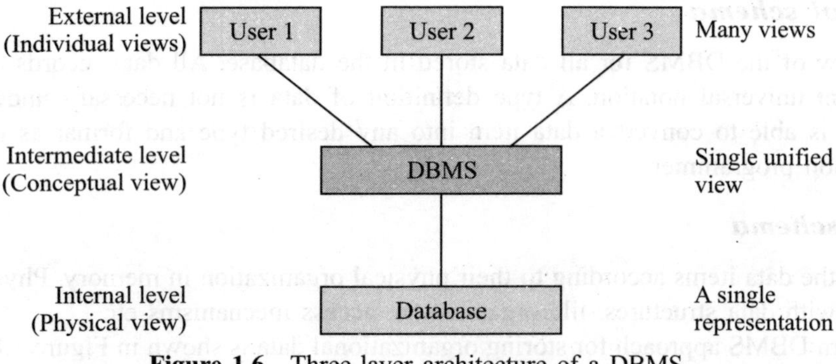

Figure 1.6 Three-layer architecture of a DBMS.

1.4.2 Schema of Different Layers

It is already mentioned that software components at different levels of the DBMS view the data in the database differently. Each application program may have a distinct view for a data item which is different from those of other applications. This view is called external view, applications view or individual user view. The DBMS has a single unified view of data for all the applications. This view is called conceptual view or common user view. The internal view or storage view of a data is the organization of data in physical memory.

In DBMS terminology, a view of a data is also called a *schema*. We, therefore, have logical schema, conceptual schema and physical schema for data items corresponding to external, intermediate and internal layers or levels. These three schema architectures are shown in Figure 1.7.

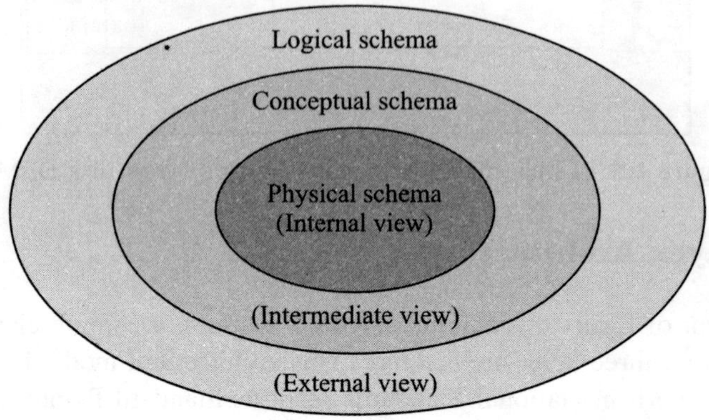

Figure 1.7 Schema at different layers of a DBMS.

Logical schema

This is the application programmers' view of the database. For each and every application, there may be a different view of the database. The DBMS allows the user (application programmer) to have a view of the required data items as per specified formats.

Conceptual schema

It is the view of the DBMS for all data stored in the database. All data records are specified in a common universal notation. A type definition of data is not necessary under this view. The DBMS is able to convert a data item into any desired type and format as requested by the application programmer.

Physical schema

It describes the data items according to their physical organization in memory. Physical schema is involved with data structures, file organization, access mechanisms etc.

A modern DBMS approach for storing organizational data is shown in Figure 1.8. Figure 1.9 depicts the centralized nature of the database system. The database server stores all data, and users can have access to data from individual terminals.

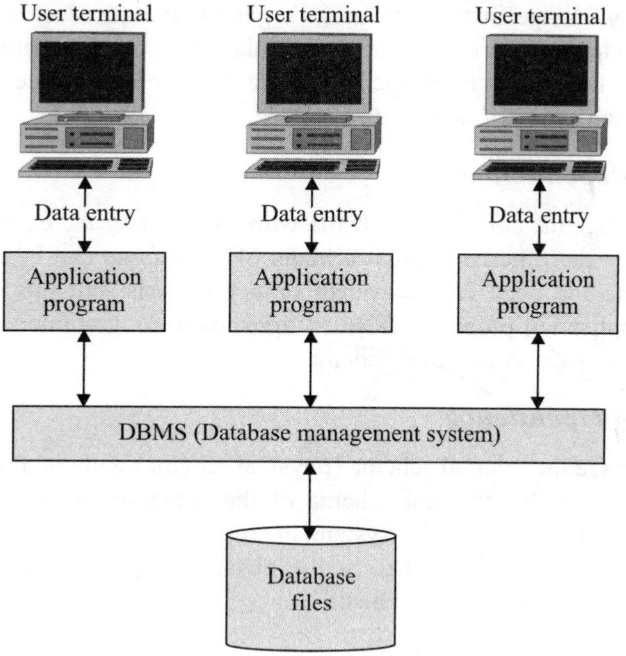

Figure 1.8 DBMS approach for database systems.

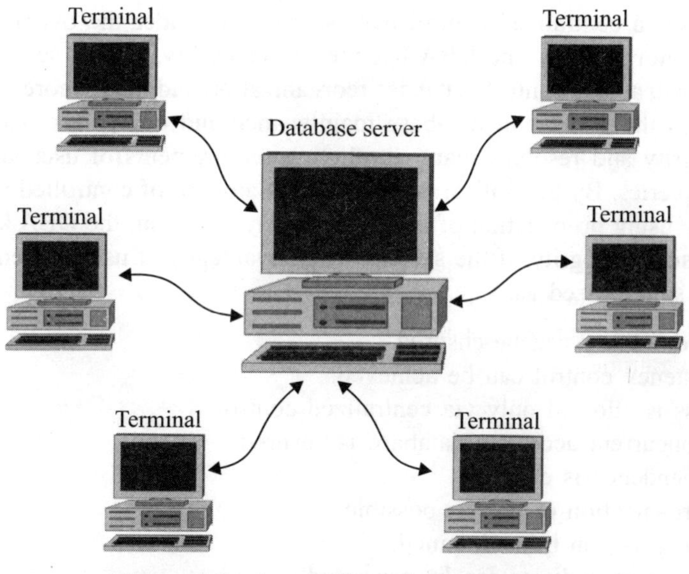

Figure 1.9 A centralized database system.

1.4.3 Data Independence

Data independence is a very important concept in database designing. In a three-layer architecture, data independence can be easily enforced. *Data independence* is the ability of the database system, such that any change in the schema at a particular layer does not affect the schema at another layer. In other words, schema at a particular layer can be changed independently of the other layers. Two types of data independence are observed in a three-layer system: *logical data independence*, and *physical data independence*.

Logical data independence

It is the ability to change the conceptual schema without affecting the external schemas (logical schemas). This means that, the conceptual schema of a database can be modified by the data manager according to the need of the system or applications, but this modification will be transparent to the application programs. That is, application programmers need not, in way, be aware of the changes in the conceptual schema.

Physical data independence

It is the ability to change the internal schema (physical schema) without affecting the conceptual schema. This means that, the physical schema of the database can be modified by the data manager according to the need of the system or applications, but this modification will be transparent to the conceptual level. That is, the physical data organization may be changed without any change in the conceptual schema.

1.4.4 Advantages of DBMS Scheme

The DBMS imposes a centralized control over stored data under the overall supervision of a database administrator (DBA). The DBA has the responsibility of data security, data back-up, authorization control, access control, database reorganization and many more. He is a key person of the enterprise in the context of database maintenance and operations. The DBA maintains the database integrity and resolves many conflicting requirements of user arising out of their applications and queries. By the utilization of a limited amount of controlled redundancy within stored data and by using propagation of the effect of any updation, the DBA keeps the database consistent and ensures integrity of the system. The advantages of using a centralized database, therefore, can be summarized as:

- Limited redundancy can be ensured.
- Full consistency control can be achieved.
- Data access is allowed only via centralized control.
- Secured concurrent access to database is ensured.
- Data independence is ensured.
- Flexible organization of data is possible.
- System Integrity can be maintained.
- Back-up/recovery policies can be exercised.

1.4.5 Database Users

It is already mentioned that a database may be used by the different categories of users. Each category has its own specific requirements. *Common users* or non-technical users expect results for some user specified query. For example, a railway passenger may type a query for his reservation status. An *application developer* may write an application program and execute it under the control of DBMS. He is a technical user and hence can avail greater access facilities over the database compared to the ordinary user. A *database manager* and the DBA have full control over the database. He can modify the organization of data in the database and allow others to use the database with limited facilities. Managerial staff of the host enterprise generally runs system level queries to generate specific aggregation reports. They are also non-technical users. All such non-technical users are generally termed *end-users*.

Among all sorts of users, DBA or database administrator is the most important person in relation to the database. Roles of DBA are illustrated in broader details in the following section.

1.4.6 Role of DBA

In Section 1.4.5, we have briefly mentioned some of the responsibilities of the DBA. A detailed description of such roles is given below.

Organizing operational data

The DBA supervises the organization of data in the database. He has to study the requirements of the organization for data and nature of data to be stored. Accordingly, he decides what data to be maintained and what to not. Also, an appropriate organization of data using necessary data structures is to be enforced. The DBA defines this data organization and develops the internal view of data or the conceptual schema for the database. The DBA also prepares all data definition metafiles which are called Data Dictionary (DD) of the database in combined form.

Defining access methodologies

Depending on the data structures used to store data, the DBA defines the data access methodologies. In other words, the mapping between the conceptual view and the internal view of data is established by the DBA. The Data Description Language (DDL) is used for this purpose.

Maintaining data security

DBA applies necessary validity checks, authentication checks etc., as a part of conceptual schema definition. He needs to grant appropriate authorization toward access of data by any user. Encryption/decryption methodologies may be applied by him when necessary.

Defining back-up/recovery policies

A database is meant for the use by many different categories of users on a regular basis. Data may be damaged or lost by any sort of malfunctioning by the user/programmer or any other human errors. It is, therefore, necessary to keep back-up of the database at regular intervals. This back-up may be taken weekly or monthly or at other frequencies as per the requirements. Also, suitable recovery strategies must be implemented to recover any loss of important data during a day's transactions.

Monitoring system performance

The DBA needs to regularly monitor the performance of DBMS after its deployment. Whenever necessary, suitable changes in data structures/organization, access mechanism etc. are applied to improve this performance.

1.5 Significance of Database Systems

Although a database is nothing but a collection of data files, it has a high significance to its owner organization. Database maintains records mainly related to the activity of the organization. Data stored in a database is expected to have long term usability, and hence it is considered a valuable resource of the concerned organization. As a database may be used by a large number of users of varying categories, it is extremely necessary to maintain it under some centralized control in order to keep it compact, consistent and integral. Compactness, consistency and integrity are three interrelated features of a database system.

Redundancy–inconsistency–lack of integrity

The primary motivation behind developing a DBMS is to ensure integral performance of a record keeping system (the database system) that provides consistent results at any circumstances. From our experience in daily life and analysis of classical record keeping systems we can arrive at the decision that duplication or redundancy of data in a database is the primary reason for data inconsistency, and data inconsistency, in turn, is the cause of anomalous or non-integral behaviour of a database system. The three terms *redundancy*, *inconsistency* and *lack-of-integrity* are thus highly interrelated in the context of a database system. We can define these terms as follows:

- **Redundancy:** Duplication of the same data in different files or tables.
- **Inconsistency:** Different values for the same data item at different occurrences.
- **Lack of integrity:** Anomalous functioning of the database system (producing incorrect results) due to inconsistent data.

While designing a database system we must, therefore, attempt to prohibit all possible chances of these vulnerable factors from appearing into the proposed system.

Exercises

1.1 What is a Database Management System (DBMS) and what are its components? In what way is a DBMS different compared to an operating system (OS)?

1.2 What are the different types of users of a DBMS and how do they interact with the system?

1.3 Who is a DBA? What is his importance in the enterprise maintaining a database?

1.4 Compare and contrast traditional File based system and a Database system.

1.5 Illustrate the three-level architecture of a DBMS with clear diagram.

1.6 What is a schema? Describe different types of schema available in a DBMS.

1.7 How are the three terms; Redundancy, Consistency and Lack of integrity are interrelated in connection with a database?

1.8 Mention advantages and disadvantages of having a database system for organizational information processing.

1.9 Define data abstraction and data independence.

1.10 List major components of a database system and describe their functions.

CHAPTER 2

Modelling a Database

A database maintains a huge amount of interrelated data. These data must be organized into suitable data structures for the purpose of efficient storage, retrieval and processing. Also, during processing, different manipulation operations need to be applied over the stored data. Requirements of data storage and data manipulation may be conflicting. It is, therefore, necessary to use a representation that can serve the applications in a better manner. In general, a common goal of a database system is to hide organizational details of data from users (applications). This is commonly done by data abstraction. A suitable data model can provide all necessary means of application independent data access by using data abstraction. A data model is thus an abstract model of data that describes how the data are organized in the physical storage and how they can be accessed. In order to find out such a suitable data representation, for a particular database system, we need to study different data models.

2.1 Representation of Data

Depending on levels of data abstraction, one can have the different types of data representation levels. A high degree of abstraction indicates human understandability, while a low degree indicates machine understandability. Human beings always have some idea about an object or entity that this is the highest degree of abstraction (conceptual). Computers can store a representation of the same object or entity in digital notation that this is the lowest degree of abstraction (physical). For conversion of conceptual representation to physical representation, we need an intermediate representation. A three-level representation scheme for data can have three different levels of abstraction. Between the conceptual and physical levels, there is a logical representation level that simplifies the conversion from conceptual to physical definition.

Different levels of data abstraction are:

- Conceptual level
- Logical level
- Physical level.

As already mentioned, conceptual representation is hypothetical in nature. We can think of this kind of representation, but these representations cannot be easily converted into a machine understandable form. Machine understands a data item only in terms of its binary string representation, its starting location in memory; and can access it only when all such data are arranged in a suitable data structure. This machine understandable form of data is also termed a physical representation of data. Therefore, before converting conceptual view of data into its physical representation, we need to organize them into logical data structures and also to develop suitable access mechanisms. A logical level of data abstraction is, therefore, very important in database technology.

Corresponding to each different level of abstraction there exists a schema or view of data. Conceptual schema provides an overall view of some data or entity. Logical schemas are application dependent, and physical schemas are related to the storage representation of data. The conceptual view contains all possible properties of an entity that describes the concerned object properly. Since a particular entity may be used in various different applications, we may have a number of logical views. Logical views are, therefore, subsets of the conceptual view.

Outcome of different levels of data abstraction are as follows:

- Conceptual schema (all possible properties of an entity)
- Logical schema (properties related to the concerned application)
- Physical schema (digital/storage representation of properties).

2.2 Data Models

Data model forms the blueprint of a database design. A data model is based on some mathematical background and maintains some rules and restrictions. Data models are highly correlated with the physical data structures being used for storage of data in the database. Therefore, a Data Model is based on some mathematical concept and represents a combined view of data representation, data access and data manipulation methodologies followed by the concerned model mentioned below:

- **Abstract models:** Hypothetical or abstract. They are used in the design phase only. An example is the Entity-relationship model.
- **Logical models:** Mathematically based models. Used for physical implementation. An example is the Relational model.
- **Physical model:** This is represented by a set of data structures used to store data, and their access methodologies. Database developers use different such structures and procedures for their own products (database packages).

In Figure 2.1, we try to depict the concept and the use of different data models in designing a database system. From this figure, it is clear that database designing is step-by-step process of conversion of data models from abstract to physical.

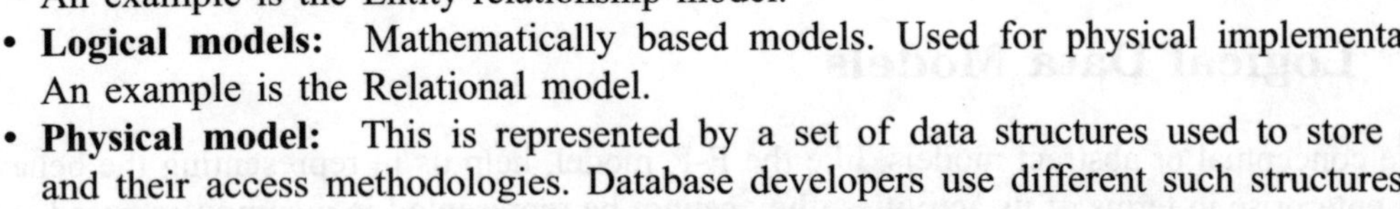

Figure 2.1 Conversion of data models into a physical database.

Abstract or conceptual models can be of two types: *object-based* models and *record-based* models. In object-based models, data or information are treated as objects having all their operating principles along with data values. Hence, object oriented programming paradigm is better suited for processing them. Although this kind of programming allows efficient processing of data, we need to associate codes of operating procedures along with each object-class. For each different category of objects we need to develop and process a different set of such procedures. Applications using object models may, therefore, be computationally intensive. Since a database contains a huge amount of data, all of which must be processed uniformly at a very high speed, relatively simpler record-based models of data are highly preferable.

2.3 Entity-Relationship Model (E-R model)

The Entity-relationship model is a record-based conceptual model for designing a database. It is based on human concepts of representing natural relationships among different entities of interest. It is relatively easy to understand, and hence, the most widely used one in designing a database. Some common features of the E-R model are:

- A perceptual model for the real world.
- Involves Entities and Relationships.
- Entities represent data records (objects) and Relationships represent link (relation) between them.
- Using the E-R model, a database (only a conceptual view) can be designed as an E-R diagram.

Generally, the E-R model is treated as a tool for designing a relational database system. The E-R model of data directly leads to an E-R diagram which can be easily converted to relational database. Since the relational data model is the very commonly used model in designing a database, we shall devote a complete chapter to study the features of the E-R based data modelling.

2.4 Logical Data Models

While conceptual or abstract models, like the E-R model, help us in representing the behaviour of an enterprise in terms of its activities, they cannot be represented in a computer-based system directly. These models must be converted into physically realizable logical models. Logical models are based on computer manageable data structures, storage and retrieval techniques. Logical models must also be supported by sufficient mathematical tools and methodologies. Some important features of logical models are:

- Physically realizable and conform to real-world situations.
- Based on mathematical principles.
- Must have well defined access methodologies.

Three such models (for handling record-based data) are:

- Hierarchical data model
- Network data model
- Relational data model.

Out of the above-mentioned record-based logical models, the relational model is very popular because of its simplicity. Uniform tabular data structures can be used here for all types of data, and efficient access methodologies are available. Major database operations can be performed very efficiently using this model. Some other features in favour of this model are:

- Relational model is the universally accepted state-of-art for database systems.
- The E-R model can be easily converted into a corresponding Relational model.

2.4.1 Hierarchical Data Model

In hierarchical model data are organized in a tree structure using parent-child relationship among data records or data blocks. This approach implies that relevant data may be found in a sequence of nodes which are parent and child in the hierarchy. Records are, therefore, connected via pointers to establish links among themselves. The relationship is one-to-many in nature, i.e. a number of children nodes are connected to a single parent node. Parent and child nodes are determined on the basis of importance of attributes they maintain as predicate.

- Data records are organized in a tree structure.
- Data are segmented in a parent-child fashion.
- Internal nodes of the tree represent predicate nodes. Leaf nodes contain actual data records.
- Depending on the nature of a higher level predicate data records may have repetition or duplication at leaf nodes.
- A two-way link exists between parent and immediate child.
- One-to-many relationship exists between parent and children.
- Accepted as IMS (Information Management System) standard of IBM in 1970s.

The major disadvantage of the hierarchical model that links between data items (records) are hard-coded into the data structure. In other words, once a particular arrangement is created, it cannot be easily changed. Reorganization of data, as may be needed by some application, involves significant processing overhead. This model, therefore, is unable to provide a common application independent view of the data. The data reorganization overhead grows heavily with size of the database. So, although we can use this model for small scale databases, it is practically unusable for very large databases.

2.4.2 Network Data Model

Network data model maintains many-to-many relationship among data records. Here also, data are linked by pointers. The organization of data is a graph using nodes and directed arcs.

- A collection of records form a network among themselves.
- Accepted at the CODASYL (Conference on Data Systems Languages) in 1971.
- Relationship is many-to-many.
- Database is organized as a collection of graphs (sub-networks).
- Relationship between records is established by links or pointers.
- Organization is complicated.
- Complicated to access and process.

The basic advantage of the network data model is that it maintains only many-to-many relationship among the records. Each record (of group of records) may be connected to a number of other records. The major disadvantage is that, this data model may contain weak links. If any such link is lost during manipulation, it is very hard to recover it. Again, as in the case of hierarchical data model, organization of the database is not flexible with respect to requirements of various applications.

2.4.3 Relational Data Model

In relational data model data (or records) are maintained in table structures. A table or relation is formed using mathematical concept of relation. Tables contain rows and columns. A row represents a record. The relationship among a number of tables is established by certain specific attributes (columns of tables) of related tables. Characteristics of relational model are given below.

- Data are organized as relations or tables.
- A collection of such relations constitute the database.
- A record is a fixed length k-tuple (with k attributes).
- Derived from the mathematical concept of relations.
- Links between different tables are established via key attributes of related tables.

2.5 Comparison of Logical Data Models

Hierarchical and Network data models have been developed earlier compared to the Relational data model. The earlier models were conceptually simple, as they were based on conventional data structures and existing procedural access methodologies. However, these models suffer from many important aspects of a database system including data independence, data integrity, uniform access methodologies, ordering constraints etc. For large databases these models became very complex and access of data also became much more complicated and could not be performed in real-time. Data needed to be reorganized for different applications differently and thus organization became inflexible. Application programs, being written in procedural languages, used to contain many high level programming details about physical data structures and suffered from portability. In the hierarchical model, strict parent child relationship caused inclusion of redundancy in data. Although the network model could avoid this by virtue of multiple links among data records, data access methods became very complex.

In the following, an example supplier database is used to illustrate organization of physical data using different logical data models. We considered a very simple database having three entities SUPPLIER, PARTS and SHIPMENTS as shown in Figure 2.2. A possible hierarchical relationship among these entities is also shown in this figure.

SUPPLIER (S#, SNAME, SADDRESS, SPHONE)

S#	SNAME	SADDRESS	SPHONE

PARTS (P#, PNAME, PWEIGHT, PCOST)

P#	PNAME	PWEIGHT	PCOST

SHIPMENT (S#, P#, QUANTITY, ORDER DATE)

S#	P#	QUANTITY	ORDER_DATE

} Database relations

SUPPLIER (S#, SNAME, SADDRESS, SPHONE)

↓

PARTS (P#, PNAME, PWEIGHT, PCOST)

↓

SHIPMENT (S#, P#, QUANTITY, ORDER_DATE)

} A possible hierarchical relationship

Figure 2.2 A sample database and hierarchy among its components.

We now consider some instances of these entities (records from different database files). In Figure 2.3, we see how these records are linked using a hierarchical data structure. The records from different relations are connected via pointers. Here, a parent child relationship among records is observed. Access of data in such a database must follow tree search mechanism.

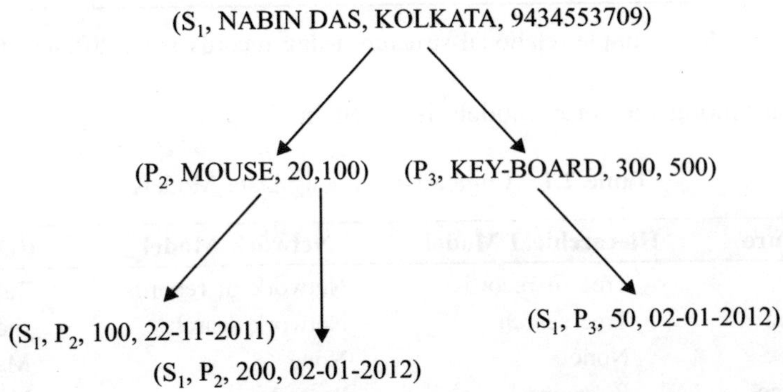

Figure 2.3 Example of hierarchy among records from different files.

In the case of a network data organization, as shown in Figure 2.4, the storage description is a more complicated one. Here, records may be connected by pointers, in a linked list fashion. The overall structure of the database is like a graph network. Access of data from such a structure is really very complicated. The relational structure, shown in Figure 2.5, enables us with a easy-to-understand organization, and simple access mechanisms.

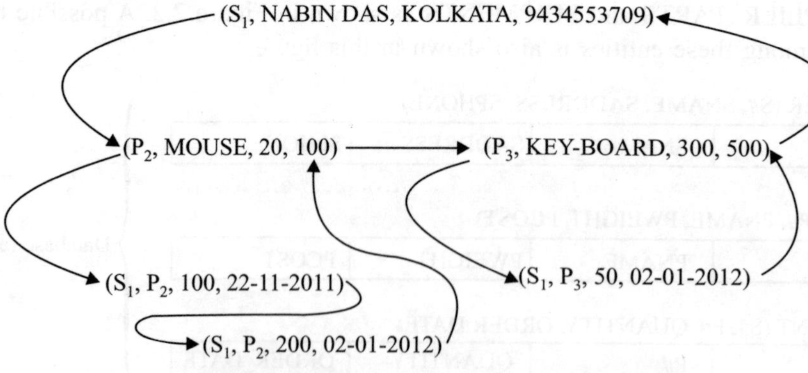

Figure 2.4 Example of a network among records from different files.

SUPPLIER

(S_1, NABIN DAS, KOLKATA, 9434553709)

PARTS

(P_2, MOUSE, 20, 100)
(P_3, KEY-BOARD, 300, 500)

SHIPMENTS

(S_1, P_2, 100, 22-11-2011)
(S_1, P_2, 200, 02-01-2012)
(S_1, P_3, 50, 02-01-2012)

Figure 2.5 Example relational structure using records from different files.

A comparison among the three models is given in Table 2.1.

Table 2.1 Comparison among Data Models

Criteria/Feature	Hierarchical Model	Network Model	Relational Model
Data structure	Tree of records	Network of records	Table of records
Access method	Tree search	Network search	Indexed search
Foundation	None	None	Mathematical
Query language	Procedural	Procedural	Non-procedural
Integrity criteria	None	None	Part of model
Updation	Difficult	Difficult	Very easy
Data independence	None	None	Part of model

2.6 Other Data Models

Besides the preceding logical data models, there exist some other data models also. One important data model, out of these, is the object-oriented data model. This data model emerges from the concept of object-oriented programming logic that has been developed in recent past. Data items are treated as objects, and common properties of objects are asserted over them. This model may be treated as a combination of the relational model and object-oriented concepts of data.

Besides the object data model, very recently other models, like XML data model, semantic data model, functional data models etc., have also been developed. A detailed description of these databases is beyond the scope of this book.

Exercises

2.1 What is a data model? What is its importance in database designing?

2.2 Names some commonly used logical data models, and mention their advantages and disadvantages.

2.3 Illustrate hierarchical data model with suitable example.

2.4 Illustrate network data model with suitable example.

2.5 What type of query language is used for relational databases? What are its advantages?

2.6 Why is relational data model considered superior compared to the other data models?

2.7 What is the role of a conceptual data model?

2.8 Write down the differences between record based data models and object based data models.

2.9 What kind of data model supports a top-down data structure to store data? What are its advantages and disadvantages?

2.10 What is logical model based mainly on linked list structures? What are its advantages and disadvantages?

CHAPTER 3

Modelling with E-R Diagram

The Entity-Relationship diagram (E-R diagram) is a tool that provides an architectural blueprint for designing a database. The E-R diagram highlights all important aspects of the design while hides the minute details. Being a real-world abstract model, the E-R model (Entity-Relationship model) helps us visualizing the database and associated applications before they are actually implemented. Modelling a database using the E-R diagrams is called E-R modelling. It is a top-down design approach for the database. Starting with only a backbone skeleton (the basic E-R diagram), we approach toward a physical realization of the database by converting the components of the diagram into their logical counterparts, and then implement the system using necessary data and applications.

3.1 E-R based Modelling

Entity-Relationship model deals with Entities and Relationships. Entities are related to other entities by relationships. Relationships, therefore, represent functionality of the concerned relations or entities. Entities are characterized by their attributes, of which one important attribute, called the *key* attribute identifies an instance of an entity uniquely. For modelling the system we, therefore, need to identify all such components and establish connections between them based on the required applications. The E-R modelling is an iterative process; it must be reviewed, modified and re-reviewed until the final model is reached. The Entity-Relationship based modelling process involves the following sequence of steps:

- **Identifying entities:** From problem definition and requirements specification, we need to find out the appropriate entities about which information will be stored. Entities are named using appropriate nouns.
- **Identifying relationships:** Relationships naturally exist among entities. This can also be realized from problem definition and requirements specification. All the entities must be connected to one or more of the other entities. An isolated entity is meaningless.
- **Drawing base E-R diagram:** A skeleton of the design is drawn which is called the base E-R diagram. This will be expanded in future as per requirements.

- **Identifying key attributes:** Each entity must have a certain number of attributes. One of them, called the key attribute, must be identified. It is the key attribute, using which we establish a link or relationship between entities.
- **Identifying other relevant attributes:** The remaining attributes must then be identified for individual entities. Care must be taken not to include any unnecessary or redundant attributes. In other words, number of attributes should be as small as possible.
- **Drawing detailed E-R diagram:** The base E-R diagram is then augmented by addition of all attributes of individual entities.
- **Reviewing the design:** The E-R diagram, thus drawn, is checked thoroughly for any missing attribute or item. If any error is detected, the model should be reviewed completely from the beginning, and this continues until a correct model is produced.

From the above description, we can summarize the concept of E-R diagrams (or E-R modelling) using the following notions:

- E-R diagram is an elegant tool for modelling databases.
- Its components are entities, relationships and attributes (of entities).
- Entities are linked via key attributes. These attributes are shared between the concerned entities in order to establish relationships.
- E-R diagram yields an abstract model only. It should be converted to a logical data model, and finally to a physical database.
- Only E-R diagram is insufficient for designing a practical database; it must also be supplemented with actual application related processes.

Different symbolic notations used in an E-R diagram are shown in Figure 3.1.

3.1.1 Entity and its Characteristics

In a database system entities represent the objects to interact with. An entity can be any real-life object or event or other specific item like bank account, job title, name of a place etc. Entities can and should be related to other entities in some manner. Meaningful information can be extracted from such inter-Entity-Relationship. For example, in the case of a banking application, we can identify two entities customer and accounts. While the former is specified personal attributes (characterizing features) like name, address, profession regarding a customer, the latter contains account number, account type, balance of customers etc. Clearly, we must relate these two entities in order to find out individual customer's account numbers. In a E-R diagram, we actually use an entity set. An entity set contains all possible entities of a certain category. If Ram and Sam have bank accounts in a certain bank, each of them is a member or instance of the entity CUSTOMER. We can summarize properties of entities as:

- An entity (an object, event, concept, etc.) is something that exists and about which we want to store information.
- A set of attributes defines an entity.
- An instance of an entity is a member of the said entity.
- An entity should have multiple instances in a database.
- Generally, an entity name is a noun and singular. Abbreviations should be avoided in naming an entity, and multiple words should be linked with underscores.

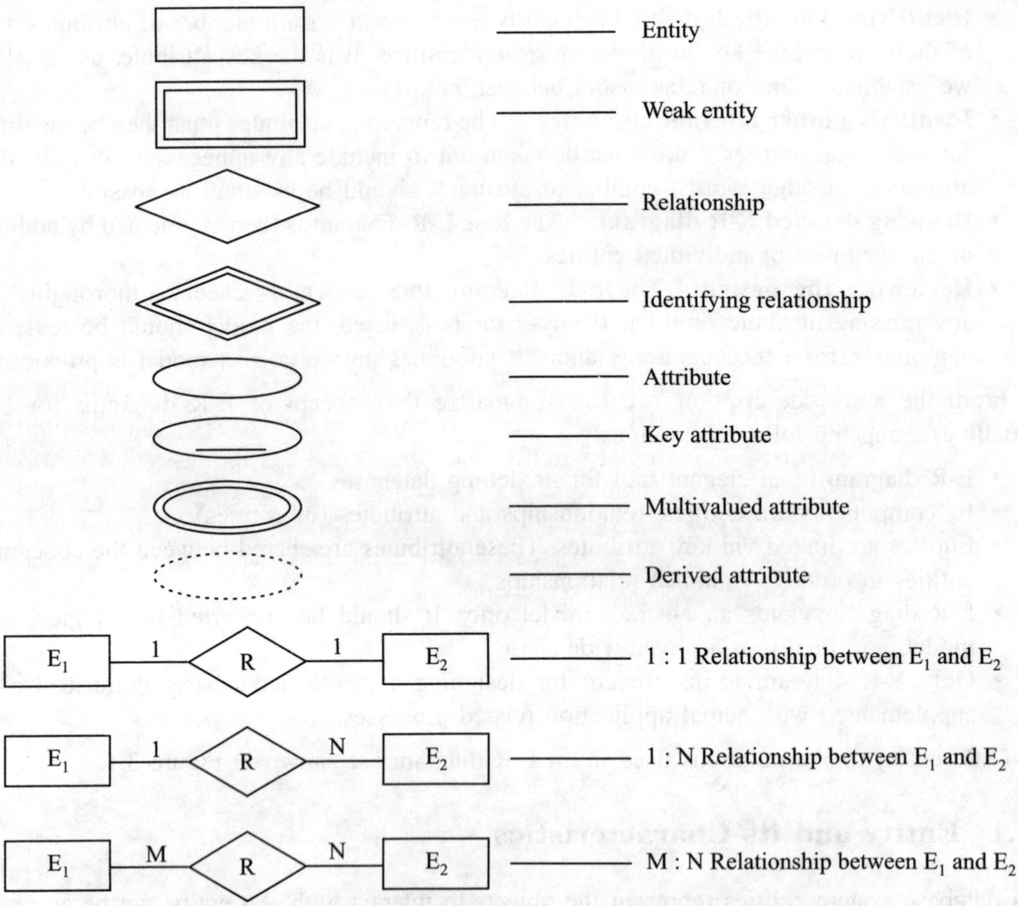

Figure 3.1 Different symbols used in an E-R diagram.

Attributes

Entities in an entity set are characterized by their attributes. In the above description, we have mentioned the attributes name, address, profession etc., for a customer entity. An entity should be represented by a small number of suitable attributes. One of attributes (or combination of attributes) should be able to distinguish one entity from others in the set. This attribute is the most important one and is termed a key attribute. Although attributes may have values which are indivisible (like, salary = 10000) or composite (name = Ram Pal; here name can be decomposed as first name and last name) in nature, it is always better to have indivisible valued attributes. If values of some attribute can be derived from other existing attributes, the former is called a derived attribute. Use of such attributes is, however, not recommended. Therefore, we can say:

- Entities are defined by a number of attributes.
- A unique-valued attribute identifies an instance of an entity unambiguously. This attribute is called a *Key* attribute.
- An attribute should have simple and indivisible values.

- Number of attributes in an entity should be limited.
- Attribute names should be nouns, multiple words should be linked by underscores when necessary.

Key attribute

A group of attributes (may be a single attribute, preferably) that identifies each member of an entity uniquely is called a *key attribute*. For example, if we consider STUDENTS to be an entity then its members (individual students) can be uniquely identified by the attribute {REGISTRATION-NUMBER} or by combination of attributes {NAME, ROLL-NUMBER}.

It should be noted that, a key has the only property that it can identify an entity member uniquely. Hence, any combination of such an attribute with any other attribute(s) will also form another key combination. For example, in the case of our STUDENTS entity, a combination of attributes {REGISTRATION-NUMBER, NAME} may also be a key. However, we can properly define a key as a subset of the minimal number of attributes that has the unique identification capability. Therefore, in our case, both {REGISTRATION-NUMBER} and {NAME, ROLL-NUMBER} may be keys. Now, when a number of keys are available for some entity set, each of them are referred to as *candidate keys*. One of the candidate keys is selected as a *primary key*. The remaining candidate keys (if any) are called *alternate keys*. A *super key* is something that has one or more extraneous attributes along with the key attribute(s). For example, {REGISTRATION-NUMBER, NAME} is a super key for STUDENTS.

Weak entity

In some cases, individual instances of an entity cannot be uniquely identified by values of its own attributes. In other words, such entities do not have a primary key of their own. These entities generally borrow a key attribute from some associated *strong entity* (that has its own primary key) to form its schema definition. Therefore, there exists a dependency of a *weak entity* over a strong entity. The strong entity, in such a case, is called a dominant entity or *identifying entity*, and the weak entity is called a subordinate entity. The relationship between a weak entity and its identifying entity is called a *identifying relationship*.

To describe the role of weak entities, let us consider an example of bank accounts of a customer in a bank. The customer may have several accounts on which several transactions are done with each transaction having a serial number (transaction number). If we have entities ACCOUNTS and TRANSACTIONS, where the former have attributes {account number, account type, customer name} and the later is having a single attribute {transaction number}, then TRANSACTIONS is a weak entity. Because transactions on different accounts may have the same number and, thus, TRANSACTIONS is a no-key entity. If we borrow the attribute account number from the ACCOUNTS entity, then the pair (account number, transaction number) may form a key for TRANSACTIONS.

Degree of an entity

The number of attributes that define an entity is referred to as the degree or arity or dimension of the concerned entity.

Cardinality of an entity

The number of members (records or tuples) that are represented by an entity, at any instant, is referred to as the cardinality of the concerned entity.

3.1.2 Relationship and its Characteristics

Relationships are natural associations that exist among entities. In other words, relationships connect one or more entities among themselves. An isolated entity has no meaning in the context of database operations. Relationships may be of varying types depending on their degrees and cardinalities.

- Relationship forms a link between entities.
- Relationships may have their own attributes and can be stored as a database table.
- Relationship names should be verbs, multiple words should be linked by underscores when necessary.

Degree of a relationship

This specifies how many entities are related by the concerned relationship. There may be three different types in general, mentioned as follows:

- **Unary relationship:** Only one entity is involved, i.e. this relationship relates instances of the same entity. For example, consider the entity TEACHERS (of some college). Some of the teachers are definitely heads of respective departments. However, the entity TEACHERS involves all teachers from all departments. So, we get a relationship that some teachers are heads of other teachers. Diagrammatically, this kind of relationship forms a self loop. This is shown in Figure 3.2.

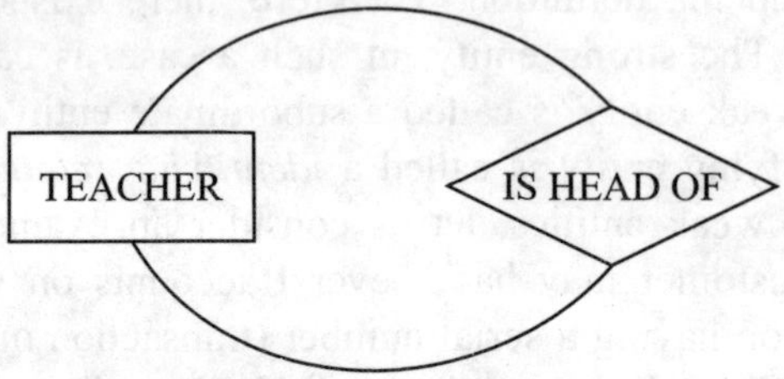

Figure 3.2 Unary relationship.

- **Binary relationship:** Two entities are involved, i.e. this relationship relates instances of one entity to instances of the other. For example, if TEACHERS and DEPARTMENTS are two participating entities, some of the teachers are definitely heads of individual departments. This example relationship is shown in Figure 3.3.

Figure 3.3 Binary relationship.

- **Ternary relationship:** Three entities are involved, i.e. this relationship relates instances from three different entities. For example, if TEACHERS, STUDENTS and DEPARTMENTS are three participating entities, instances from both TEACHERS and STUDENTS may be members of the same department. This example relationship is shown in Figure 3.4.

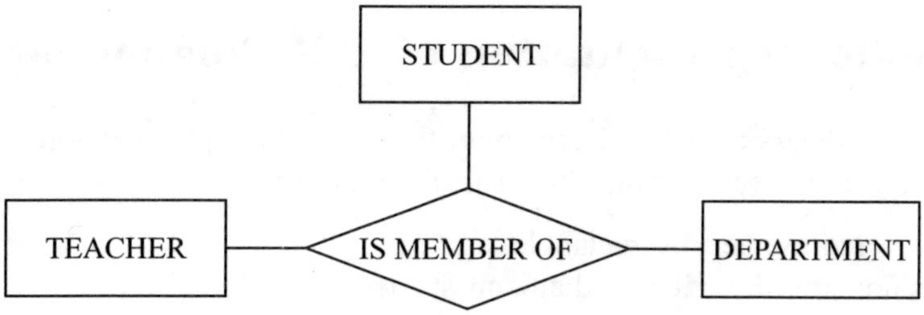

Figure 3.4 Ternary relationship.

There may be relationships of higher degrees, but these relationships will have theoretical interest only. Practically, it is always better to limit degrees within three.

Cardinality ratio of a relationship

The type of a relationship among entities is specified by its cardinality ratio. Relationship maps records (instance of an entity) from one entity (relation) to records of the other participating entity. Relationships can be of the following types:

- **One-to-one (1:1):** One instance from an entity is related to one instance from the other entity. For example, if TEACHERS and DEPARTMENTS are two participating entities, the concerned relationship will be one-to-one when we are concerned with headship. Because only one of the teachers can be head of a department and vice versa.
- **One-to-many (1:N):** One instance from an entity set is related to multiple instances from the other entity set. For example, a number of teachers are members of a certain department.
- **Many-to-one (N:1):** An one-to-many relationship, if viewed from the opposite direction, it becomes the many-to-one relationship. It is essentially the same as the earlier one.
- **Many-to-many (M:N):** Multiple instances from an entity is related to multiple instances from the other entity set. For example, if we consider another entity called STUDENTS, relationship between teachers and students is found to be many-to-many. Because, a teacher can teach a number of students and a student may be taught by a number of teachers.

Like entities, relationships may have attributes. In general, binary many-to-many relationships or ternary relationships come with attributes. Let us consider a many-to-many relationship between entities EMPLOYEES and PROJECTS: a person may be assigned to more than one project, and many persons work in a single project. We may consider a relationship WORKS-ON between these two entities. Some of the attributes of the relationship may be START-DATE, HOURS-WORKED, TASK-ASSIGNED, etc. A given task-assignment or start-date is common only to an instance of assignment of a PERSON in a particular PROJECT, and it is multi-valued when considering either the PERSON or the PROJECT entity alone. For a one-to-one or a one-to-many relationship such attributes are unnecessary. Because, at least one side of the relationship there is a single entity and there cannot be any ambiguity in assigning the attribute to the entity instead of assigning it to a relationship.

3.2 Symbolic Representation of E-R Components

Before drawing E-R diagrams, let us learn about the symbolic representations of different items or components that are used in it (as shown in Figure 3.1).

- Entities are represented by rectangles.
- Relationships are identified as diamond shapes.
- Attributes are denoted by oval shapes.
- Weak entities are represented by two rectangles, one embedded within the other.
- Relationship cardinalities are represented by numeric annotations (of the cardinality values) on the respective links of the relationships.

3.2.1 Relationship

These establish links among entities. Different types of relationships are described below using Figures 3.2 to 3.4.

Unary relationship

- Relationship of degree 1
- Represented by a self loop.

Binary relationship

- Relationship of degree 2
- Representing relationship between two entities.

Ternary relationship

- Relationship of degree 3
- Representing relationship among three entities.

3.3 Mapping between Entities

A relationship maps a subset of members from one entity set to a subset of another. Depending on the ratio of number of members from the two related sets, mapping functions (relationships themselves) can be classified as one-to-one, one-to-many, many-to-one and many-to-many.

Mapping abilities of some relationship is also referred to as its cardinality or cardinality ratio. One-to-one, one-to-many and many-to-one mapping are very commonly found among entities. Many-to-many mapping is, however, a little complicated to implement.

3.3.1 Different Types of Mapping

Different types of mappings are illustrated in Figures 3.5 to 3.8 with the help of entities DEPARTMENT, TEACHER and STUDENTS.

One-to-one relationship

If TEACHERS and DEPARTMENTS are two participating entities, they are connected by the relationship 'IS HEAD OF'. It is a one-to-one mapping because only one of the teachers can be head of a department and vice versa.

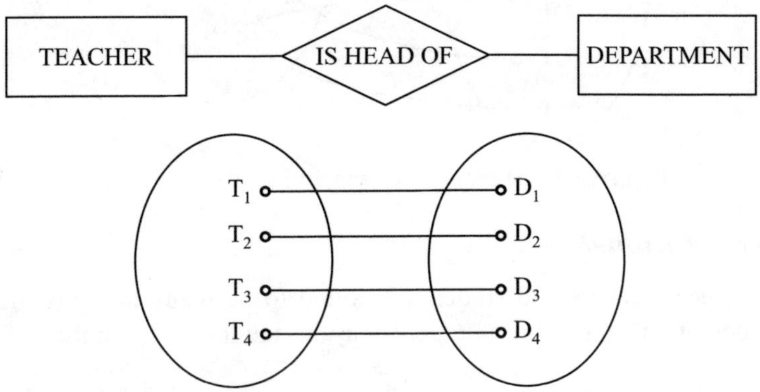

Figure 3.5 One-to-one mapping between entities.

One-to-many relationship

TEACHERS and DEPARTMENTS may also be connected by a one-to-many or many-to-one relationship 'IS MEMBER OF'. Here, a number of teachers are the members of a certain department, and on the contrary, a department has a number of teachers.

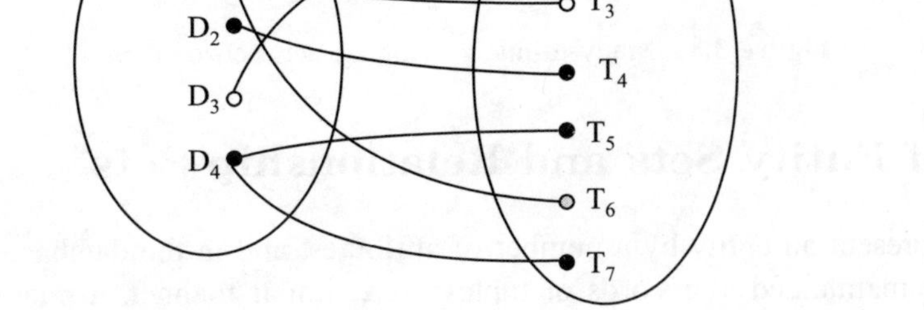

Figure 3.6 One-to-many mapping between entities.

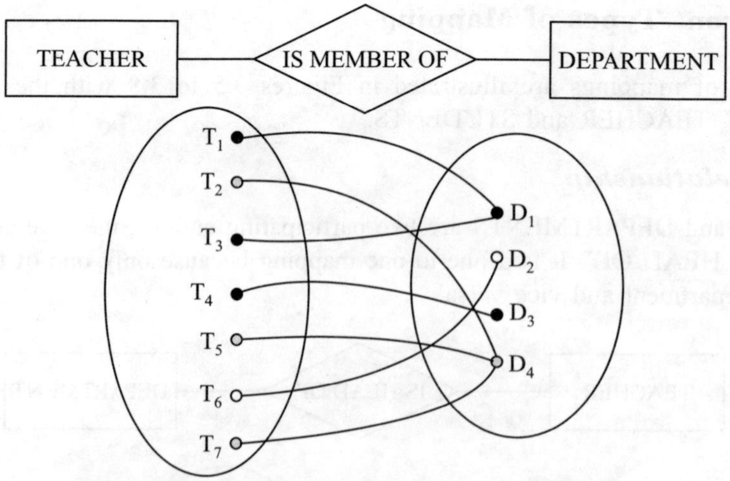

Figure 3.7 Many-to-one mapping between entities.

Many-to-many relationship

A relationship between teachers and students is found to be many-to-many, because a teacher can teach a number of students, and a student may be taught by a number of teachers.

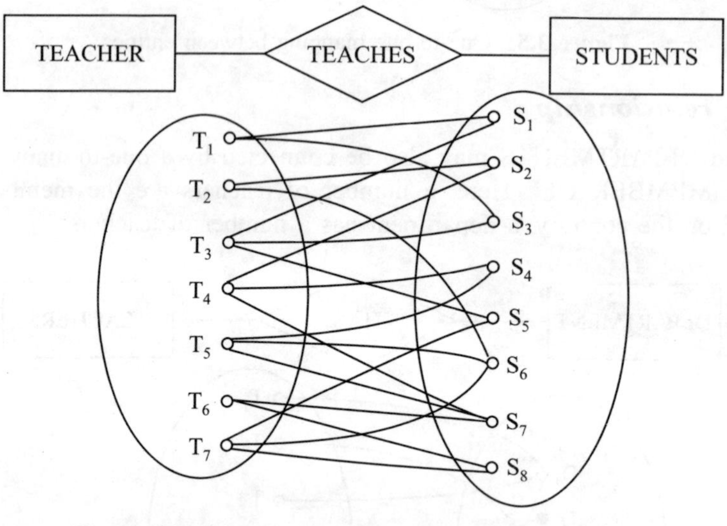

Figure 3.8 Many-to-many mapping between entities.

3.4 Use of Entity Sets and Relationship Sets

We generally represent an entity by a number of attributes, and in the database table, instances of the entity are maintained as records or tuples. In a similar manner, a relationship can also have attributes and can be stored as relationship-tables. Generally, relationship attributes are descriptive in nature. The primary key combination of the participating entities becomes the key of the relationship set. Besides, the relationship set may have its own descriptive attributes. Let us consider an example of two entities *customer* and *account* participating in the relationship *deposits*. Here, *customer#* and *account#* may act as primary keys of the participating entities. But none of the above two entities can stores the details of deposit transactions properly. How to store information like date and amount of deposit, name(s) of depositors, number of deposits? Hence, relationships may need to be maintained as separate tables for keeping transactional data.

A general practice is to use a relationship set to describe actions between entities. After determining this, we can decide what attributes can represent a relationship set, and what others can constitute an entity set.

It is notable here that, although primary keys of the participating entities act as a key of the concerned relationship set, they must not be mentioned in the E-R diagram as specific attributes of the relationship; their participation is implicit.

3.5 Modelling with E-R Diagram

In earlier sections, we have demonstrated the role of E-R diagram in database design process, its components and their representations, properties of different components etc. We can summarize our knowledge as follows:

- E-R diagram is an elegant tool for modelling databases.
- Its components are entities, relationships and attributes (of entities).
- Entities are linked via key attributes. These attributes are shared between the concerned entities.
- E-R diagram yields an abstract model only.
- Only E-R diagram is insufficient for designing a practical database; it must also be supplemented with actual application related processes.

3.5.1 E-R based Design Process

Designing a database for some enterprise is a very complicated process that requires understanding of the applications to be handled. The developer may need to collect information regarding the above from requirements specification documents, by interviewing managers, stakeholders of the enterprise, and also the ordinary system users. We can summarize the steps as follows:

- **Requirements analysis:** The existing system and all necessary documents as supplied by the enterprise must be studied thoroughly and new requirements are recorded. After prolonged discussion with the client and users preparation of requirements-specifications for the new system is to be completed.
- **Identifying entities:** Entities to be represented in the new system must be identified then.
- **Identifying relationships:** Relationships among the attributes and their cardinalities, etc. are to be determined.

- **Identifying entity attributes:** We need to identify a minimal set of attributes for the entities, only those that are needed for running applications concerned. Presence of extraneous attributes not only complicates the design but also causes error and undesired redundancy in the system.
- **Identifying relationship attributes:** It is necessary to identify relationships among entities and their types, i.e. to determine whether the relationship is a one-to-one or one-to-many or many-to-many in nature. At every point, a decision should be taken after a detailed discussion with the managers and users of the system.
- **Drawing the base E-R diagram:** The base E-R diagram is developed from entities and relationships. The underlying authority from the enterprise must conform to the basic design.
- **Drawing the detailed E-R diagram:** The E-R diagram is augmented by the inclusion of attributes for entities and relationships.

After going through the above steps, one can design only a preliminary prototype of the system. This prototype may have to be refined many times as per requirements. After a well agreed E-R diagram is found, the designer starts conversion of the E-R diagram into a logical (Relational) model.

3.5.2 E-R based Design Examples

Here, we shall apply our knowledge in modelling database systems for some practical applications. We shall consider only very simple applications with limited scopes.

ILLUSTRATION 3.1 E-R diagram for Bank

Problem statement

We are to design a bank transaction system for all the banks and their branches in a city. The following specifications, for transactions, are available to us.

- A bank has a number of branches at different cities.
- Each branch has multiple customers.
- Customers have different types of accounts.
- Customers can avail different types of loans from the concerned branch.
- Multiple account and loan facilities available.

Design steps

- Studying problem statement.
- Identifying Entities.
- Identifying entity attributes.
- Identifying key and non-key attributes.
- Identifying Relationships and their cardinalities.
- Identifying relationship attributes.
- Drawing the base E-R diagram.
- Drawing the detailed E-R diagram.

Identifying entities

- Entities are represented by entity sets. Thus, each entity has multiple instances.
- Here, the entities are:
  - BANK
  - BRANCH
  - LOAN
  - ACCOUNT
  - CUSTOMER

Identifying entity attributes

- Here, entity attributes may be:
  - BANK (bank_code, bk_name, bk_address)
  - BRANCH (bank_code, branch#, br_name, br_address)
  - LOAN (loan#, loan_type)
  - ACCOUNT (account#, account_type)
  - CUSTOMER (customer#, cm_name, cm_tel#, cm_address)

Identifying relationships

- Relationships are determined based on the types of transactions needed.
- Here, the relationships are:
  - Each bank has a number of branches, and each branch belongs to a single bank (1 : N).
  - Each branch offers many loans, and each loan is associated to a single branch (1 : N).
  - Each branch maintains multiple accounts, and each account belongs to a single branch (1 : N).
  - Each branch have multiple customers, and each customer belongs to a single branch (1 : N).
  - A loan can be sanctioned to multiple customers, and a customer can avail multiple loans (M : N).
  - An account can be opened jointly by multiple customers, and a customer can have multiple accounts (M : N).

Relationship attributes

- These may be identified as:
  - BANK_LOAN_DETAILS (Bank_code, Branch#, Loan#)
  - BRANCH_ACCOUNT_DETAILS (Bank_code, Branch#, Account#)
  - BRANCH_CUSTOMER_DETAILS (Branch#, Customer#)
  - LOAN_CUSTOMER_DETAILS (Loan#, Customer#, Date_of_Sanction, Interest_rate, Amount, Duration)
  - CUSTOMER_ACCOUNT_DETAILS (Customer#, Account#, Date_of_Opening)

The base E-R diagram for banking system:

The base E-R diagram is shown in Figure 3.9.

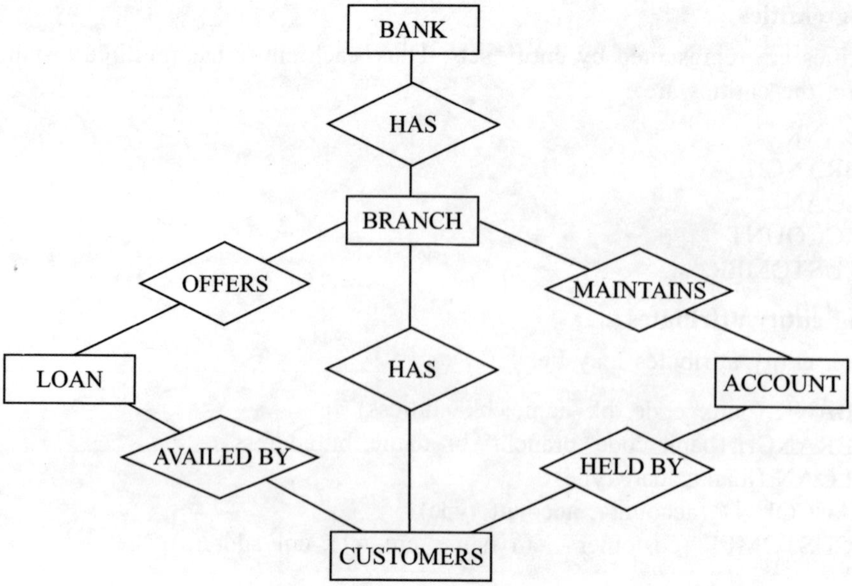

Figure 3.9 Basic E-R diagram for a banking database.

Complete E-R diagram

The complete E-R diagram is shown in Figure 3.10.

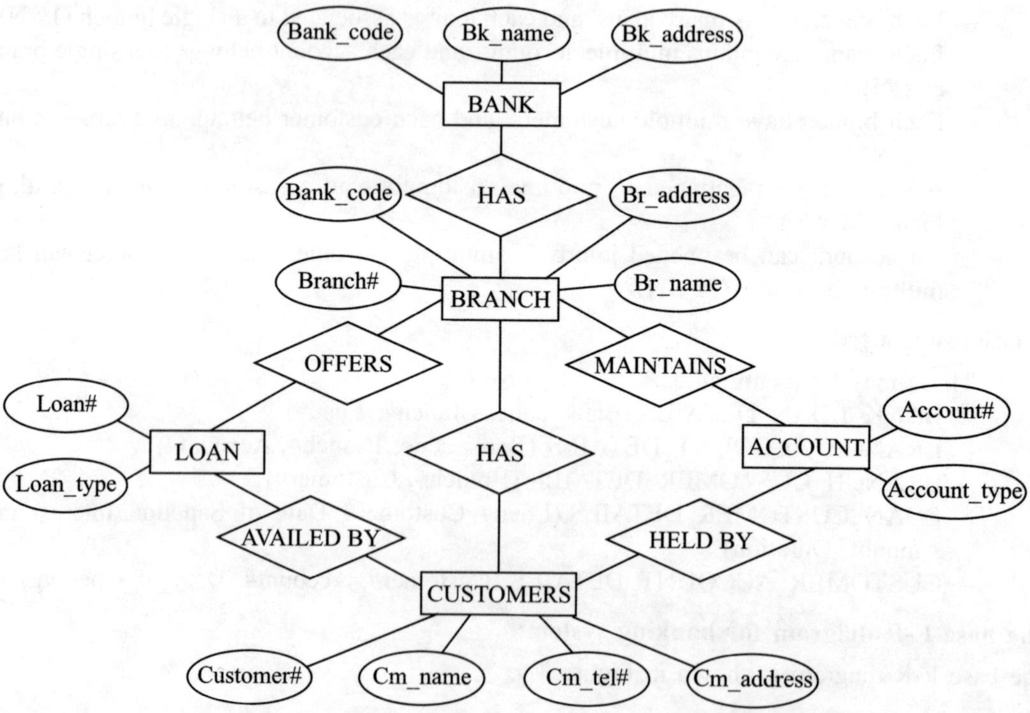

Figure 3.10 Complete E-R diagram for a banking database.

Conceptual to logical design

- Each entity is converted to a Relation (table).
- A Relationship may be stored as a separate relation (table). This table must contain the key attributes of the related entities among others.
- In the case of one-to-one or one-to-many relationships, we may not maintain separate relationship tables.
- This is mandatory for many-to-many situation.

Example sets of entity and relationship tables are shown in Figures 3.11 and 3.12 respectively.

Tables for entities

BANK

Bank_code	Bk_Name	Bk_Address

BRANCH

Bank_code	Branch#	Br_Name	Br_Address

LOAN

Loan#	Loan_type

ACCOUNT

Account#	Account_type

CUSTOMER

Customer#	Cm_Name	Telephone#	Cm_Address

Underlined attributes indicate primary keys

Figure 3.11 Relations for example banking applications.

Tables for relationships

BRANCH_LOAN_DETAILS

Bank_code	Branch#	Loan#

BRANCH_ACCOUNT_DETAILS

Bank_code	Branch#	Account#

BRANCH_CUSTOMER_DETAILS

Branch#	Customer#

LOAN_CUSTOMER_DETAILS

Loan#	Customer#	Date_of_Sanction	Interest_rate	Amount	Duration

CUSTOMER_ACCOUNT_DETAILS

Customer#	Account#	Date_of_Opening

Figure 3.12 Relationships for example banking applications.

Note:

- Base tables are those concerned with different entities.
- These tables contain basic information regarding entities and are relatively fixed in nature.
- Relationship tables are designed and maintained according to the need of the application.
- For the banking application, in our example, the loan_customer_details table is very important because of its many-to-many mapping.
- A single customer can avail a number of loans, and a particular loan may be sanctioned to a number of customers.
- The above is true for customer_account_details also.
- loan_customer_details table has two foreign keys, taken from the concerned base tables. These two foreign keys, in combination, act as the primary key for the relationship table.
- The above is true for customer_account_details also.
- The other attributes in these tables depend on the need of the application.

It is worthwhile to mention here that, actual design of a database may be somewhat different from the E-R diagram based design. Need of the applications to be run may have something that cannot be represented in the E-R diagram itself. Such aspects must be learned from experience. Nature of certain applications may not be fixed always. They may have to be changed from time to time. However, in majority of the cases, only minor modifications need to be incorporated in the design.

It may also be noted that, in general, relationship (along with their attributes) are stored in a relational system as tables. These tables contain primary key attributes of the participating entities plus attributes of the relationship itself (as are specified by the applications concerned). In the case of one-to-one and one-to-many relationships, it may not be very essential to store relationships as separate table. However, for many-to-many relationship it is mandatory. An application is nothing but transaction between entities; and transaction details (time dependent data) should be stored in separate tables other than entity tables.

ILLUSTRATION 3.2 E-R diagram for University

Problem statement

A university requires a database to be designed using its course, teachers and students to manage its regular activities. Problem specifications as available are mentioned below (All the steps are not shown for this example).

- A university has a number of departments.
- Each department offers different courses.
- Students can enroll in different courses.
- Teachers teach different courses of the concerned department.
- A course can be taught by more than one teacher.
- A student can enroll in more than one course offered by different departments.

In this case, some designers may be prompted to start a design using the university itself as an entity. However, it must be remembered that university is the authority.

The base E-R diagram for a university:

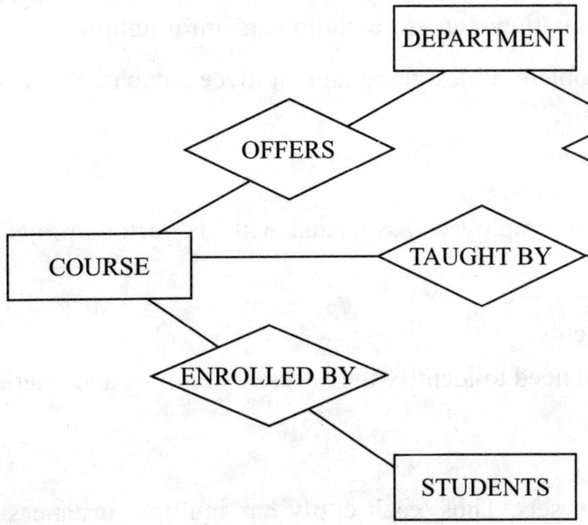

Figure 3.13 Basic E-R diagram for a university database.

The base E-R diagram for a university is shown in Figure 3.13. It contains only entities and relationships interconnecting them. By associating attributes for the entities (attribute name are not shown here), we can get the complete E-R diagram as shown in Figure 3.14.

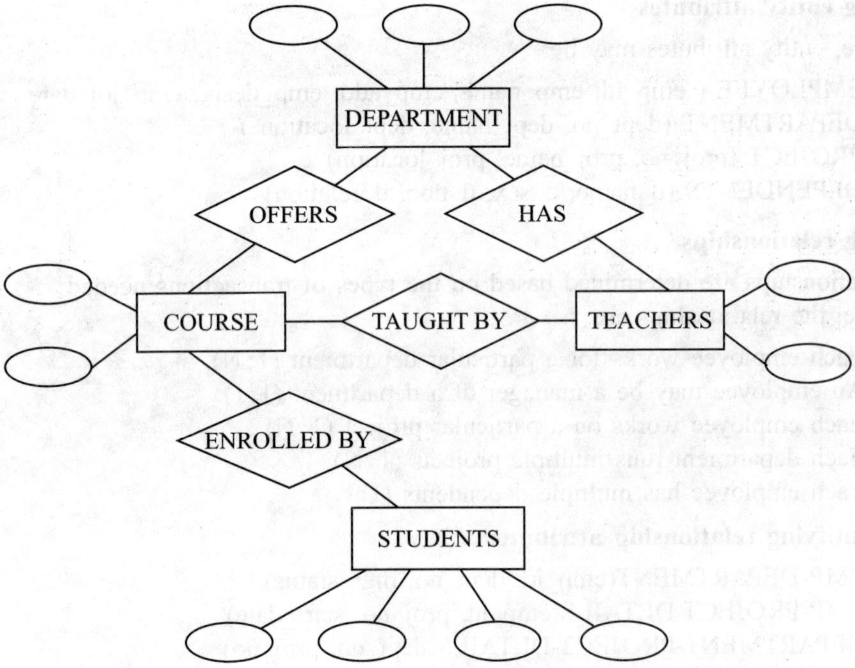

Figure 3.14 Complete E-R diagram for a university database.

It should be noted that, the design is not complete here. We must specify the data structures for different relations and relationships by identifying attributes, key fields etc. Many-to-many relationships must be treated specially, as they can store significant information.

ILLUSTRATION 3.3 Consider the problem of designing an employee database for a company where the following details are available:

- A company has several departments.
- Each department runs several projects.
- Each department has a number of employees associated with its various projects.
- Each department has a manager.
- Each project has a project leader.
- Employees have several dependents.

Before drawing the E-R diagram, we need to identify the necessary entities and relationships, and their attributes.

Identifying entities

- Entities are represented by entity sets. Thus, each entity has multiple instances.
- Here, the entities are:
  - EMPLOYEE
  - DEPARTMENT
  - PROJECTS
  - DEPENDENTS

Identifying entity attributes

- Here, entity attributes may be:
  - EMPLOYEE (emp_id, emp_name, emp_add, emp_desig, emp_joindate, emp_sal)
  - DEPARTMENT (dept_no, dept_name, dept_location)
  - PROJECT (proj_no, proj_name, proj_location)
  - DEPENDENTS (d_name, d_sex, d_dob, d_relation)

Identifying relationships

- Relationships are determined based on the types of transactions needed.
- Here, the relationships are:
  - Each employee works for a particular department (1:N).
  - An employee may be a manager of a department (1:1).
  - Each employee works on a particular project (1:N).
  - Each department runs multiple projects (1:N).
  - Each employee has multiple dependents (1:N).
- **Identifying relationship attributes**
  - EMP-DEPARTMENT(emp_id, dept_no, mgr_status)
  - EMP-PROJECT-DETAILS(emp_id, proj_no, start_date)
  - DEPARTMENT-PROJECT-DETAILS(dept_no, proj_no)
  - EMP-DEPENDENT()

Basic and completed E-R diagram are shown in Figures 3.15 and 3.16 respectively.

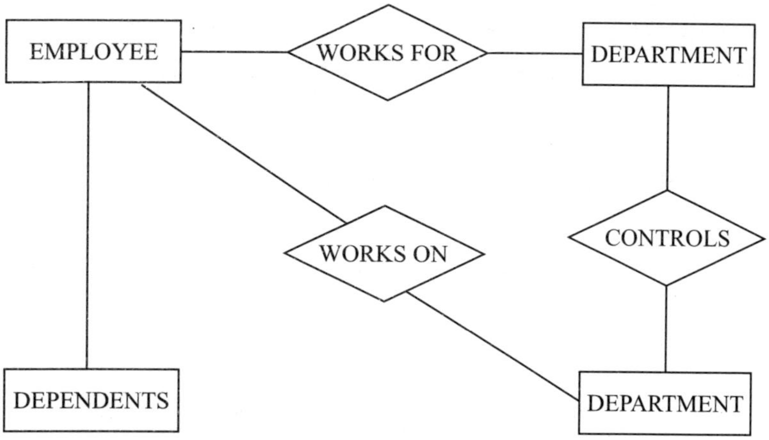

Figure 3.15 Basic E-R diagram for an employee database.

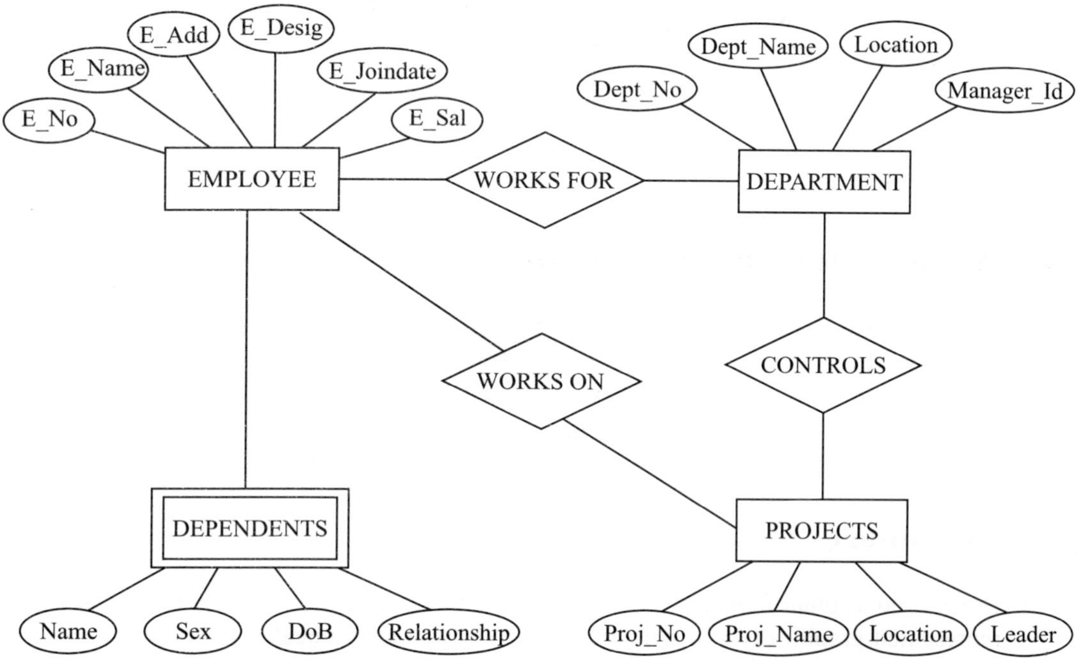

Figure 3.16 Complete E-R diagram for an employee database.

ILLUSTRATION 3.4 Draw the E-R diagram of a departmental store that sales different items. Each department has a number of employees. Items are supplied by a number of suppliers.

E-R diagram for a Departmental Store is shown below in Figure 3.17. Students are advised to complete the design with all necessary details (as shown for earlier examples).

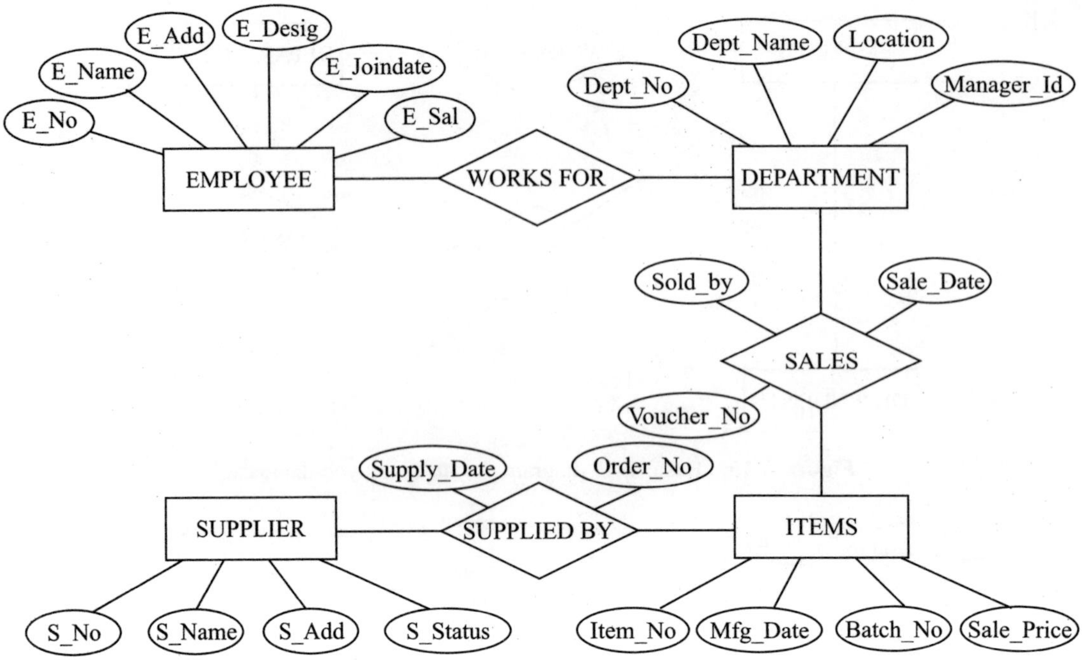

Figure 3.17 Complete E-R diagram for a departmental store database.

3.6 Advantages and Disadvantages of E-R Model

The E-R model is extensively used as a tool in the database design process. Although it is very easy to understand (as it has enough similarity with the real world events and relationships), it is not that straightforward as it is believed to be. There may be important conceptual gaps between any two different designs for the same system. Potential advantages and disadvantages of this modelling tool are mentioned below.

3.6.1 Advantages of E-R Model

- Being a conceptual model, it is easy to understand. Real-life business problems can be represented graphically and hence understood by non-technical persons also.
- It displays entities and relationships in the most natural way. Therefore, it can be realized physically with little efforts.
- Easy to redesign based on the changed need of applications.
- Enhances the database design process.
- Being a higher level abstraction of the system to be designed it serves as an important document for any future upgradation.

3.6.2 Disadvantages of E-R Model

- Before physical realization, conversion into a logical model (relational model) is needed.
- Interpretation of components of the E-R model may lead to some form of ambiguity regarding how to implement the relationship components.
- Without a proper understanding of the system to be designed and applications to be handled, E-R diagram is likely to be misinterpreted leading to an incorrect design.

Exercises

3.1 Define an entity and mention its characteristics.

3.2 What are the roles of a relationship in an E-R diagram? How are they stored in a database?

3.3 What is the role of a E-R diagram in designing a database? What are its components?

3.4 Why do we call the E-R diagram a conceptual model of a database?

3.5 What are the differences between super keys and primary keys? In a relation, there are four attributes. One of them is the primary key. How many super keys can you define?

3.6 Consider a Hospital Management System with the following entities: DEPARTMENTS, DOCTORS, PATIENTS and MEDICINES. A patient can be admitted in one department only but may be treated by doctors of other departments as well. A number of medicines can be prescribed to a patient.

Draw a E-R diagram of the system. Write down attributes of entities, relationships and their primary and foreign keys.

Write down a scheme to find out a list of doctors who did not treat a patient named 'X'.

3.7 What is meant by cardinality of a relationship? What can be the possible attributes of a relationship table when its cardinality ratio is 1:1?

3.8 A relationship is designated as a *m*:*n* one in an E-R diagram. Should you store it in the database as a separate table? Why?

3.9 What are the reasons that we must maintain a table for a relationship having many-to-many mapping between concerned entities?

3.10 How do you transform a many-to-many relationship into a relation?

3.11 Convert the E-R diagram of Exercise 3.3 into a corresponding relational schema.

3.12 What are strong and weak entities? Explain with examples.

3.13 How the schema of an weak entity may be specified? Give an example.

3.14 How can we identify individual instances of a weak entity set? Describe how schema for a weak entity can be defined. How can we convert a weak entity set into a strong entity set?

3.15 Write down the advantages and disadvantages of E-R based modelling.

CHAPTER 4

Principles of Relational Database Management Systems

A Relational Database Management System (RDBMS) is based on Relational Data Model. In this model data are presented to the user in tabular forms (called Tables or Relations). Each row of a table represents a record of information regarding a certain entity of concern, and each column represents an attribute or characteristic property of that entity. Although a base relation may be large and could contain many records and attributes, application users may create their own views by the selection of desired records and attributes.

RDBMS is based on strong mathematical foundations of relational algebra and relational calculus which enable us to manipulate information systematically. An ideal RDBMS should maintain some desirable properties defined by its developer, Dr. E.F. Codd. Using relational mathematics and maintaining characteristic properties allows us to develop robust and useful relational database systems for real-life applications.

4.1 Foundations of Relational Model

The relational model is direct descendant of the so called E-R model, and is based on strong theoretical and mathematical foundations. This model was proposed by Dr. E.F. Codd and he defined its organization, constraints and manipulation strategies. These properties of a relational database make it different from those based on the E-R model.

4.1.1 Relation

Mathematically, a Relation is a subset of the Cartesian product of two or more sets of values from some Domains.

Cartesian product of two sets S_1 and S_2 of cardinality n_1 and n_2 respectively contains all possible $(n_1 \times n_2)$ 2-tuples formed by concatenation of a value from S_1 and a value from S_2, in that order.

The following example clarifies the notion of relations.

Consider two sets N (name) and R (roll no) where N = {X, Y, Z} and R = {1, 2, 3}. Find Cartesian product of N and R, and form a relation having distinct attribute values for all instances.

- The Cartesian product of sets R and N is
  R × N = {(1, X), (1, Y), (1, Z), (2, X), (2, Y), (2, Z), (3, X), (3, Y), (3, Z)}.
- A subset of the product that contains 2-tuples having different values for each position is
  S = {(1, X), (2, Y), (3, Z)}.
- Subset S is a relation between R and N.

Tabular presentation:

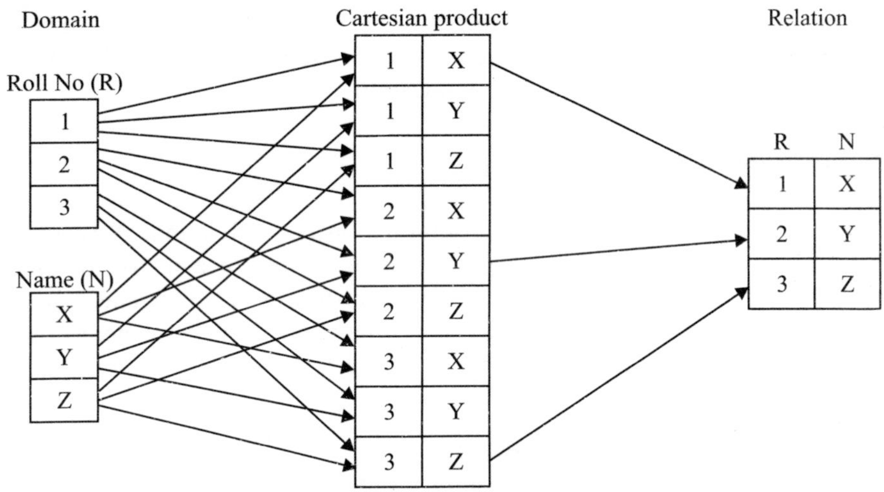

Figure 4.1 Cartesian product and formation of a relation.

4.1.2 Relational Schema and Instances

A relation is, therefore, formed by the process of Cartesian product followed by the selection of tuples from the product. In preceding example, we have developed a product by taking elements from two domains, viz., **Roll Number (R)** and **Name (N)**. After that we have selected three suitable tuples to get the final relation called **Students**. Here, the relation Students has two attributes **Roll Number (R)** and **Name (N).** These two attribute names constitute what is called a schema for the relation. Therefore, the schema for the relation **Students** is represented as

Roll No	Name

The current contents of a relation are called an instance of the relation. In our case, the three tuples (as shown below) present in the relation **Students** constitutes an instance of **Students**.

1	X
2	Y
3	Z

As already mentioned in Chapter 3, schema may be of three different categories, conceptual and physical, we can elaborate this concept here with our example. Let the database stores more attributes regarding a student, such as **Address, Age, Class, Year Admitted** etc. Then the overall or conceptual schema for relation **Students** may be represented as

Roll No	Name	Address	Age	Class	Year admitted

In this case, the former schema is a logical schema, and the latter is the conceptual schema. The former one consists of a subset of attributes from the set of all attributes. Since different application programs need different subset of attributes of some entity, we have many different logical schemas, one corresponding to each application.

4.1.3 Organization of a Relation

The basic structure, for the presentation of information, is a Relation. A relation contains information in rows and columns, in a manner similar to that of a matrix or tabular chart. The difference is that in a matrix data structure we can store only homogeneous data (data of the same type), while a relation (or database table) may contain heterogeneous data (data of different types) as well. The organization of data in a relation or table can be specified by the following properties:

- Data are organized in rows and columns.
- Each row contains a data record for some entity of concern.
- Each row contains a distinct record.
- Each column represents an attribute of the entity of concern.
- Each column has a distinct name (attribute name).
- Each column maintains homogeneous data only.
- Ordering of rows is unimportant.
- Ordering of columns is unimportant.
- Each cell of the table contains isolated atomic values only.

The structure of an example relation (table) is shown below.

NAME	YEAR	ROLL-NO	ADDRESS	CATEGORY

This relation is named "Students" relation, as it contains students' information. This relation has five columns corresponding to attributes "NAME", "YEAR", "ROLL-NO", "ADDRESS" and "CATEGORY" respectively. Note that, while attributes "YEAR" and "ROLL-NO" contains numeric values the other attributes represent character (string) values. In the above shown form the relation is empty, i.e., it contains no records. Now, one may insert any number of records into the relation. For example, if we insert the record

<NAME = "Ram"; YEAR = 2; ROLL-NO = 6; ADDRESS = "Kolkata"; CATEGORY = "General">

the relation looks like

NAME	YEAR	ROLL-NO	ADDRESS	CATEGORY
Ram	2	6	Kolkata	General

The "Students" table now contains the information that Ram is a student of 2nd year having roll number 6 and residing in Kolkata. In similar fashion, any number of records can be inserted into the table.

4.1.4 Data Manipulation

A relational database system provides sufficient facilities for processing data stored in it. Such facilities includes convenient data structures, easy access methodologies, data definition and manipulation languages, query languages, library routines, control program constructs etc. The relational system supports two types of languages based on *relational algebra* and *relational calculus*. The most commercially available language SQL (Structured Query Language) is based on the relational algebra.

4.1.5 Data Independence

Schemas are abstract views of the data stored physically in a computer's storage. Depending on the varying requirements of different application programs, physical data may be reorganized in memory using different data structures. But this modification of physical data structure should be transparent to the application programs or the DBMS, i.e., modification of physical data structure should not imply any change in the logical or conceptual views. In other words, physical schema should be independent of logical or conceptual schemas. This is called *physical data independence.*

In some cases, the conceptual view may be redefined by the administrator by addition of a new attribute or relocation of attributes. Such modification in the conceptual view should not, in any way, prohibit the existing applications to have earlier logical views. In other words, conceptual views should be altered without affecting existing logical schemas. This is called *logical data independence.*

4.1.6 Integrity Constraints

Integrity constraints are applied over a database in order to maintain consistency of data. Any modification of data by authorized users must satisfy these constraints. Two types of restrictions are generally employed.

- **Entity integrity**
  — Implies that no primary key attribute value can be NULL. Attribute values of a primary key (PK) are used for unique identification of a record in a relation. A NULL value does not have the capacity of unique identification.
- **Referential integrity**
  — If a non-key attribute (NK) of some relation R_1 plays the role of primary key of another relation R_2, then no value of attribute NK in relation R_1 can be NULL. In such a situation, R_1 is called a referred relation and R_2 is called a referring relation. Here NK is a foreign key of R_1.

A *foreign key*, in a relation R_1, is a set of attributes of R_1 which acts as primary key in another relation R_2. If we consider a SUPPLIER-PARTS database, that contains two relations SUPPLIER (SUPPLIER#, PART#, QUANTITY) and PARTS (PART#, PCOST), then the attributes SUPPLIER# and PART# are primary keys of SUPPLIER and PARTS respectively. And PART# also acts a foreign key of the relation SUPPLIER. Therefore, a foreign key can be used to identify records in another relation in which it is a primary key.

4.2 Application Areas of RDBMS

RDBMS finds its applications in almost all enterprises/organizations running real-life transactions on a regular basis. Examples are:

- Bank, insurance, finance
- Airlines, railways, telecom
- Universities, institutions
- Hospitals, Health care
- Manufacturing, marketing, sales
- Management
- And others.

4.3 Advantages of RDBMS

Following are the advantages of RDBMS.

- **Flexible organization:** Data are presented in tabular form. Physical organization of data supports access of data in many different forms according to the needs of varying applications.
- **Security:** Security restrictions can be applied to specific tables or records and attributes.

- **Data independency:** Data can be served to applications in desired forms without regard to its physical organization.
- **Data manipulation:** Data retrieval and manipulation are supported by mathematical operations of relational algebra and relational calculus.
- **Easy to use:** Logical views of data are presented in tabular forms consisting of rows and columns. Each component of a row or a column can be easily accessed by the user.

4.4 RDBMS Packages and their Developers

The details of software packages and their developers are shown in Table 4.1.

Table 4.1 RDBMS Packages and Developers

Software package	Developer
Ingress	Computer Associates Intl. Inc.
Oracle	Oracle Corporation
Informix	Informix Software Inc.
Sybase	Sybase Inc.
DB2	IBM
SQL Server	Microsoft
MYSQL	MYSQL AB, Sweden

4.5 CODD's Rules for RDBMS

The developer of the concept of RDBMS, Dr. E. F. Codd, defined some characteristic features for an ideal relational database system. There are 12 such characteristics or rules mentioned below.

- **Information rule:** All data in a relational system should be represented only in exactly one form, i.e., in tabular form only.
- **Guaranteed access rule:** All data items should be accessible to the user without ambiguity. Appropriate references should be made using table name, primary key and column names.
- **Systematic treatment of NULL values:** The RDBMS should appropriately handle NULL values for some attribute. NULL values should not be treated as ZEROS or SPACES.
- **Dynamic online catalog rule:** The DBMS should maintain a system catalog. This catalog holds names, structures and links for tables and other items of the database.
- **Comprehensive data sublanguage rule:** The DBMS should support at least one clearly defined language for the purpose of data definition, data manipulation and transaction control operations.
- **View updation rule:** All views that are theoretically updatable should also be updatable by the relational system.
- **High level insert, update and delete rule:** The capability of handling a database table or a derived table as a single operand applies not only to the retrieval of data, but to insertion, deletion and updation of data also.

- **Physical data independence rule:** Application programs and terminal activities should remain logically unimpaired whenever any changes are made either to the storage structure or access methodologies.
- **Logical data independence rule**: Application programs and terminal activities should remain logically unimpaired whenever any changes are made to the database table descriptions (conceptual views).
- **Integrity rule:** Integrity restrictions (constraints) specific to any particular relational database must be definable in the relational data sub-language and storable in the catalog, not in the application programs.
- **Distribution independence rule:** A user should be completely unaware of the fact that a database is distributed (applicable when a distributed database is in use).
- **Non-subversion rule:** If a relational system has a low level (single record at a time) language, that low level cannot be used to subvert or bypass the integrity rules and constraints expressed in the higher level relational language (multiple records at a time).

Besides these individual rules, Dr. Codd also proposed an overall rule regarding a relational system which states that, *if a system claims or advertised to be a relational DBMS system, it must be able to manage database entirely through its relational capabilities only.*

4.6 Relational Operations

Relational mathematics is the underlying mathematical tool behind execution of a relational query. Generally, query languages are non-procedural languages—an instruction or statement that does reveal what will be the expected result, but not how to achieve the result. However, each query must be treated as a combination of mathematical operations that are performed in sequence to obtain the result. Hence, we can express a query in mathematical notation as expression. Since tables or relations are nothing but the sets of records, and columns are nothing but the sets of attribute values, set theoretic relational operations are applied to solve queries. Query languages are, therefore, based on set theoretic relational mathematics. Query languages can be classified into two broad categories:

- **Algebraic languages:** Here queries are expressed using specific algebraic operators to the concerned relations. Underlying mathematics is relational algebra.
- **Predicate calculus languages:** Here queries generate a set of tuples from one or more relations that satisfy some specific predicate. Underlying mathematics is relational calculus.

4.6.1 Relational Algebra

In Relational algebra there are several specific operations for processing of queries. These operations accept one or two relations as inputs and produce a new relation as output. Depending on one or two relations are used as inputs, the operations may be unary or binary. There are five basic or fundamental operations; *union, set difference, Cartesian product, selection* and *projection*. Besides, a number of composite operations that can be implemented as combinations of the basic operations are also very commonly used. These operations include *intersection, quotient* and *join* operations.

Basic operations

- Set union: Union of items from two or more different sets.
- Set difference: Difference of items between two different sets.
- Cartesian product: Combination of items from two or more different sets.
- Projection: Isolation of selective attributes from a set of attributes.
- Selection: Isolation of selective records from a set of records.

Additional operations

- Set intersection
- Quotient/Set division
- Join
- Natural join

Now, we will discuss these operations one by one

- Set union → $R \cup S$
- Set difference → $R - S$
- Cartesian product → $R \times S$
    - — R is of arity $k_1 \rightarrow R^{(k_1)}$
    - — S is of arity $k_2 \rightarrow R^{(k_2)}$
    - — $R \times S$ is of arity $(k_1 + k_2)$
    - — $R \times S$ contains all attributes of R followed by those of S.
- Projection → $S = \Pi_{i_1, i_2, \ldots, i_m}(R)$
    - — Projection on the specified attributes of R.
    - — $i_1, i_2, \ldots, i_m$ are serial numbers of the specified attributes.
- Selection → $S = \sigma_F(R)$
    - — F is a formula of the following forms:
        - $S = \sigma_{i_1='x', i_2='y', \ldots, i_m='z'}(R)$
          i_1th attribute has value '*x*', i_2th attribute has value '*y*', and so on.
        - $S = \sigma_{1='x', 2='y', \ldots, m='z'}(R)$
          1st attribute has value '*x*', 2nd attribute has value '*y*', and so on.
        - $S = \sigma_{1='x' \vee 2='y', \ldots, m!='z'}(R)$
          arithmetic and logical operations are allowed in the formula.
    - — F may contain arithmetic and logical operators.
- Set Intersection → $R \cap S \rightarrow R - (R - S)$
    - — Tuples that are in R but not in S.

- Quotient → R ÷ S

— Arity of R and S are '*r*' and '*s*' respectively.
— $S \neq \emptyset$
— R ÷ S is the set of $(r - s)$-tuples '*t*' such that for all *s*-tuple '*u*' in S, '*tu*' is a tuple in R.
— Let $m = r - s$.

Step by step description of the Quotient or Set division operation

— Let, $T = \Pi_{1,2,\ldots,m}(R)$
— Let, $V = \Pi_{1,2,\ldots,m}((T \times S) - R)$
— Then, $R \div S = T - V$
— $R \div S = \Pi_{1,2,\ldots,m}(R) - \Pi_{1,2,\ldots,m}((T \times S) - R)$
— $R \div S = \Pi_{1,2,\ldots,m}(R) - \Pi_{1,2,\ldots,m}((\Pi_{1,2,\ldots,m}(R) \times S) - R)$

- Join → $R \underset{i\theta j}{\bowtie} S$

— θ is an arithmetic comparison operator
— Can be expressed as $\sigma_{i\ \theta\ (r+j)}(R \times S)$
— Where '*r*' is the arity of R.

- Natural Join → R ⋈ S
— Applicable when R and S have one or more common attributes.

Steps to compute natural join

— Compute R × S
— For each common attribute A, select from R × S, those tuples whose values agree the relation R · A = S · A
— For each attribute A above, project out the column S · A
— $R \bowtie S = \Pi_{i_1, i_2, \ldots, i_m}(\sigma_{R \cdot A_1 = S \cdot A_1 \wedge \ldots \wedge R \cdot A_k = S \cdot A_k}(R \times S))$

- Here, $i_1, i_2, \ldots, i_m$ is the list of all components of R × S in order, except the components $S \cdot A_1, \ldots, S \cdot A_k$.

We have seen that the set of basic relational algebraic operators {X, ∪, –, σ, Π} is a *complete set.* This implies that, all other relational algebraic operators can be implemented as combination of some of the basic operators.

ILLUSTRATION 4.1 Consider the following two relations. Find the union and intersection of R_1 and S_1.

R_1 =

A	B	C
a	*b*	*c*
b	*c*	*a*
c	*a*	*b*
c	*b*	*a*

S_1 =

A	B	C
b	*a*	*c*
c	*b*	*a*
c	*a*	*b*
a	*b*	*c*

Solution Set union means combination of all distinct tuples. Hence we arrive at

$R_1 \cup S_1$ =

A	B	C
a	*b*	*c*
b	*c*	*a*
c	*a*	*b*
c	*b*	*a*
b	*a*	*c*

Set difference of R and S means combination of all different tuples that are in R but not in S. Hence we arrive at

$R_1 - S_1$ =

A	B	C
b	*c*	*a*

ILLUSTRATION 4.2 Consider the following two relations R and S. Find the Cartesian product of R and S.

R_2 =

A	B	C
a	*b*	*c*
b	*c*	*a*
c	*a*	*b*

S_2 =

A	B	C
b	*a*	*c*
c	*b*	*a*

Solution Cartesian product means concatenation of all different tuples from R and S. Hence we arrive at

$R_2 \times S_2$ =

R·A	R·B	R·C	S·A	S·B	S·C
a	*b*	*c*	*b*	*a*	*c*
b	*c*	*a*	*b*	*a*	*c*
c	*a*	*b*	*b*	*a*	*c*
a	*b*	*c*	*c*	*b*	*a*
b	*c*	*a*	*c*	*b*	*a*
c	*a*	*b*	*c*	*b*	*a*

ILLUSTRATION 4.3 Consider the relations R_1. Find projection of R over the first two attributes, and perform selection of tuples from R where the second attribute has value '*a*'.

Solution Result of projection $\Pi_{1,2}(R_1)$ is

P =

A	B
a	*b*
b	*c*
c	*a*
c	*b*

Result of selection $\sigma_{2='b'}(R_1)$ is

Q =

A	B	C
a	*b*	*c*
c	*b*	*a*

ILLUSTRATION 4.4 Find intersection of R_1 and S_1 using set difference only.

Solution We know that Set intersection: $R \wedge S = R - (R - S)$
Here,

$P_1 = R_1 - S_1 =$

A	B	C
b	*c*	*a*

and

$P_2 = R_1 - P_1 =$

A	B	C
a	*b*	*c*
c	*a*	*b*
c	*b*	*a*

ILLUSTRATION 4.5 Find quotient of the following relations R_3 and S_3.

$R_3 =$

A	B	C	D
a	*b*	*c*	*d*
a	*b*	*e*	*f*
b	*c*	*e*	*f*
e	*d*	*c*	*d*
e	*d*	*e*	*f*
a	*b*	*d*	*e*

$S_3 =$

C	D
c	*d*
e	*f*

Solution We know that, quotient of relations R and S is defined by the following relational steps, where arity of R and S are *r* and *s* respectively and that of $R \div S$ is $m = r - s$.

1. $T = \Pi_{1,2,\ldots,m}(R)$
2. $V = \Pi_{1,2,\ldots,m}((T \times S) - R)$
3. $R \div S = T - V$

Here, ignoring attribute names, we get

T =

a	*b*
b	*c*
e	*d*

T × S =

a	*b*	*c*	*d*
b	*c*	*c*	*d*
e	*d*	*c*	*d*
a	*b*	*e*	*f*
b	*c*	*e*	*f*
e	*d*	*e*	*f*

T × S − R =

b	*c*	*c*	*d*

V =

b	*c*

R ÷ S = T − V =

a	*b*
e	*d*

ILLUSTRATION 4.6 Consider the following two relations R and S. Compute $\sigma_{A=C}$ (R × S).

R =

A	**B**
a	*b*
c	*b*
d	*e*

S =

B	**C**
b	*c*
e	*a*
b	*d*

Solution

R × S =

a	*b*	*b*	*c*
a	*b*	*e*	*a*
a	*b*	*b*	*d*
c	*b*	*b*	*c*
c	*b*	*e*	*a*
c	*b*	*b*	*d*
d	*e*	*b*	*c*
d	*e*	*e*	*a*
d	*e*	*b*	*d*

$\sigma_{A=C}$ (R × S) =

a	*b*	*e*	*a*
c	*b*	*b*	*c*
d	*e*	*b*	*d*

ILLUSTRATION 4.7 Entities of the relational database are:

Consider the following schema of an EMPLOYEE database.

Employee(e_no, e_name, e_address, e_sal)

Department (d_no, d_name, d_location)

Project (p_no, p_name)

Relationships of the employee database are:

Works_for (e_no, d_no)

Works_on (e_no, p_no, duration)

Write the relational algebraic expressions for the following queries related to the above EMPLOYEE database.

1. List names of employees who are working for the "Production" department.
2. List names of employees who are not working in any project.
3. List names of employees who are members of the "Production" department but not associated to any project.
4. List names of employees who are associated to projects "P_1" and "P_2".

Solution

1. Π_{e_name}(Employee ⋈ ($\sigma_{d\_name=\text{"PRODUCTION"}}$ (Department)) ⋈ Works_for)
2. Π_{e_name}(Employee) – Π_{e_name} (Employee ⋈ Works_on)
3. Π_{e_name} (Employee – $\sigma_{d\_name=\text{"PRODUCTION"}}$ (Π_{e_name} (Employee ⋈ Works_on)) ⋈ Works_for)
4. This problem can be solved using the following four steps. 'A' denotes the project numbers for "P_1" and "P_2". 'B' represents the employee numbers who works on projects "P_1" or "P_2". 'C' represents the employee numbers who are not working on projects "P_1" or "P_2". 'D' is the required set of names.

   A = Π_{p_no}($\Pi_{p\_name=\text{"}P_1\text{" OR } p\_name=\text{"}P_2\text{"}}$(Projects)

   B = Π_{e_no}((Π_{e_no} (Works_on) – A) ⋈ Works_on)

   C = Π_{e_no} (Works_on) – B

   D = Π_{e_name} (Employee ⋈ C)

4.6.2 Relational Calculus

Relational calculus is a mathematical tool that follows the principles of first order predicate calculus derived from the field of logic.

Query expressions in tuple relational calculus takes the following general form:

$$\{t \mid \Psi\ (t)\}$$

where t is a tuple variable representing a tuple of some fixed length (generally a tuple of length or arity k is written as $t^{(k)}$), and Ψ is a formula built from the atoms and a collection of tuple calculus operators. Atoms of formula Ψ are of the following three types:

1. $R(s)$ is an atom, where R is a relation name and s is a tuple variable. This atom asserts the fact that s is a tuple in relation R.

2. $s[i]\ \theta\ u[j]$ is an atom, where s and u are tuple variables and θ is an arithmetic comparison operator like =, <, >, ≤ etc. This atom asserts the fact that the ith component of s maintains the relation θ with the jth component of u.
3. $s[i]\ \theta\ a$ and $a\ \theta\ s[i]$ are atoms, where s is a tuple variable, a is a constant and θ is an arithmetic comparison operator, as before. These atoms assert the fact that the ith component of s maintains the relation θ with the constant a.

Free and bound occurrence of tuple variables

Free variables are free from any restrictions to be applied over them. They are similar to global variables in programming languages. Bound variables, on the other hand, bound by some restrictions. They have similarity with local variables in programming languages. The occurrence of a variable may be free or bounded depending on whether or not they are introduced with *for all* (∀) or *there exists* (∃) quantifiers.

Formulae are defined as:

1. Every atom is a formula.
2. If Ψ_1 and Ψ_2 are formulas, then $\Psi_1 \wedge \Psi_2$, $\Psi_1 \vee \Psi_2$, and $!\Psi_1$ are formulae. The above formulae imply "Ψ_1 and Ψ_2 are both true" , Ψ_1 or Ψ_2 is true , and "Ψ_1 is not true" respectively. The occurrences of tuple variables in $\Psi_1 \wedge \Psi_2$, $\Psi_1 \vee \Psi_2$, and $!\Psi_1$ are free or bound as they are free or bound in Ψ_1 or Ψ_2, depending on where they occur. It is important to note that an occurrence of tuple variable s could be free in Ψ_1 while another occurrence of s may be bound in Ψ_2, or conversely.
   If Ψ is a formula, then $(\exists s)\ (\Psi)$ is a formula. The occurrences of s that are bound in Ψ are also bound to $(\exists s)$ in $(\exists s)\ (\Psi)$.
   If Ψ is a formula, the $(\forall s)(\Psi)$ is a formula. Free occurrences of s in Ψ are bound to $(\forall s)$ in $(\forall s)(\Psi)$ and other occurrences of s in Ψ are treated as in (3) above.
3. Parentheses may be placed formulae as needed. The relevant order of operator precedence is; at first arithmetic comparison operators, then quantifiers ∃ and ∀, and then !, ∧, ∨, in that order.
4. Nothing else is a formula.

A tuple relation calculus expression is an expression of the form

$$\{t \mid \Psi(t)\}$$

Where t is the only free tuple variable in Ψ.

Transforming universal and existential quantifiers

A universal expression containing quantifier can be transformed into an equivalent expression containing an existential quantifier and vice versa. The following steps are needed for this purpose.

- Replace one type of quantifier into the other and precede the quantifier by NOT (!) operator.
- Replace AND (∧) with OR (∨) operator and vice versa.
- Formula is preceded by NOT (!) operator and, hence, negated formula becomes affirmed and vice versa.

The following are some examples of such transformation:

$(\exists t)\ (\Psi) \equiv !(\exists t)\ (!\Psi)$
$(\forall t)\ (\Psi) \equiv !(\forall t)\ (!\Psi)$
$(\exists t)\ (\Psi_1 \wedge \Psi_2) \equiv !(\forall t)\ (!\Psi_1 \vee !\Psi_2)$
$(\forall t)\ (\Psi_1 \vee \Psi_2) \equiv !(\exists t)\ (!\Psi_1 \wedge !\Psi_2)$
$(\exists t)\ (!\Psi_1 \vee !\Psi_2) \equiv !(\forall t)\ (!\Psi_1 \wedge !\Psi_2)$
$(\forall t)\ (!\Psi_1 \wedge !\Psi_2) \equiv !(\exists t)\ (!\Psi_1 \vee !\Psi_2)$

The '≡' symbol represents equivalent to.

Conversion of basic expressions between relational algebra and relation calculus

- **Union:** $R \cup S \rightarrow \{t \mid R(t) \vee S(t)\}$
  The above expression implies the set of all tuples t such that t is in R or in S.
- **Set difference:** $R - S \rightarrow \{t \mid R(t) \wedge !S(t)\}$
  The above expression implies the set of all tuples t such that t is in R but not in S.
- **Cartesian product:** $R \times S \rightarrow \{t^{(r+s)} \mid (\exists u^{(r)})\ (\exists v^{(r)})\ (R(u) \wedge S(v) \wedge ((t[1] = u[1]) \wedge (t[2] = u[2]) \wedge \ldots \wedge (t[r] = u[r])) \wedge ((t[r+1] = v[1]) \wedge (t[r+2] = v[2]) \ldots \wedge (t[r+s] = v[s]))\}$
  The above expression implies the set of all tuples t of arity $(r + s)$, such that there exist tuples u and v where the first r components of t form u and the next s components of t form v.
- **Projection:** $\Pi_{i_1, i_2, \ldots, i_k}(R) \rightarrow \{t^{(k)} \mid (\exists u)\ (R(u) \wedge ((t[1] = u[i_1]) \wedge (t[2] = u[i_2]) \wedge \ldots \wedge (t[k] = u[i_k]))\}$
- **Selection:** $\sigma_F(R) \rightarrow \{t \mid R(t) \wedge F'\}$
  where F′ is the formula F with each operand i, denoting the ith component, replaced by $t[i]$.

ILLUSTRATION 4.8 Write down the tuple relational expression for natural join operation.

Solution This can be treated as a three-step process as described below.

Step 1: $Q = R \times S = \{t^{(r+s)} \mid (\exists u^{(r)})\ (\exists v^{(r)})\ (R(u) \wedge S(v) \wedge ((t[1] = u[1]) \wedge (t[2] = u[2]) \wedge \ldots \wedge (t[r] = u[r])) \wedge ((t[r+1] = v[1]) \wedge (t[r+2] = v[2]) \ldots \wedge (t[r+s] = v[s]))\}$

Step 2: $T = \sigma_F\ (Q) = \{t \mid (\forall t)Q(t) \wedge (t[i] = t[j])\}$.

Step 3: $W = \Pi_{i_1, i_2, \ldots, i_k}(R) = \{t^{(k)} \mid (\exists u)\ (R(u) \wedge ((t[1] = u[i_1]) \wedge (t[2] = u[i_2]) \wedge \ldots \wedge (t[k] = u[i_k])$ where W is the result of the desired join operation.

ILLUSTRATION 4.9 Assuming R and S are of arity 3 and 2 respectively, convert the expression $\Pi_{1,5}(\sigma_{2=4 \wedge 3=4}\ (R \times S))$.

Solution We can solve the conversion problem in a stepwise fashion.

$$R \times S = \{t^{(5)} \mid (\exists u^{(3)})\ (\exists v^{(2)})\ (R(u) \wedge S(v) \wedge (t[1] = u[1]) \wedge (t[2] = u[2]) \wedge (t[3] = u[3]) \wedge (t[4] = v[1]) \wedge (t[5] = v[2])\}$$

$$\sigma_{2=4 \wedge 3=4}(R \times S) = \{t^{(5)} \mid (\exists u^{(3)})(\exists v^{(2)})(R(u) \wedge S(v) \wedge (t[1] = u[1]) \wedge (t[2] = u[2]) \wedge (t[3] = u[3]) \wedge (t[4] = v[1]) \wedge (t[5] = v[2]) \wedge (t[2] = t[4]) \wedge (t[3] = t[4])\}$$

$$\Pi_{1,5}(\sigma_{2=4 \wedge 3=4}(R \times S)) = \{w^{(2)} \mid (\exists t^{(5)})(\exists u^{(3)})(\exists v^{(2)})(R(u) \wedge S(v) \wedge (t[1] = u[1]) \wedge (t[2] = u[2]) \wedge (t[3] = u[3]) \wedge (t[4] = v[1]) \wedge (t[5] = v[2]) \wedge (t[2] = t[4]) \wedge (t[3] = t[4]) \wedge (w[1] = u[1]) \wedge (w[2] = v[2])\}$$

The above expression can also be expressed as, by removing the extra tuple variable t as

$$\Pi_{1,5}(\sigma_{2=4 \wedge 3=4}(R \times S)) = \{w^{(2)} \mid (\exists u^{(3)})(\exists v^{(2)})(R(u) \wedge S(v) \wedge (u[2] = v[2]) \wedge (u[3] = v[2])(w[1] = u[1]) \wedge (w[2] = v[2])\}$$

ILLUSTRATION 4.10 Write down the relational algebra expression for the following relational calculus expression.

$$\{t^{(2)} \mid R(t) \Psi (\exists u^{(2)})(S(u) \Psi \wedge !\ (u[1] = (t[2])\}$$

Solution Here, tuples are extracted from relation R only. Relation S used for defining a condition among attributes of R and S. Hence, the desired expression will be:

$$\sigma_{S.1 \neq R.2}(R)$$

Exercises

4.1 Write the mathematical basics of a relational database design.

4.2 Write down integrity rules for database design.

4.3 What is data independence? What is its importance?

4.4 Write down Codd's rules for relational database.

4.5 What are relational algebra and relational calculus? What are their importance?

4.6 Write down expressions for five basic operations of relational algebra. Can we say that these operations form a universal set for relational operators?

4.7 Given two relational schema R = (A, B, C) and S = (D, E, F). Tuples over R and S are denoted as r and s respectively. Write down expressions in relational algebra to compute the following:

(i) List attribute A from R.
(ii) List all tuples of R where attribute B has value 17.
(iii) Compute Cartesian of R and S.
(iv) Select first and fifth attributes from the Cartesian Product of R and S.

4.8 Write down expression for the queries in Exercise 4.1 using relational calculus.

4.9 Consider the following relations P and Q.

P =

A	B	C	D
a_1	b_2	c_2	d_2
a_2	b_1	c_1	d_2
a_1	b_1	c_2	d_1
a_2	b_1	c_2	d_2

Q =

A	B	C	D
a_1	b_1	c_1	d_2
a_2	b_3	c_1	d_2
a_1	b_2	c_2	d_1
a_1	b_1	c_2	d_1

Compute the following:

(i) P union Q
(ii) P intersection Q
(iii) P join Q
(iv) P minus Q

4.10 Consider the following relations R_1, R_2 and R_3. Compute $R_1 \div R_2$ and $R_1 \div R_3$.

R_1

A	B
a_1	b_1
a_1	b_2
a_1	b_3
a_1	b_4
a_2	b_1
a_2	b_1
a_2	b_2
a_3	b_2
a_4	b_2
a_4	b_4

R_2

B
b_1

R_3

B
b_2
b_4

4.11 Consider the relations R = (A, B, C) and S = (D, E, F). Write down relation calculus expressions corresponding relational algebra expressions

(i) $\pi_A(R)$
(ii) $R \times S$
(iii) $\pi_{A,F}\ (\sigma_{C=D}(R \times S))$

4.12 A relational database contains the following relations: EMPLOYEE, DEPARTMENT, PROJECTS and a many-to-many relationship WORKS_ON. Express the following queries in relational algebra.

(i) Find names of employees working in project P_2.
(ii) Find names and departments of employees working in project P_2 and P_3.
(iii) Find names of employees working in at least one project, employee "Bablu" once worked in.

4.13 Express the division operation in relational algebra in terms of Cartesian product and set difference.

4.14 Express the natural join operation in relational algebra in terms of projection, Cartesian product and selection.

4.15 What are the use of relational algebra and tuple relational calculus? Describe with example.

4.16 Explain the concept of safe expressions in tuple relational calculus. Why is it needed?

4.17 Write a query involving a division operation and express it in tuple relational calculus.

CHAPTER 5

Relational Database Design

The database designer generally starts the design process starting with a conceptual data model which we call the Entity-Relationship model (E-R model). The E-R model leads to identification of necessary relations, relationships, their attributes and mapping (establishing relationships) procedures. The above model leads to a natural and conceptual design. In most of the cases, such a design suffers from many drawbacks due to lack of application of logical and mathematical rules and restrictions. Therefore, the initial intuitive design of a database must pass through some formal testing procedures.

5.1 Designing a Database

The goodness of a relational design (schema design) can be analyzed at two important levels. These are the logical or conceptual level and the implementation or physical level. At the logical level, good design supports properties like understandability, completeness and irreducibility of schema definition, accessibility of data in different forms etc. At the physical level, we require efficient storage representation for faster access and updation facilities.

5.1.1 Properties of a Good Design

Although, it is very difficult to measure the quality of a database design without analyzing its performance after deployment, several guidelines may be followed as rules of thumb. Maintaining these guidelines during the design steps may protect the system from malfunctioning to a large extent. Some of the guidelines are mentioned below:

- Each relational schema should properly describe a single entity type and no more. Attributes should clearly describe instances of that particular category of entities only.
- Relations should be checked very carefully so that insertion, deletion and updation anomalies may not occur during operation. These anomalies generally occur due to improper selection of attributes for relations as mentioned in the earlier statement.
- Relation schema should be such that we may not have to insert records with NULL values in it. Occurrence of NULL values causes integrity problems and causes anomalous behaviour of the system.

- Relations should be joined, when necessary, only with equijoin mode, and the concerned attributes should be only primary key or foreign keys of relations. This condition will ensure that no spurious tuples are generated unfortunately.

5.2 Functional Dependency

A database is a repository of related data. In an E-R diagram, we have seen that, entities are interrelated by certain relationships. But attributes of individual entities are also dependent on other attributes of the same entity. In other words, attributes of an entity are not independent. In case of a relational database system, entities are denoted by relations. Therefore, we can say that attributes of a relation are interrelated. In relational database terminology, this kind of relationship among attributes of a relation is denoted by *functional dependency*.

Every relation in a database system is properly specified by a set of functional dependencies (FDs). FDs determine the relationship among the attributes of a relation. It may be seen that some of the attributes in a relation are automatically implied by some others. Keeping all such attributes in the relation not only complicates the structure of the relation but also lead to fatal malfunctioning of the database. Hence, we need to select a minimum set of attributes for a relation in order to eliminate redundancy and chance of inconsistency. A thorough analytical evaluation of the set of functional dependencies is, therefore, needed during design of a database. The following are some intuitive concepts about functional dependencies.

- Some of the attributes in a relation may determine the values of other attributes.
- Suppose R (X, Y, Z) is a relation. If X → Y ("X determines Y"), then Y is functionally dependent on X.
- Here X is a called a determinant of Y.
- An attribute that determines all other attributes is a Primary Key of the concerned relation.

Let us consider the following relation SPO concerning Supplier, Product and Order. A supplier is located in a certain city and ordered for certain products with specific quantities. An instance of the SPO relation is shown in Table 5.1.

Table 5.1 SPO Relation

S#	CITY	P#	QTY
S_1	London	P_1	100
S_1	London	P_2	100
S_2	Paris	P_1	200
S_2	Paris	P_2	200
S_3	Paris	P_2	300
S_4	London	P_2	400
S_4	London	P_4	400
S_4	London	P_5	400

In the SPO relation, each supplier has a unique number represented by S#, and each product has unique code P#. A close observation of the tuples of SPO (only present instances of SPO) may reveal the following FDs:

- {S#} → {CITY}
- {S#, P#} → {QTY}
- {S#, p#} → {CITY}
- {S#, P#} → {CITY, QTY}
- {S#, p#} → {S#, p#, CITY, QTY}
- {S#, p#} → {S#}
- {S#} → {QTY}
- {QTY} → {S#}
- Etc.

In the preceding expression, we have identified several of the many possible functional dependencies present in relation SPO. It is found that, for a particular S#, we can identify the corresponding CITY, i.e. S# functionally determines CITY. Or, in other words, CITY is functionally determined by S#. Similarly, the combination of attributes {S#, p#} functionally determines order quantity QTY. It should be noted that, all of the above listed dependencies may not be generally true; they seem to be true after investigation of the existing instances of relation SPO. For example, {S#} → {QTY} cannot be true in general; it is not correct to say that a particular supplier will be ordered only for a very specific quantity every time he is ordered.

Note that, in the above list of functional dependencies, many redundancies are present. For example, FD 3 tells us that CITY is determined by {S#, p#} combination. However, we already know that CITY can be determined by S# only (FD 1). So, definitely there is redundancy in FD 3. As FDs are treated as important system specification, we need to identify a complete yet minimum set of FDs. We call such a set an irredundant set of FDs.

ILLUSTRATION 5.1 For the given relation R, which of the following functional dependencies are satisfied by the instances?

Relation R

X	Y	Z
1	4	2
1	5	3
1	6	3
3	2	2

(a) XY → Z and Z → Y
(b) YZ → X and Y → Z
(c) YZ → X and X → Z
(d) XZ → Y and Y → X

Solution Z → Y, X → Z are incorrect because attributes Z and X do not contain unique values. Similarly, XZ → Y is incorrect because the pair {X, Z} has the same values {1, 3} at multiple records (tuples). Therefore, the only set of FDs that are satisfied by R is (c).

ILLUSTRATION 5.2 For the given relation R, find out the functional dependencies that are satisfied by the given instances?

Relation R

A	B	C
a1	b1	c1
a1	b1	c2
a2	b1	c1
a2	b1	c2

Solution Table 5.2 shows the results of testing of candidate FDs for their correctness.

Table 5.2 Table of Illustration 5.2

Candidate FD	Test result	Reason
A → B	Success	$a_1 \rightarrow b_1$ and $a_2 \rightarrow b_2$ are only possible; it is a one-to-one mapping
A → C	Failure	One-to-many and many-to-one mapping found
B → C	Failure	One-to-many mapping found
B → A	Failure	One-to-many mapping found
C → A	Failure	Many-to-many mapping found
C → B	Success	Many-to-one mapping found
AB → C	Failure	One-to-many mapping found
AC → B	Success	Many-to-one mapping found
BC → A	Failure	Many-to-many mapping found

Trivial and non-trivial dependencies

Dependencies that are satisfied by all relations, in general, are called trivial dependencies. For example, the dependency X → X is satisfied by any relation having attribute X. Again, XY → X is satisfied by any relation having attribute X. In general, a dependency X → Y is trivial if Y ⊆ X. Trivial dependencies are not concerned with database consistency, and hence they do not have much significance. Non-trivial dependencies, however, are very significant as they correspond to essential integrity constraints of the database. Trivial dependencies are only of theoretical interest.

5.2.1 Closure of a Set of Functional Dependencies

In order to get a complete and minimum set of FDs, we need to do the following:

- To derive the complete set of FDs (result is a closure of FDs).
- To minimize the complete set of FDs (result is a canonical set of FDs).

The complete set of FDs can be obtained from closure of FDs. Closure of some set of FDs, $\mathcal{F}$, is defined as the set of FDs that are implied by $\mathcal{F}$ including $\mathcal{F}$ itself. To compute the closure of a set of FDs, computation of closure of attributes of each FD is very important. Closure of an attribute can be similarly defined as that of the closure of FDs. That is, closure of an attribute is the set of all attributes that can be derived from the concerned attribute.

Algorithm to compute closure of a set of FDs

Let $\mathcal{F}$ be a set of FDs and A is a subset of attributes. Closure $[\mathcal{F}, A]^+$ of A is the set of all attributes that are functionally dependent on attribute A over $\mathcal{F}$.

```
begin
    closure [𝓕,A]+ = {A};
    do forever
    begin
        for each FD X→Y 𝓕 do
            if X is a subset of [𝓕,A]+
            then [𝓕, A]+ = [𝓕, A]+ ∪ Y;
        if [𝓕, A]+ did not change
        then exit loop;
    end
end
```

For a given set of FDs $\mathcal{F}$, we can say whether $X \to Y$ follows from $\mathcal{F}$ or not. The above is true only if $Y \in X^+$. Thus, we can now decide whether a given FD: $X \to Y$ is in closure $\mathcal{F}^+$ of $\mathcal{F}$. We can also compute $\mathcal{F}^+$. By computing all possible FDs, followed by rejection of redundant ones, we can compute a minimal or canonical set of FDs.

ILLUSTRATION 5.3 Let R be a relation: R = (A, B, C, D, E, F) having the functional dependencies.

(a) $A \to BC$
(b) $B \to E$
(c) $C \to EF$
(d) $E \to CF$

Find the closure of {A, B} over the given set of FDs.

Solution We start with the initial closure for {A, B} and proceed by extending the set in steps.

$$
\begin{aligned}
[AB]^+ &= \{A, B\} \\
&= \{A, B, C\} \text{ (as } A \to BC) \\
&= \{A, B, C, E\} \text{ (as } B \to E) \\
&= \{A, B, C, E, F\} \text{ (as } C \to EF) \\
&= \{A, B, C, E, F\} \text{ (as } E \to CF)
\end{aligned}
$$

All the FDs are considered, and no more inclusion in the set $[AB]^+$ is possible.
Hence, $[AB]^+ = \{A, B, C, E, F\}$ is the result.

ILLUSTRATION 5.4 Let R be a relation: R = (A, B, C, D, E, F) having the functional dependencies

(a) $C \to F$
(b) $E \to A$
(c) $EC \to D$
(d) $A \to B$

Which of the following is a key for R?

(a) CD (b) EC (c) AE (d) AC

Solution

$[CD]^+ = \{C, D\} = \{C, D, F\}$

$[EC]^+ = \{E, C\} = \{E, C, A, F\} = \{E, C, A, F, D, B\}$

$[AE]^+ = \{A, E\} = \{A, E, B\}$

$[AC]^+ = \{A, C\} = \{A, C, F, B\}$

That is, only the combination EC determines all other attributes of R. Hence {E, C} is the primary key for relation R.

ILLUSTRATION 5.5 Let R be a relation: R = (A, B, C, D, E) having the functional dependencies.

(a) $AB \rightarrow C$
(b) $DE \rightarrow B$
(c) $CD \rightarrow E$

Is AB a candidate key for R? If not, is ABD? Explain your answer.

Solution

$$[AB]^+ = \{A, B\}$$

Since $AB \rightarrow C$, we can update as $[AB]^+ = \{A, B, C\}$

No more expansion of $[AB]^+$ is possible. Hence AB can't be a key of R.

Now, $[ABD]^+ = \{A, B, D\}$

From earlier arguments, we get $[ABD]^+ = \{A, B, C, D\}$

Since $CD \rightarrow E$, we can update as $[AB]^+ = \{A, B, C, D, E\}$. Hence ABD is a candidate key.

ILLUSTRATION 5.6 Let R be a relation: R = (A, B, C, D, E, F, G) having the functional dependencies.

(a) $A \rightarrow B$
(b) $BC \rightarrow D$
(c) $BC \rightarrow E$
(d) $AEF \rightarrow G$
(e) $B \rightarrow G$

Find out candidate keys of R.

Solution Here, $[A]^+ = \{A, B, G\}$, $[B]^+ = \{B, G\}$, $[BC]^+ = \{B, C, D, E, G\}$, $[AEF]^+ = \{A, B, E, F, G\}$

Hence, $[ACEF]^+ = \{A, B, C, E, F, G\} = \{A, B, C, D, E, F, G\}$

Since, $A \rightarrow B$ and $BC \rightarrow E$ imply $AC \rightarrow E$, we can write

$$[ACF]^+ = \{A, B, C, D, E, F, G\}$$

Therefore, {A, C, F} is a candidate key.

ILLUSTRATION 5.7 Given a relation R = {A, B, C, D, E}, and the corresponding set of FDs: $\mathcal{F} = \{A \rightarrow BC, CD \rightarrow E, B \rightarrow D, E \rightarrow A\}$. Find out candidate keys of relation R.

Solution Here,

$$[A]^+ = \{A\} = \{A, B, C\} = \{A, B, C, D, E\}$$
$$[B]^+ = \{B\} = \{B, D\}$$
$$[C]^+ = \{C\}$$
$$[D]^+ = \{D\}$$
$$[CD]^+ = \{C, D\} = \{C, D, E\} = \{C, D, E, A\} = \{A, B, C, D, E\}$$
$$[E]^+ = \{E\} = \{E, A\} = \{A, B, C, D, E\}$$

Therefore, A, E and CD are candidate keys of the relation R.

5.2.2 Armstrong's Inference Rules

Armstrong's inference rules help us in identifying equivalence of FDs. Hence applying these rules we can eliminate redundant FDs. These rules are described below with the help of a sample relation.

Let A, B, C, D be attributes of a relation R. Then, the following rules hold.

— Self Determination: $A \to A$
— Reflexivity: if B is a subset of A, i.e. $B \leq A$ then $A \to B$
— Augmentation: if $A \to B$ then $AC \to BC$
— Transitivity: if $A \to B$ and $B \to C$ then $A \to C$
— Decomposition: if $A \to BC$ then $A \to B$ and $A \to C$
— Union: $A \to B$ and $A \to C$ implies $A \to B\ C$
— Composition: if $A \to B$ and $C \to D$ then $AC \to BD$
— Pseudo-transitivity: if $A \to B$ and $BC \to D$ then $AC \to D$
— General unification: if $A \to B$ and $C \to D$ then $A \cup (C - B) \to BD$

Use of the above rules help simplify the database design process by generation or elimination of required or redundant FDs.

ILLUSTRATION 5.8 Consider the following set of FDs: $A \to B$, $ABCD \to E$ and $EF \to G$. Determine whether the FD: $ACDF \to G$ is implied by the given set or not.

Solution

$A \to B$ and $ABCD \to E$ implies $ACD \to E$ (pseudo-transitivity rule)
Also, $ACDF \to EF$ (Augmentation rule)
and $ACDF \to G$ (Transitivity rule: since $EF \to G$)
Hence, we arrive at $ACDF \to G$.

5.2.3 Equivalence of Sets of Functional Dependencies

Two sets of FDs are said to be equivalent if they cover each other. FD $\mathcal{F}_1$ covers FD $\mathcal{F}_2$ means that every FD in $\mathcal{F}_2$ can be inferred from those of $\mathcal{F}_1$. In other words, two sets of FD $\mathcal{F}_1$ and $\mathcal{F}_2$ are equivalent if $[\mathcal{F}_1]^+ = [\mathcal{F}_2]^+$.

ILLUSTRATION 5.9 Consider the following two sets of FDs:

$\mathcal{F}_1$ = {A → C, AC → D, E → AD, E → H} and $\mathcal{F}_2$ = {A → CD, E → AH}.

Check whether $\mathcal{F}_1$ and $\mathcal{F}_2$ are equivalent.

Solution Here, from $\mathcal{F}_1$ we get, A → C, AC → D implies that A → D. Therefore, we can write A → CD.

Also, E → AD, E → H implies that E → AH.

Therefore, $\mathcal{F}_1$ covers $\mathcal{F}_2$.

Again, from $\mathcal{F}_2$ we get, A → CD implies that A → C, A → D and AC → D.

Also, E → AH implies that E → A and E → H. Since we already have shown that A → D, therefore, we can write E → AD.

Therefore, $\mathcal{F}_2$ covers $\mathcal{F}_1$.

This proves that $\mathcal{F}_1$ and $\mathcal{F}_2$ are equivalent.

Alternative approach

From $\mathcal{F}_1$,

$[A]^+ = \{A, C\}$;

$[AC]^+ = \{A, C, D\}$;

Which implies that $[A]^+ = \{A, C, D\}$

$[E]^+ = \{A, D, H\}$ implies that $[E]^+ = \{A, C, D, E, H\}$

From $\mathcal{F}_2$,

$[A]^+ = \{A, C, D\}$ and $[AC]^+ = \{A, C, D\}$

$[E]^+ = \{A, E, H\} = \{A, C, D, E, H\}$

Therefore, $[\mathcal{F}_1]^+ = [\mathcal{F}_2]^+$

5.2.4 Minimal or Canonical Cover of Functional Dependencies

For designing a database from user specifications we need to gather information regarding entities, relationships, attributes that are essentially needed for the database. However, the designer must also ensure to maintain all data without any unnecessary redundancy. This can be performed by a comprehensive study of different attributes of relations and their interrelationships. Such relationship between attributes of a relation is generally expressed as functional dependencies. Very commonly it is found that a relation may support many such relationships while a majority of them are actually redundant, i.e. they are implied by others. The designer needs to consider only the minimum set of FDs.

When a database relation is updated we must be careful so that none of the existing functional dependencies are violated, i.e. all FDs must be preserved. Checking for possible violation FDs can be performed easily if we have a minimal equivalent set of FDs. This minimal set can be obtained by elimination of extraneous FDs or extraneous attributes from given FDs. Extraneous attributes may appear either on the left or right side of a FD. Extraneous FDs or attributes can be identified as follows. Here, we assume that X and Y represent group of attributes, and A, B represent individual attributes only.

- **Extraneous FD:** If $\{\mathcal{F} - \{X \to A\}$ is equivalent to $\mathcal{F}$ then FD $X \to A$ is extraneous.
- **Extraneous right attribute:** If $\{\{\mathcal{F} - \{X \to Y\}\} \cup \{X \to (Y - A)\}\}$ is equivalent to $\mathcal{F}$, then attribute A is extraneous in FD $X \to Y$.
- **Extraneous left attribute:** If $\{\{\mathcal{F} - \{X \to A\}\} \cup \{(X - B) \to A\}\}$ is equivalent to $\mathcal{F}$ then attribute B is extraneous in FD $X \to A$.

Now observe that, if we reduce all the given FDs into a form like $X \to A$, then there will be no extraneous attributes on the right side. This will further simplify the procedure.

The following algorithm enables the designer to find out a complete yet minimal set of FDs $\mathcal{F}_2$ starting with an arbitrary initial set of FDs $\mathcal{F}_1$. These initial FDs are generally user supplied or determined by the designer after initial observation. The algorithm performs two tasks. It eliminates redundancy present in any determinant, as well as eliminates any extraneous FD.

Algorithm for minimal cover of FDs

```
begin
    set F2 := F1;
    replace an FD X→{A1, A2, …, An} in F2 by following smaller FDs X→A1, X→A2, … , X→An;
    for each FD X→A in F2 do
    begin
        for each attribute B that is an element of X do
        begin
            if {{F2 - {X→A}} ∪ {(X - B)→A}} is equivalent to F2
               then replace X→A with (X - B)→A in F2;
        end
    end
    for each remaining FD X→A in F2 do
        begin
            if {F2 - {X→A} is equivalent to F2 then remove FD X→A from F2;
        end
end
```

After finding out the minimal set of FDs (or minimal cover of FDs), the designer can start designing a proper set of irredundant relations.

ILLUSTRATION 5.10 Given a relation R = {A, B, C, D, E, F, G, H, I}, and the corresponding set of FDs :{ABCD→ E, AB → G, B → F, C → J, CJ → I, G → H}. Minimize the set of FDs. Determine the primary key for R, and then find out a minimal cover for the given FDs.

Solution Here, in the FD: CJ → I, the determinant CJ is found to have a redundancy because C → J is already available. Hence CJ → I should be replaced by J → I. There is no other FD or determinant having a similar characteristic. Hence we get the minimal cover as

{ABCD→ E, AB → G, B → F, C → J, J → I, G → H}

It is found that $[ABCD]^+$ = {A, B, C, D, E, F, G, H, I, J}. Therefore, {A, B, C, D} is the primary key.

The above problem can be solved in the following tabular approach, in which case, the steps will be clearer.

Steps	Old FD Set	New FD Set	Reason
1	ABCD → E AB → G B → F C → J CJ → I G → H	ABCD → E AB → G B → F C → J J → I G → H	{𝓕 – {CJ → I}} ∪ {J →I} is equivalent to 𝓕
2	ABCD → E AB → G B → F C → J J → I G → H	ABCD → E AB → G B → F C → J J → I G → H	No other reduction is possible (This 2nd step is not needed at all)

Therefore, the minimal cover is {ABCD → E, AB → G, B → F, C → J, J → I, G → H}.

ILLUSTRATION 5.11 Given a relation R = {A, B, C, D}, and the corresponding set of FDs: {A → BC, AC → D, D → B, AB → D}. Find out A^+, B^+, C^+, D^+ and hence determine the primary key for R. Minimize the set of FDs.

Solution

A^+= {A} = {A, B, C} = {A, B, C, D}
B^+ = {B}
C^+ = {C}
D^+ = {D} = {D, B}

Therefore, {A} is the primary key.
Input set of FDs = {A → BC, AC → D, D → B, AB → D}
This can be written as: {A → B, A → C, AC → D, D → B, AB → D}

In FD: AC → D, the determinant AC is found to have a redundancy because A → C is already available. Hence AC → D should be replaced by C → D. Similarly, AB → D should be replaced by B → D

Hence we get, equivalent set of FDs = {A → B, A → C, C → D, D → B, B → D}

Therefore, we arrive at the minimal cover as {A → B, A → C, C → D, D → B, B → D}

The above problem can be solved in the following tabular approach, in which the steps will be clearer.

Steps	Old FD Set	New FD Set	Reason
1	A → BC AC → D D → B AB → D	A → B A → C AC → D D → B AB → D	A → BC → A → B, A → C Decomposition

(Contd.)

Steps	Old FD Set	New FD Set	Reason
2	A → B A → C AC → D D → B AB → D	A → B A → C A→ D D → B AB → D	{𝓕 – {AC → D}} ∪ {A → D} is equivalent to 𝓕
3	A → B A → C A→ D D → B AB → D	A → B A → C A→ D D → B B → D	{𝓕 – {AB → D}} ∪ {B → D} is equivalent to 𝓕

Therefore, we arrive at the minimal cover as {A → B, A → C, A → D, D → B, B → D}

Alternatively,

Steps	Old FD Set	New FD Set	Reason
1	A → BC AC → D D → B AB → D	A → B A → C AC → D D → B AB → D	A → BC → A → B, A → C Decomposition
2	A → B A → C A → D D → B AB → D	A → B A → C C → D D → B AB → D	{𝓕 – {AC → D}} ∪ {C → D} Is equivalent to 𝓕
3	A → B A → C C → D D → B AB → D	A → B A → C C → D D → B B → D	{𝓕 – {AB → D}} ∪ {B → D} is equivalent to 𝓕

Therefore, we arrive at the minimal cover as {A → B, A → C, C → D, D → B, B → D}. It, therefore, can say two different solutions are possible for the given minimization problem

ILLUSTRATION 5.12 Given a relation R = {A, B, C, D}, and the corresponding set of FDs: 𝓕 = {A → BC, B → C, A → B, AB → C}. Minimize the set of FDs.

Solution

Steps	Old FD Set	New FD Set	Reason
1	A → BC B → C A → B AB → C	A → B A → C B → C A → B AB → C	A → BC → A → B, A → C Decomposition

(*Contd.*)

Steps	Old FD Set	New FD Set	Reason
2	A → B A → C B → C A → B AB → C	A → B A → C B → C AB → C	A → B was present in duplicate
3	A → B A → C B → C AB → C	A → B A → C B → C A→ C	{𝓕 – {AB →C}} ∪ {A →C} is equivalent to 𝓕
4	A → B A → C B → C A→ C	A → B A → C B → C	A → C was present in duplicate
5	A → B A → C B → C	A → B B → C	A → B, B → C → A → C

Therefore, {A → B, B → C} is the minimal set of FDs.

ILLUSTRATION 5.13 Given a relation R = {A, B, C, D}, and the corresponding set of FDs: 𝓕 = {A → BC, B → AC, C → AB}. Minimize the set of FDs.

Solution

Steps	Old FD Set	New FD Set	Reason
1	A → BC B → AC C → AB	A → B A → C B → A B → C C → A C → B	A → BC → A → B, A → C B → AC → B → A, B → C C → AB → C → A, C → B Decomposition
2	A → B A → C B → A B → C C → A C → B	A → B B → A B → C C → A C → B	A → B, B → C → A → C
3	A → B B → A B → C C → A C → B	A → B B → C C → A C → B	B → C, C → A → B → A

Therefore, {A → B, B → C, C → A, C → B} is the minimal set of given FDs. There are more canonical covers for the above set of FDs. The reader should tryout.

ILLUSTRATION 5.14 Given a relation R = {A, B, C, D, E}, and the corresponding set of FDs:

$\mathcal{F}$ = {A → BC, CD → E, B → D, E → A}. Minimize the set of FDs.

Solution

Steps	Old FD Set	New FD Set	Reason
1	A → BC CD → E B → D E → A	A → B A → C CD → E B → D E → A	A → BC → A → B, A → C Decomposition
2	A → B A → C CD → E B → D E → A	A → B A → C A → E B → D E → A	E → A A → B, B → D → A → D A → C, A → D → A → CD Therefore, replace CD → E with A → E

Therefore, {A → B, A → C, A → E, B → D, E → A} is the minimal set of given FDs.

5.3 Relational Decomposition

When we design a relational database, we generally start with a single flat relational schema having all the required attributes. Such a relation is called a universal relation. During the design process, we generally need to decompose a universal relation (or relational schema) into a number of fragment relations, leading to different normal forms. However, definitions of normal forms are not sufficient enough to preserve many important properties of a relation during decomposition. Accordingly, decomposition processes may be lossy or lossless.

In general, design of a relational database schema starts with a single universal relational schema R = {A_1, A_2, ..., A_n}. Schema R includes all necessary attributes for the database. A set of functional dependencies should hold over the attributes of R as per specifications supplied by the user or designer of the database. In order to achieve a better design, the universal schema may need to be decomposed into fragments R_1, R_2, ..., R_k (not all disjoint). During such splitting of a relation we, generally, do not have a basis to determine that the original relation can be reconstructed from the fragments. So, a good decomposition process should incorporate some restriction over itself. Some of the desirable properties of a good decomposition are

- Attribute preservation
- Dependency preservation
- Lossless-join decomposition

Attribute preservation and dependency preservation are relatively easy to understand. The join decomposition property is related to information preservation. Sometimes, terms like *lossy-join decomposition* and *lossless-join decomposition* are also used to indicate lossy and lossless decomposition respectively. The *loss-less* join property is also referred to as *non-additive* join property. This means that, after a relation R is decomposed into its fragments R_1 and R_2 (say), the original relation R should be recovered exactly by natural join of R_1 and R_2. Stated differently, the said property specifies that, the natural join of the fragments should neither lose any existing tuple nor add any spurious tuple. To achieve a lossless decomposition is very important in order to preserve database information. These properties are described below in detail.

5.3.1 Attribute Preservation

This is an obvious requirement that all attributes in the parent relation must also be present in the decomposed or fragmented relations. Fragments may not be disjoint totally, and in general, they form child relations, such that the following equation holds over their attributes.

$$\bigcup_{i=1}^{k} R_i = R$$

The above is called the criteria for *attribute preservation* of decomposition. Therefore, decomposition of a relation into its fragments $R_1, R_2, \ldots, R_k$ (not all disjoint) must ensure that each attribute of R will appear in at least one of the fragments R_i so that no attribute of R is lost.

5.3.2 Dependency Preservation

A good decomposition must also satisfy the *dependency preservation condition.* This condition states that the union of functional dependencies for all fragment relations must be equivalent to the set of FDs F of the original relation R.

Each relation has its own set of dependencies among its attributes. When a relation is broken into fragments R_1 and R_2, it may be the case that we lose some important functional dependency. Let us consider a simple example. Let R is a relation such that the schema of R = (A, B, C, D). Suppose, the dependencies in R are F = {A → B, A → C, B → D}. If schemas of fragments are R_1 = (A, B) and R_2 = (A, C, D), then we lose the dependency B → D, because B and D are now in different relations. Therefore, dependencies are not preserved in such decomposition. This is not desirable as dependency is an important constraint on a database.

For preserving dependency, we must ensure that for each original dependency X → Y, both the attributes *X* and *Y* appear in the same relation (at least one of the fragments).

General dependency preservation

The principle of dependency preservation can be applied to explain the general case of relational decomposition. Let F be the set of functional dependencies or R to be decomposed into fragments $R_1, R_2, \ldots, R_k$. The dependency preservation restriction of F over R_i is the set F_i of all functional dependencies in F^+ that include only attributes of R_i.

Let a set of dependencies X → Y is in F^+, the closure of FDs in R. Now, if after decomposition, all the attributes in X → Y are in a fragmented schema R_i, then the set of dependencies X → Y in F^+ must be supported by R_i. In other words, if $\Pi_{R_i}(F)$ represents the projection of F in R_i where R_i is a fragment of R, then we must have

$$((\Pi_{R_1}(F)) \cup (\Pi_{R_2}(F)) \cup \cdots \cup (\Pi_{R_k}(F))^+ = F^+$$

Here, $\Pi_{R_i}(F)$ is the set of functional dependencies that include only attributes of R_i.

5.3.3 Lossless-join Decomposition

A good decomposition must be *lossless-join decomposition.* The conditions related to attribute and dependency preservation must also be considered. In addition, this should ensure that after joining the fragments we are able to recover complete information stored in the original relation. Sometimes, due to careless decomposition, we may lose one or more important functional dependencies. As a result the original non-fragmented relation can never be recovered fully by joining the fragments.

If a relation R is decomposed into fragments R_1, R_2, ..., R_k, then the decomposition is said to be lossless if the following constraint holds:

$$\Pi_{R_1}(R) \bowtie \Pi_{R_2}(R) \bowtie \ldots \bowtie \Pi_{R_k}(R) = R$$

or simply,

$$R_1 \bowtie R_2 \bowtie \ldots \bowtie R_k = R$$

In other words, if the original relation can be recovered fully by combining the projections of the original relation (fragments) using natural join, the decomposition is lossless; otherwise it is a lossy decomposition.

Binary decomposition: In many cases, a relation is broken into only two fragments. This is called a binary decomposition. These kinds of decompositions are relatively easy to handle.

For a binary decomposition (which is often the case), we decompose a relation R (having set of functional dependencies F) into its fragments R_1 and R_2. It can be shown that, R_1 and R_2 form a lossless decomposition of R if at least one of the following functional dependencies

$$R_1 \cap R_2 \rightarrow R_1$$
$$R_1 \cap R_2 \rightarrow R_2$$

is in F^+, the cover of F. Here, $R_1 \cap R_2$ represents all attributes in $R_1 \cap R_2$. In other words, if $R_1 \cap R_2$ form a superkey of either R_1 or R_2, the decomposition is a lossless one. For example, if we consider that

R = (customer_id, loan_number, amount) and its fragments are
R_1 = (customer_id, loan_number) and
R_2 = (loan_number, amount), then
$R_1 \cap R_2$ = loan_number and loan_number → amount, which satisfies the condition for lossless decomposition.

The lossless decomposition property (of R) is also satisfied if at least one of the following functional dependencies

$$R_1 \cap R_2 \rightarrow R_1 - R_2$$
$$R_1 \cap R_2 \rightarrow R_2 - R_1$$

is in F^+, the cover of F. This can be easily verified with our example.

This is, however, difficult to prove for a general category of decompositions (into many sub-schemas). The decomposition of a relation into multiple fragments is a difficult problem.

ILLUSTRATION 5.15 Consider the relational schema R = {A, B, C, D, E}. The functional dependencies defined over R are given by the set F: {A → CD, B → D, CD → E, E → A}. Determine whether the following decomposition of R is lossless or not.

Decomposed relations are: R_1 = {A, B, C} and R_2 = {A, D, E}. Is dependency preserved in this case?

Solution Here, $R_1 \cap R_2$ = {A}.

From the FD set F, we see that $[A]^+$ = {A, C, D, E}. Therefore, A is a superkey of R_2, and the decomposition is lossless.

However, after decomposition the FD; B → D is no longer implied. Hence, the decomposition is not dependency preserving.

ILLUSTRATION 5.16 Consider the relational schema R = {A, B, C, D}. The functional dependencies defined over R are given by the set F: {A → B, C→ D}. Determine whether the following decomposition of R is lossless or not.

Decomposed relations are: R_1 = {A, B} and R_2 = {C, D}

Solution Here, $R_1 \cap R_2 = \varnothing$. Therefore, the decomposition is not lossless.

From the FD set F, we see that the dependencies A → B, C → D hold even after decomposition. Therefore, the decomposition is dependency preserving.

ILLUSTRATION 5.17 Consider the relational schema R = {U, V, X, Y, Z}. The functional dependencies defined over R are given by the set F: {Z → U, V→ Y, XY → Z, U → VX}. Determine whether the following decomposition of R is lossless or not.

Decomposed relations are: R_1 = {U, V, X} and R_2 = {U, Y, Z}.

Solution

Here, $R_1 \cap R_2$ = {U}. The closure of U is

$[U]^+$ = {U} = {U, V, X} since U → VX. Hence, we can write, $R_1 \cap R_2 \rightarrow R_1$.

Therefore, the decomposition is lossless.

From the FD set F, we see that the dependencies V→ Y, XY → Z does not hold after decomposition. Therefore, the decomposition is not dependency preserving.

5.4 Normalization

Generally, at the beginning of database design, we start with a single *universal relation* having all necessary attributes, and a set of user supplied functional dependencies. Later on, the universal relation is decomposed into fragments applying various design principles. After a thorough analysis of the supplied functional dependencies, we arrive at a set of irreducible set of functional dependencies for each base relation along with their key attributes. We now need to study what should be the proper semantic of a relation in connection with achieving a proper and desirable normal form. Normal forms ensure some technical standards over a database.

5.4.1 Need for Normalization

E-R model based ad-hoc designs may need some refinement for maintaining consistency and integrity. Normalization process helps in such refinement and also to maintain some industry standard. It helps simplify database design process. Five Normal Forms: 1NF (first normal form), 2NF (second normal form), 3NF (third normal form), 4NF (fourth normal form), and 5NF (fifth normal form) are commonly used. A Designer conforms to a certain normal form (NF). Generally, 2NF or 3NF is used industry standards. Another common form is BCNF (Boyce-Codd Normal Form). BCNF is assumed to lye somewhere between 3NF and 4NF in the normalization hierarchy. Normalization is required due to following reasons:

- Ad hoc designs may sufficient redundancy.
- Ad hoc designs may suffer from the following problems:
  - Insertion anomaly
  - Updation anomaly
  - Deletion anomaly.
- Normalization process helps eliminating these problems.
- A Normal database is a standard one.
- A Normal database contains lesser redundancy.

5.4.2 Mathematical Foundation of Normalization

Normalization theory stands on strong mathematical foundation. Several mathematical concepts/constraints are commonly involved in connection with different normal forms. These constraints are:

- Atomicity (1NF)
- Functional dependency (2NF)
- Transitive dependency (3NF)
- Multi-valued dependency (4NF)
- Join dependency (5NF)

However, achieving a higher degree of normalization may not guarantee a better design. In fact, too much normalization results in inefficient design due to higher processing overhead.

Let us consider a sample database containing information related to supplier, parts and orders (shipments). It is assumed that a supplier is located only at a single city, every supplier has a unique status depending on the city he resides in, a supplier is ordered for one or more parts in varying quantities. We also assume that all information related to this application are stored in a single table called SUPPLIER-ORDER. Attributes of SUPPLIER-ORDER are assumed to be supplier number (S#), supplier's city information (CITY-INFO), parts number ordered (P#), parts name (PNAME), parts colour (PCOLOR), parts weight (PWEIGHT), city produced (PCITY), and quantity ordered (QTY). So we may arrive at an initial view of the database as

S#	CITY-INFO	P#	PNAME	PCOLOR	PWEIGHT	PCITY	QTY

5.4.3 First Normal Form (1NF)

We may observe that attributes PNAME, PCOLOR, PWEIGHT and PCITY are related only to associated parts and not in any way with suppliers or shipments. Hence, in order to simplify analysis, we may keep them aside for the time being. The CITY-INFO attribute is assumed to contain city name and its status jointly (as pairs). Let, after above simplification, Table 5.3 shows instances of records present in SUPPLIER-ORDER.

Table 5.3 SUPPLIER-ORDER

S#	CITY-INFO	P#	QTY
S_1	London 20	P_1	300
S_1	London 20	P_2	200
S_1	London 20	P_3	400
S_1	London 20	P_4	200
S_1	London 20	P_5	100
S_1	London 20	P_6	100
S_2	Paris 10	P_1	300
S_2	Paris 10	P_2	400
S_3	Paris 10	P_2	200
S_4	London 20	P_2	200
S_4	London 20	P_4	300
S_4	London 20	P_5	400

In the above database (an ad-hoc design), each city information is a tuple; it has two parts *city name* and *city* (or *supplier*) *status*. Since the status of a city is solely dependent on the city itself and nothing else, it is quite natural to encapsulate them as a single item. However, the field CITY-INFO is not an atomic attribute; it has two separable components: *city* and *status*. According to the principle of relational database systems, we should decompose it into two indivisible attributes. Therefore, after above mentioned decomposition, we get a new Table 5.4 (let us call it FIRST) as shown below.

Table 5.4 FIRST Table

S#	CITY	STATUS	P#	QTY
S_1	London	20	P_1	300
S_1	London	20	P_2	200
S_1	London	20	P_3	400
S_1	London	20	P_4	200
S_1	London	20	P_5	100
S_1	London	20	P_6	100
S_2	Paris	10	P_1	300
S_2	Paris	10	P_2	400
S_3	Paris	10	P_2	200
S_4	London	20	P_2	200
S_4	London	20	P_4	300
S_4	London	20	P_5	400

It is clear that FIRST is in first normal form (1NF). All the attributes have atomic and indivisible scalar values, which is the only determining criteria for a relation being in first normal form.

- **Definition:** A relation is in 1NF if and only if all underlying domains contain scalar values only (Scalar values are atomic values).

The relation FIRST satisfies the above condition, hence FIRST in is 1NF. FIRST can be defined as

FIRST(S#, CITY, STATUS, P#, QTY): PRIMARY KEY {S#, P#}

Functional dependency diagram (FDD) of relation FIRST is given below in Figure 5.1.

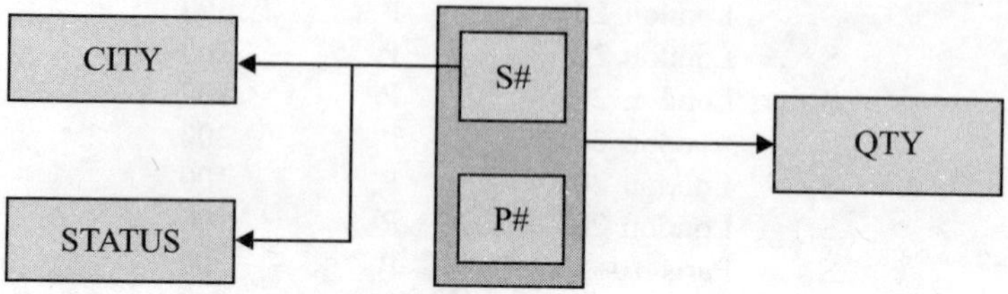

Figure 5.1 Functional dependency diagram of relation FIRST.

From this FDD, it is clear that {S#, P#} pair is the primary key of relation FIRST because QTY is determined only by this pair of attributes. Although {S#, P#} pair also determines the other attributes, i.e. CITY and STATUS, we see that these attributes are only partially dependent on the primary key. In other words, CITY and STATUS are dependent only on S#, and not on P# in any way.

From the above example, we observe the following:

- A primary key may be a subset of the attributes of relation R.
- A non-key attribute may be fully or partially dependent on the primary key.

Suppose, R(X, Y, Z, W) is a relation with primary key {X, Y}. If $X \rightarrow Z$ or $Y \rightarrow W$, then Z or W are partially dependent on the primary key.

The relation FIRST has several drawbacks in its organization. We can enlist them as:

- FDD for FIRST is relatively complicated.
- FIRST is having a lot of redundancy.
- Attributes of FIRST are not irreducibly dependent on the primary key, i.e. it contains partial dependency.
- Presence of redundant information causes various updation anomalies (as specified below):

  Insertion anomaly: We can't insert the fact that a supplier is located in a particular city until he supplies at least one part. The reason is that, without a part the primary key becomes undefined, leading to a violation of Entity Integrity.

  Deletion anomaly: If we delete the only FIRST tuple for a particular supplier, we destroy not only the corresponding shipment contract, but also destroy the information that the concerned supplier is located at a particular city. For example, if we delete the tuple for S_3, we will lose the information that S# is located in Paris.

Updation anomaly: The city value for a given supplier appears redundantly in FIRST (i.e., many times). Now, if S1 is shifted from London to Amsterdam, we will have to modify all tuples connecting S_1 and London.

5.4.4 Second Normal Form (2NF)

It has been observed that all anomalies in FIRST arise due to the following FDs (partial dependencies):

FD : **{S#, p#} → CITY**
FD : **{S#, p#} → STATUS**

We also note that:

- CITY is partially dependent on the primary key.
- LHS of FD: **{S#, p#} → CITY** is reducible.
- Entity Integrity condition is not satisfied.
- Similar are the cases with FD **{S#, p#} → STATUS.**

A Possible approach to eliminate the anomalies caused by relation FIRST may be to:

- Make each attribute fully dependent on the primary key
- Make LHS of all FDs irreducible
- Maintain entity integrity

The above can be done by breaking FIRST into two components SECOND (S#, CITY, STATUS) and SP (S#, P#, QTY). The new relations are shown in Tables 5.5 and 5.6.

Table 5.5 SECOND Table

S#	CITY	STATUS
S_1	London	20
S_2	Paris	10
S_3	Paris	10
S_4	London	20

Table 5.6 SP Table

S#	P#	QTY
S1	P1	300
S1	P2	200
S1	P3	400
S1	P4	200
S1	P5	100
S1	P6	100
S2	P1	300
S2	P2	400
S3	P2	200
S4	P2	200
S4	P4	300
S4	P5	400

FD diagrams for SECOND and SP are shown below in Figure 5.2.

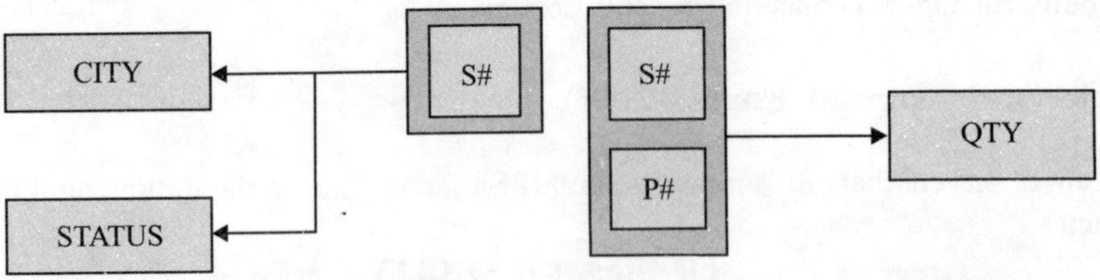

Figure 5.2 Functional dependency diagrams of relation SECOND and SP.

These FDDs indicate that SECOND and SP are in 2NF because there is no partial dependency.

- **Definition:** A relation is in 2NF if and only if it is in 1NF and every non-key attribute is irreducibly dependent on the primary key.

Since SECOND is in 2NF, we realize the following advantages:

- We can now insert the fact that supplier S_5 is located in Athens, even if he is not supplying any part.
- We can delete shipment tuple for S_3 (supplying P_2) from SP without losing his location information.
- City for one supplier appears once in SECOND and hence updation becomes simpler (any change of city can be easily incorporated).

Our initial schema contains parts information like part name (pname), part color (pcolor), part weight (pweight) and part city (pcity), then we could have three decomposed relation as shown below. In this case, we assume that status of a supplier is independent of his city. Also, we assume that a supplier has different warehouses in different cities. Hence, parts may be supplied from different cities. Therefore, the initial table would have the following structure.

S#	CITY	STATUS	P#	PNAME	PCOLOR	PWEIGHT	PCITY	QTY

Following the above mentioned procedure, we could have decomposed the relation into the following three 2NF relations (supplier S, parts P and shipments SP).

S (S#, SNAME, STATUS, CITY) primary key S#;
P (P#, PNAME, COLOR, WGT, CITY) primary key P#;
SP (S#, p#, QTY) primary key (S#, p#), foreign key S# references S, foreign key P# references P;

Functional dependency diagram for the above database would be as follows (Figure 5.3).

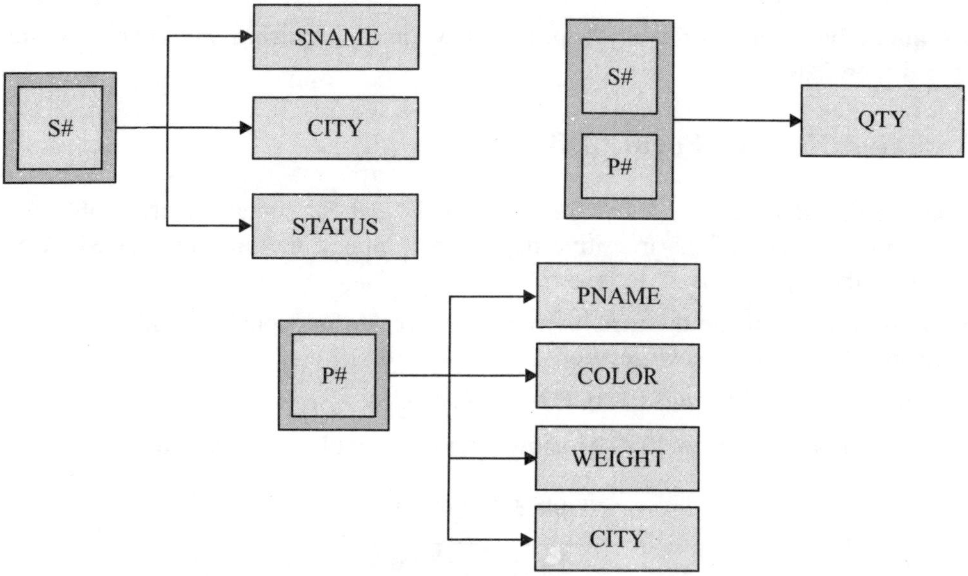

Figure 5.3 Functional dependency diagram for the supplier-parts database.

How to convert from 1NF to 2NF: A rule of thumb

Given a 1NF relation R(A, B, C, D) with primary key {A, B} and A $\rightarrow$ D as an FD. Break R into R_1 and R_2 such that

R_1 (A, D) Primary Key {A}

and

R_2(A, B, C) Primary key {A, B} and Foreign Key {A} References R_1.

Non-loss decomposition

We have noticed that, during conversion of a relation from one normal form into another, we need to decompose the relation into fragments. However, it is desirable that the decomposition be non-loss in nature. An arbitrary decomposition may be either lossy or non-loss; but only non-loss decompositions are desirable. In our example, R is the join of R_1 and R_2 over *foreign-to-matching-primary-key*, hence it is non-loss. We shall discuss different aspects of a non-loss decomposition later in this chapter.

In our example, 2NF relations SECOND and SP we may find out the following problems:

- SECOND-SP pair has some redundancy problems.
- FD diagram for SECOND contains a transitive dependency.
- We face the following anomalies due to the presence of transitive dependency.

Insertion anomaly: We can't insert the fact that a city has a particular status unless a supplier is located there.

Deletion anomaly: We can't delete the only SECOND tuple of a supplier without losing his city information.

Update anomaly: Status of a city appears many times, requiring any change of status be propagated thoroughly.

5.4.5 Third Normal Form (3NF)

We observed that the second normal form SECOND and SP contain many problems. These are due to the presence of the transitive dependency among the attributes of SECOND. We can eliminate these problems as follows:

- We need to eliminate the transitivity present in the functional dependencies.
- Break SECOND into two relations
  - SC (S# → CITY) and CS (CITY → STATUS)
- The relations are SC and CS as shown below in Tables 5.7 and 5.8.

Table 5.7 SC Table

S#	CITY
S_1	London
S_2	Paris
S_3	Paris
S_4	London

Table 5.8 CS Table

CITY	STATUS
London	20
Paris	10

- **Definition:** A relation is in 3NF if and only if it is in 2NF and every non-key attribute is non-transitively dependent on the primary key.

The FDD for the new relations will be as follows (Figure 5.4):

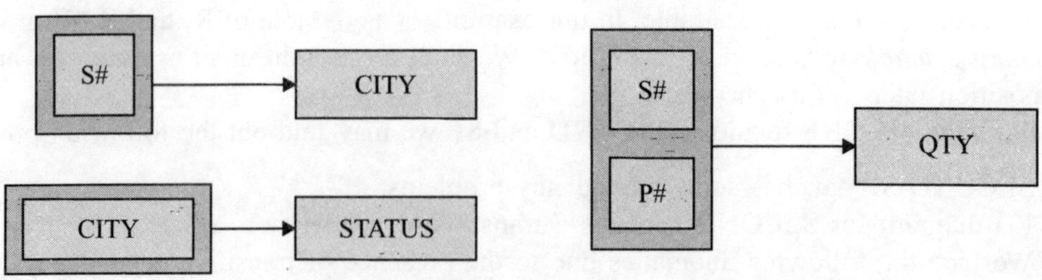

Figure 5.4 Functional dependency diagrams of relation SC, CS and SP.

How to convert from 2NF to 3NF: A rule of thumb

Given a 2NF relation R(A, B, C) Primary key {A} and FD, B $\rightarrow$ C. Break it as

R_1(B, C) Primary key {B}
and
R_2(A, B) Primary key {A}, Foreign key {B}, and references R_1

The 3NF can be achieved by considering functional dependency properties (partial dependency and transitive dependency) only. These two properties ensure preservation of functional dependencies as well as losslessness. In other words, a third normal form can be achieved without sacrificing the above two preservation conditions. However, the 3NF cannot ensure the chances of occurrences of anomalies, and the presence of data redundancy and NULL values in relations.

5.4.6 Boyce-Codd Normal Form (BCNF)

The next higher normal form after 3NF should be 4NF. However, Boyce and Codd found the presence of another normal form in between 3NF and 4NF. This is called the Boyce-Codd normal form (BCNF). In some cases, it is also referred to as yet another normal form that is somewhat stronger than the 3NF. BCNF is conceptually simpler than the 2NF and 3NF because it does not make any explicit reference to the so called partial dependency and transitive dependency. Therefore, one may attempt to get a BCNF relation directly from a 1NF relation.

- **Definition:** A relation R is said to be in BCNF if and only if every determinant is a candidate key.

The second and third normal forms assume that all attributes that are not the part of a candidate key, depend only on the candidate key, but they do not deal with dependencies *within the key*. BCNF takes these dependencies into account. It should be noted that in majority of the situations, a 3NF relation and the corresponding BCNF relation are the same. They differ only when the following three conditions occur:

- Candidate keys are composite in nature (more than one attribute),
- There are more than one candidate keys, and
- Candidate keys are overlapped, i.e. not disjoint.

Let us consider a modified supplier relation S_1(S#, SNAME, CITY, STATUS) where every S# are SNAME are unique, and STATUS does not depend on CITY. Here, S_1 has two candidate keys S# and SNAME, and S_1 is in BCNF.

However, if we modify the SP relation to get an augmented relation SP_1(S#, SNAME, P#, QTY), we see that there exist two overlapping candidate keys, viz., (S#, P#) and (SNAME, P#) where P# is a common attribute. The relation SP_1 is not in BCNF, because we have two determinants S# and SNAME, which are not candidate keys of SP_1. But SP_1 is in 3NF as there are no partial or transitive dependencies of the non-key attributes over the candidate key. The fact that SNAME depends only on S# is ignored here as SNAME is a component of the other candidate key. However, due to the presence of two overlapping candidate keys, we observe a kind of redundancy in SP_1 which causes updation anomalies. Note that the redundancy is due to S# and SNAME, and any modification of name of particular supplier may left the database inconsistent (if updation is not propagated). To solve this problem, we may decompose the relation SP_1 in any of the following pairs:

$$SS(S\#, SNAME) \text{ and } SP_2(S\#, P\#, QTY)$$
or
$$SS(S\#, SNAME) \text{ and } SP_3(SNAME, P\#, QTY)$$

Each of the resultant decomposed relation pairs $\{SS, SP_2\}$ or $\{SS, SP_3\}$ are in BCNF. Note that, after decomposition into a set of BCNF relations, we need to check for the lossless-join and dependency preservation properties of the fragments. Since it is very hard to achieve a set of relations that are BCNF, lossless and dependency preserving simultaneously, one may be forced to choose a form between lossless BCNF and dependency preserving 3NF.

5.4.7 Some Conversion Algorithms

Although it may be difficult to satisfy all the desirable preservation criteria in a particular normal form, we have some specific algorithms in this regard. Since, very commonly, a relation is converted into a 3NF or a BCNF, we shall present algorithms in relation to these normal forms only.

Algorithm to convert a universal relation into dependency-preserving 3NF

Let us consider a universal relation R. We need to decompose it into a number of dependency preserving 3NF relations. The following algorithm may be followed for this purpose.

Input: The universal relation R and the set of functional dependencies F on attributes of R.

Step 1: Compute a minimal cover of dependencies G for relation R.
Step 2: For a determinant X in G, create a new relational schema that contains attributes A_1, A_2, ..., A_k, where $X \rightarrow A_1$, $X \rightarrow A_2$, ..., $X \rightarrow A_k$ are the only dependencies in G with X as the left hand side. X will be the key of the new relation.
Step 3: Put all other attributes (that are not already put in any fragment relation) in a separate relation R′. Rename R′ as R.
Step 4: Repeat steps 1 to 3 until no more new relations are possible.

All the fragmented relations, that are the outcome of the above algorithm, will be in 3NF and dependency preserving.

Algorithm to convert a universal relation into loss-less join BCNF

Let us consider a universal relation R. We need to decompose it into a number of loss-less join BCNF relations. The following algorithm may be followed for this purpose.

Input: The universal relational schema R.

Step 1: If there exists a dependency $X \rightarrow Y$ in R that violates BCNF criteria, decompose schema R into two sub-schemas R_1 and R_2, where R_1 contains attributes $\{R - Y\}$, and R_2 contains attributes $\{X \cup Y\}$.
Step 2: Repeat step 1 for each of the fragments R_1 and R_2 by treating them as the initial relation R separately.

All the fragmented relations, that are the outcome of the above algorithm will be in BCNF and satisfy loss-less join dependency criteria.

5.4.8 Fourth Normal Form (4NF)

Even if a relation is in 3NF or BCNF, redundancy may still be present. The necessity of a fourth normal form arise when attributes represent sets of values. Whenever an entity contains several *set valued attributes*, a join dependency results. In a relation, join dependency incorporates some redundancy. Multi-valued dependency (MVD) results from binary join dependency. These are of the form

$$A = A_1 \bowtie A_2$$

where A, A_1 and A_2 are attribute sets. The presence of such join dependency leads to a fourth normal form (4NF) to reduce redundancy.

Definition: A relation R is said to be in 4NF if and only if, whenever there exists a MVD $X \rightarrow\rightarrow Y$, then either

1. The dependency is trivial, or
2. X is a candidate of R.

A MVD $X \rightarrow\rightarrow Y$ is trivial if either Y is a subset of X, or X and Y together form the table R.

Let us consider the relation CTX, standing for Course-Teacher-Text. It has three attributes, of which teacher and text are multi-valued, i.e. for a given course, we get multiple teachers and multiple texts (Table 5.9).

Table 5.9 Initial Form of CTX

COURSE	TEACHER	TEXT
Physics	Prof. X, Prof. Y, Prof. Z	Mechanics, Optics
Math	Prof. W	Algebra, Geometry

As seen from the table entries, the relation contains multiple values in some of its columns. When each column contains individual values only, the relation attains the following form. Individual instances of CTX are shown below in Table 5.10.

Table 5.10 CTX Table

COURSE	TEACHER	TEXT
Physics	Prof. X	Mechanics
Physics	Prof. X	Optics
Physics	Prof. Y	Mechanics
Physics	Prof. Y	Optics
Physics	Prof. Z	Mechanics
Physics	Prof. Z	Optics
Math	Prof. W	Algebra
Math	Prof. W	Geometry

From the instances of the relation CTX, we cannot identify a primary key attribute. Here, the attribute COURSE multi-determines the other attributes TEACHER and TEXT, which can be denoted as

$$\text{COURSE} \rightarrow\rightarrow \text{TEACHER}$$
$$\text{COURSE} \rightarrow\rightarrow \text{TEXT}$$

Actually, CTX is a *all key* relation, i.e. combination of all the attributes only can form a key, and the corresponding FD is a trivial one.

We can arrive at the following conclusions regarding the relation CTX:

- CTX is in BCNF, and it is '*all-key*'.
- CTX cannot be decomposed using FD.
- An attribute determines a set of values for other attribute.
- CTX has enough redundancy.
- We need to use the concept of Multi-valued dependency, i.e. MVD, to decompose this relation (in order to eliminate redundancy).

Whenever there exist more than one MVD in a relation, we need to decompose into fragments where only a single MVD is present in each fragment. Therefore, we can decompose CTX into CT and CX as shown below in Tables 5.11 and 5.12, in order to eliminate data redundancy.

Table 5.11 CT Table

COURSE	TEACHER
Physics	Prof. X
Physics	Prof. Y
Physics	Prof. Z
Math	Prof. W

Table 5.12 CX Table

COURSE	TEXT
Physics	Mechanics
Physics	Optics
Math	Algebra
Math	Geometry

After decomposition, fragment tables CT and CX remain all-key relations, but now they are in 4NF form as only trivial MVDs are present in each of them.

In the following illustration, we shall describe the process of converting an initial database relation into different normal forms. This step by step decomposition process may help students to deal with similar problems. Here we have followed the classical conversion scheme, i.e. 1NF to 2NF, 2NF to 3NF, and so on. For direct conversion to a particular normal form, above mentioned algorithms may be used.

ILLUSTRATION 5.18 A university is running a training course in its CSE, ECE and IT branches. Students from these branches can enroll for at most any two of the following courses (one with duration 15 days, and the other with duration 7 days):

- CSE branch: runs courses on 'Software Design' having course-id CS-1 of duration 15 days, and 'Hardware Design' having course-id CS-2 of duration 7 days.
- ECE branch: runs courses on 'Digital Design' having course-id EC-1 of duration 15 days, and 'VLSI Design' having course-id EC-2 of duration 7 days.
- IT branch: runs courses on 'Database Design' having course-id IT-1 of duration 15 days, and 'Interface Design' having course-id IT-2 of duration 7 days.

University maintains the following grading system.

- A grade: for marks 80 and above.
- B grade: for marks between, 70–79.
- C grade: for marks between, 50–69.
- D grade: for marks below 50.

The university keeps all records regarding course, enrolment and marks in a single table named TRAINING-DATA and an instance of the table is given below in Table 5.13.

Table 5.13 TRAINING-DATA

STUD-ID	STUD-NAME	STUD-BRANCH	COURSE-ID	COURSE-NAME	COURSE-DURATION	MARKS-OBTAINED	GRADE-OBTAINED
01	Kiran	CSE	CS-1	Software design	15	85	A
02	Anindya	ECE	CS-1	Software design	15	75	B
03	Dinesh	ECE	EC-1	Digital design	15	73	B
01	Kiran	CSE	CS-2	Hardware design	7	61	C
02	Anindya	ECE	IT-2	Interface design	7	71	B
04	Priti	IT	IT-1	Database design	15	81	A
04	Priti	IT	EC-2	VLSI design	7	63	B
05	Lipika	IT	EC-1	Digital design	15	66	C
05	Lipika	IT	EC-2	VLSI design	7	69	C
03	Dinesh	ECE	CS-2	Hardware design	7	76	B

Determine in which Normal Form (NF) the given table is in? Find out its potential problems and also, convert it into higher order Normal Forms to remove those problems.

Solution Since all the attributes of table TRAINING-DATA contain atomic values only it is in 1NF. The primary key of the given relation is the combination (<u>STUD-ID, COURSE-ID</u>). The functional dependency diagram is given below.

It is seen that Table 5.13 contains many redundancies, and from the dependency diagram, we see that TRAINING-DATA contains partial dependencies. We have to face insertion, deletion and updation anomalies with this design. For example, if the only CSE student withdraws from the course, we will lose the fact that CS-1 and CS-2 courses have been offered by the CSE department. Also, we cannot insert a new subject offered by a department unless a student enrols for that subject. Hence we should decompose it into a number of 2NF relations. Here, 2NF relations will be

- STUDENTS(<u>STUD-ID</u>, STUD-NAME, STUD-BRANCH)
- COURSES(<u>COURSE-ID</u>, COURSE-NAME, COURSE-DURATION)
- RESULTS(<u>STUD-ID, COURSE-ID</u>, MARKS-OBTAINED, GRADE-OBTAINED)

Underlined attributes represent key attributes.

The corresponding relations after decomposition are shown below in Tables 5.14, 5.15 and 5.16.

Table 5.14 STUDENTS Table

STUD-ID	STUD-NAME	STUD-BRANCH
01	Kiran	CSE
02	Anindya	ECE
03	Dinesh	ECE
04	Priti	IT
05	Lipika	IT

Table 5.15 COURSES

COURSE-ID	COURSE-NAME	COURSE-DURATION
CS-1	Software design	15
EC-1	Digital design	15
CS-2	Hardware design	7
IT-2	Interface design	7
IT-1	Database design	15
EC-2	VLSI design	7

Table 5.16 MARKS

STUD-ID	COURSE-ID	MARKS-OBTAINED	GRADE-OBTAINED
01	CS-1	85	A
02	CS-1	75	B
03	EC-1	73	B
01	CS-2	61	C
02	IT-2	71	B
04	IT-1	81	A
04	EC-2	63	B
05	EC-1	66	C
05	EC-2	69	C
03	CS-2	76	B

The functional dependencies (STUDENTS, COURSES and RESULTS) are as follows:

- In STUDENTS: STUD-ID → STUD-NAME, and STUD-ID → STUD-BRANCH
- In COURSES: COURSE-ID → COURSE-NAME, COURSE-ID → COURSE-DURATION, and COURSE-NAME → COURSE-DURATION
- In RESULTS: (STUD-ID, COURSE-ID) → MARKS-OBTAINED, (STUD-ID, COURSE-ID) → GRADE-OBTAINED, and MARKS-OBTAINED → GRADE-OBTAINED

Note that, in the above form, there is no partial dependency. Hence it is in 2NF. However, we are facing many anomalies in this NF structure. For example, if Kiran left the course in the midway, we may lose the fact that students of CSE may enrol for the training course (as there is a single record with a CSE student). There is no record in RESULT involving grade D. Also, there is no information about how marks are converted to grades. From the dependency diagrams, we see that, there exist transitive dependencies which need to be eliminated.

We may observe that, in the above mentioned FDs, there exist transitive dependencies (in COURSES and RESULTS). In order to achieve 3NF relations, we need to remove these transitive dependencies. We can do this by decomposing COURSES (into CN, CD) and RESULTS (into SCM, SCG) as shown in Tables 5.17 to 5.20.

Table 5.17 CN Table

COURSE-ID	COURSE-NAME
CS-1	Software design
EC-1	Digital design
CS-2	Hardware design
IT-2	Interface design
IT-1	Database design
EC-2	VLSI design

Table 5.18 CD Table

COURSE-ID	COURSE-DURATION
CS-1	15
EC-1	15
CS-2	7
IT-2	7
IT-1	15
EC-2	7

Table 5.19 SCM Table

STUD-ID	COURSE-ID	MARKS-OBTAINED
01	CS-1	85
02	CS-1	75
03	EC-1	73
01	CS-2	61
02	IT-2	71
04	IT-1	81
04	EC-2	63
05	EC-1	66
05	EC-2	69
03	CS-2	76

Table 5.20 SCG Table

STUD-ID	COURSE-ID	GRADE-OBTAINED
01	CS-1	A
02	CS-1	B
03	EC-1	B
01	CS-2	C
02	IT-2	B
04	IT-1	A
04	EC-2	B
05	EC-1	C
05	EC-2	C
03	CS-2	B

In the above illustration, we have followed conventional method for conversion from 1NF to 3NF or BCNF. Students should try to achieve results directly using the appropriate algorithms starting with the initial universal relation.

5.5 Importance of Normalization

Normalization process allows the database designer to achieve a standard database by virtue of maintaining well established mathematical principles and rules. The more such rules are satisfied by a design, the more standard the database becomes. However, only achieving a normal database of a certain degree should not be the only target of a practical database designer. Normalization to a certain degree may produce a mathematically stronger database design, but in practice, many other satisfying criteria need to be met. In a nutshell, we can say that normalization process provides designers with the following facilities:

- A set of formal specifications for developing relational schema by selection of proper sets of entity attributes, key attributes and necessary functional dependencies among them.

- A set of standard testing methodologies to verify the goodness of a design to a certain degree.
- To attain a certain degree of normalization as per the requirement of the organization.

It is, however, not always true that achieving the highest possible normal form ensures the best possible database design. The designer must also conform to existing organizational rules, procedures, practices and performance restrictions. Sometimes, normalization to higher normal forms, leads to complicated and inefficient designs. While decomposing an existing relation for normalization purposes, it is always necessary to ensure *non-loss decomposition*. The *preservation of functional dependencies*, as supplied by the organization, is another desirable property.

5.6 Limitations of Normal Forms

Although normal forms of a relational schema puts the concerned relation(s) in some desired industry standards, and eliminates chances of data redundancy and inconsistency they have some difficulties also. These are listed below.

- It is difficult to determine which normal form should be the best for some relational schema.
- Normal forms of higher orders may add complexity to query generation and query processing.
- Definitions of normal forms are not sufficient to specify all desirable properties to be maintained by a set of decomposed relations. These properties include preservation of functional dependency and lossless-join property.
- In many cases, developers try to normalize a relational schema using ad hoc approaches leading to an incorrect solution.

In spite of the above mentioned limitations, normal forms prove to be very important and valuable assets to a database designer. They simplify the design process and provide sufficient guidelines for structuring the database following some industry standards.

Exercises

5.1 What is the significance of relational algebraic forms of relational operations? How are relational algebra and relational calculus related?

5.2 What is meant by Normal Form of a database? Why is it needed?

5.3 Write down the significance of functional and multi-valued dependencies in database design.

5.4 Consider the following relations R_1, R_2, and R_3 (from left to right).

A	B	C
a	*b*	*c*
b	*c*	*a*
c	*a*	*b*

A	B	C
c	*b*	*a*
b	*a*	*c*
b	*c*	*a*

D
d
e
f

Perform the following relational algebraic operations.

(i) $P \cup Q$ (ii) $P \cap Q$
(iii) $P - Q$ (iv) $Q - P$
(v) $P \times Q$ (vi) $Q \times R$

5.5 Compute the closure of the set of functional dependencies F of the relation R = (A, B, C, D, E), where
$F = \{A \rightarrow BC, B \rightarrow D, CD \rightarrow E, E \rightarrow A\}$.

5.6 Describe the first and second normal forms. Define and explain functional dependency with a suitable example.

5.7 Explain different normal forms and the motivation behind achieving them. Write some disadvantages of normalization.

5.8 Define BCNF. Why BCNF is more desirable than 3NF?

5.9 Define lossless-join and dependency preservation. Consider the relation R and set of FDs F as given in Illustration 5.4 above. If we decompose R into R_1(A, B, C) and R_2(A, D, E), do we get a lossless decomposition?

5.10 Discuss Multi-valued dependency and 4NF. How can you decompose a 3NF into a 4NF?

5.11 Let R = (V, W, X, Y, Z) is a relational schema, and let F be the set of following FDs, such that $F = \{Z \rightarrow V, W \rightarrow Y, XY \rightarrow Z, V \rightarrow WX\}$. Determine whether the following decompositions are lossy or lossless.

(i) R_1 = (V, W, X), R_2 = (V, Y, Z) and
(ii) R_1 = (V, W, X), R_2 = (X, Y, Z).

5.12 Let R = (A, B, C, D, E) is a relational schema, and let M be the set of following MVDs: $M = \{A \rightarrow\rightarrow BC, B \rightarrow\rightarrow CD, E \rightarrow\rightarrow AD\}$. List all nontrivial dependencies in M^+.

5.13 Discuss Join dependency and the 5NF. Why the 5NF is also called the Projection Join normal form?

5.14 What is Join dependency? How is it different from Functional dependency and Multi-valued dependency?

5.15 "A decomposition of a 3NF relation into a BCNF, one may be lossless and dependency preserving." Is this statement correct? Justify your answer with a suitable example.

CHAPTER 6

Structured Query Language

Structured Query Language (SQL) is the most widely used data manipulation language for a relational database system. It is a non procedural query language, i.e., statements of this language specify what to do only, and not how to do. However, the instructions or statements of SQL can be very effectively used for generating answers for any specific queries. Since it has simple English like syntax, a novice may also be expected to write a query and get answer. In this chapter, we shall describe fundamental features of SQL, and the types and syntax of statements it supports.

6.1 SQL—A Query Language

SQL is a programming language and supports a number of data types. SQL commands work on relations (tables), their records and attributes. Each table has a unique name table_name , and its attributes are identified as column_name1, column_name2, column_name3, ... etc. The structure of a table called table_name having n attributes or columns is shown below. Each row of a table represents a record or tuple.

Table 6.1 table_name

column_name1	column_name2	...	column_name*n*

Attributes or columns contain values from heterogeneous domains. A specific attribute contains values from only one domain and have a specific data type. Generally, domain data are numeric (number), alphanumeric (character or string) and date data types. A table can have as many as 254 columns. The column or attribute data type descriptions are shown below.

- **Char (*n*):** fixed length (*n*) character values(strings). The maximum value of *n* is 255 bytes, in general. For example, char(20) indicates a string variable of length 20.

If the concerned string is less than 20 characters, the rightmost positions are filled with space/blank characters.

- **Varchar2(*n*):** variable length character string in varchar2(*n*) notation. The maximum value of *n* is 2000 bytes, in general.
- **Number(*t*):** numeric (integer) values having *t* number of digits.
- **Number(*t*, *d*):** numeric values having *t* number of total digits with *d* digits after the decimal point.
- **Long:** character data up to a length of 2GB. Only one long attribute is supported per table.
- **Date:** date in dd-mm-yy notation as default format. For example, the 30th January, 2011 is represented as '30-JAN-11'.
- **Null:** an indicator that an attribute is having a missing value. It is neither a numeric 0 nor an empty string. This type indicates an unknown value only.

6.2 Data Sub Languages

SQL is the default language for relational database management system. It supports not only data retrieval and manipulation operations, but also assists in data definition and control operations. Hence, SQL may be assumed to have three sub-languages. These three different sub-languages are:

- **DDL:** data definition language (includes statements like CREATE, ALTER, DROP, TRUNCATE, COMMENT etc.).
- **DML:** data manipulation language (includes statements like SELECT, INSERT, UPDATE, DELETE, CALL, EXPLAIN PLAN, LOCK TABLE etc.).
- **DCL:** data control language (includes statements like GRANT, REVOKE, COMMIT, SAVEPOINT, ROLLBACK, SET TRANSACTION etc.).

A part of the data control sub-language is also termed transaction control language (TCL), as their purpose is to control the different operations during execution of a database transaction.

6.2.1 Data Definition Language (DDL)

Data Definition Language (DDL) is used to create a new table, change structure of a table or removing a table existing in a database. The above mentioned operation can also be applied to individual rows and columns of a table. That is, using DDL statements, we can insert a new record in a table, delete a record from a table, update or modify an existing record by changing some of its attribute values (columns) etc. After creation of a table, its structure can be displayed by a DDL statement. Addition or deletion of attributes and changing their data types are also possible using DDL statements. Constraints can be imposed on specific attributes whenever necessary.

- The CREATE TABLE command creates a new table.
- The ALTER TABLE command is for the purpose of modifying a table structure.

- To delete a table from a database, the DROP TABLE command is used. This can also be done using the TRUNCATE TABLE command.
- The DESC TABLE command is used to view (describe) the structure of a table.
- DELETE command removes a record from a table.
- CONSTRAINT command is used to impose a constraint on some attribute.
- COMMENT adds comments to the data dictionary.
- The CREATE INDEX command is used to create an index over a table on an attribute.
- The DROP INDEX command is used to remove an existing index.

Syntax of DDL statements

The following are the syntaxes of the commonly used data definition statements.

- CREATE TABLE table_name (column name1 datatype, column_name2 datatype, ..., column_name*n* datatype);
- DESC table_name;
- DROP TABLE table_name;
- TRUNCATE TABLE table_name;
- CONSTRAINT constraintname <CONSTRAINT TYPE> constraintattribute;
- ALTER TABLE table_name ADD/DROP column_name;
- ALTER TABLE table_name MODIFY column_name datatype format;
- DELETE FROM table_name WHERE column_name = value;
- CREATE [UNIQUE] INDEX indexname ON table_name (column_name);
- DROP INDEX indexname;

The ALTER TABLE command is used to modify structure of a Table. A new column can be added; an existing column can be renamed, dropped, or its name, data type and width can be changed.

Examples of DDL statements

In this section, we shall try to illustrate the use of DDL statements. For citing examples of such statements, we shall use the EMP_DETAILS table as the base table over which statements will be applied.

Create statement: Let us consider creation of a table called EMP_DETAILS, containing details information of employees of some organization.

```
CREATE TABLE EMP_DETAILS
   (E_ID CHAR(5),
    E_NAME VARCHAR2(15),
    E_ADD VARCHAR2(20),
    E_DESIG CHAR(5),
    E_JOINDATE DATE,
    E_SAL NUMBER(5));
```

The following data structure will be created by execution of the above statement.

E_ID	E_NAME	E_ADD	E_DESIG	E_JOINDATE	E_SAL

A table, along with its DESCRIPTION can be copied into another table, i.e., a new table can be created by copying an old table. The following is an example of this operation.

```
CREATE TABLE EMPLOYEE_DETAILS AS SELECT * FROM EMP_DETAILS;
```

or,

```
CREATE TABLE EMPLOYEE_DETAILS AS SELECT E_ID, E_NAME, E_ADD, E_DESIG, E_JOINDATE
FROM EMP_DETAILS;
```

Note that, in the second statement of the above two examples, we have used only a subset of attributes from table EMP_DETAILS.

Insert statement: Now let us insert two records in the empty EMP_DETAILS table using the following statements.

```
INSERT INTO EMP_DETAILS VALUES
   ('E1', 'RAM', 'KOLKATA', 'CLERK', '10-JAN-2010', 5000);
INSERT INTO EMP_DETAILS VALUES
   ('E2', 'SAM', 'KALYANI', 'GR-D', '15-JUN-2009', 3000);
```

After insertion of above mentioned two records, the EMP_DETAILS table becomes

E_ID	E_NAME	E_ADD	E_DESIG	E_JOINDATE	E_SAL
E1	RAM	KOLKATA	CLERK	10-JAN-2010	5000
E2	SAM	KALYANI	GR-D	15-JUN-2009	3000

Alter statement: Once a database table is created, we may want to modify its structure. One can change the name of the table, add or drop attributes, reformat or rename attributes, add or remove constraints etc. using the ALTER statement.

The following statement can be used to alter the name of an existing table from `EMP_DETAILS` to `EMPLOYEE_1`.

```
ALTER TABLE EMP_DETAILS RENAME EMPLOYEE_1;
```

We can use the following statement for changing the structure of the table. Here, type of the salary attribute (SAL) will be changed.

```
ALTER TABLE EMP_DETAILS MODIFY E_SAL NUMBER (8, 2) ;
```

During creation of the table, E_SAL was declared to of data type NUMBER of length 5 digits only. After execution of the above statement it will be of length 8 having two positions after the decimal point.

One can change an attribute name by using the ALTER statement. Example is

```
ALTER TABLE EMP_DETAILS RENAME E_JOINDATE TO E_JD;
```

It is possible to remove an attribute from the table or to remove the entire table from the database. Examples of such statements (called DROP statements) are shown below.

```
ALTER TABLE EMP_DETAILS DROP E_JOINDATE;
```

After execution of the above drop statement the table structure becomes

E_ID	E_NAME	E_ADD	E_DESIG	E_SAL
E1	RAM	KOLKATA	CLERK	5000
E2	SAM	KALYANI	GR-D	3000

Delete statement: The `DELETE` statement can be used to remove records from table. Generally, the `DELETE` statement is used along with the where clause.

```
DELETE FROM EMP_DETAILS WHERE E_SAL <5000;
```

After execution of the above `DELETE` statement, the table `EMP_DETAILS` becomes

E_ID	E_NAME	E_ADD	E_DESIG	E_JOINDATE	E_SAL
E1	RAM	KOLKATA	CLERK	10-JAN-2010	5000

Drop statement: Database tables can be removed by using this statement. An example statement is

```
DROP TABLE EMP_DETAILS;
```

And after execution of the last statement, the EMP-DETAILS table will disappear from the database.

Index statement: Indexing is used to facilitate search and access operations from physical database files. An index is created on some attribute of the concerned base table. In the index there are two fields, index value and a block pointer, and thus, it is very small in size compared to the base table. It can be read into main memory quickly, sorted according to the index values in ascending or descending order, and binary search can be applied over it. After the desired block from storage is read, it is searched linearly for the requested record.

An index file can be created in SQL using the CREATE INDEX statement. Examples of INDEX creation and dropping are given below.

```
CREATE UNIQUE INDEX emp_ndx ON EMP_DETAILS(E_ID);
```

Using the above statement we can create the index emp_ndx for the EMP_DETAILS table over the primary key attribute E_ID. Hence, the created index will be a primary index. It is notable here that, majority of the relational database systems maintains an index for a table using the primary key automatically. This is based on the assumption that frequent data accesses are made by application programs using the primary key. If the primary key of the concerned table is dropped somehow, the corresponding index will also be dropped automatically.

A composite index, over a combination of attributes, can be created. For example, if we like to order employee records according to the attributes E_ID and E_JOINDATE, we can use the following statement:

```
CREATE UNIQUE INDEX id_jd_ndx ON EMP_DETAILS(E_ID, E_JOINDATE);
```

Indexes over non-key attributes are called secondary indexes. An index can be dropped explicitly, after its creation, by using the DROP INDEX statement. This is generally done when the indexes are created over non-primary-key attributes. Example is

```
DROP INDEX id_jd_ndx;
```

Indexes enhance search efficiency, but they may complicate the updation of tables. Hence, it is not wise to maintain many indexes for a table.

Constraints

A data type can properly identify the kind of data to be stored in a certain column of a database table. However, only data type is not sufficient to ensure the logical category of a data item. For example, numeric type data (NUMBER) can hold any number; but when an attribute like AGE (of a person) is used in a table having numeric data type, it is unable to specify that only positive values are acceptable in this column. Again, there are situations where each record in a table should have only UNIQUE values, no duplication is allowed; but we cannot specify this feature during column declaration. Similarly, database integrity restrictions, i.e., non-NULL values for primary key attributes, and non-existent foreign key attributes, must also be ensured during creation of a database table. SQL provides with a CONSTRAINT statement by which the above mentioned restrictions over column data can be specified during data definition.

Generally, constraints can be applied over a column (attribute) or the table itself. Accordingly, we get:

1. **Column constraint:** It is specified as a part of column definition and applies only over the particular column.
2. **Table constraint:** A table constraint applies over more than one column of a table, and it is specified as a part of table definition.

Column constraint syntax: <column_name> datatype CONSTRAINT <constraint_name> <default_value>;

In the above syntax, the use of *constraint_name* is optional. It is, however, suggested to use a separate constraint name for each constraint. While defining a new constraint, the existence of another constraint with the same name may be verified by checking *constraint_name*. This may also be followed while dropping an already defined constraint.

ILLUSTRATION 6.1 We consider that the attribute ROLL_NO (roll number) in a STUDENTS table should have Non-NULL values only. This can be specified in the column definition as

```
ROLL_NUMBER NUMBER(3) CONSTRAINT Nnull NOT NULL;
```

Here, Nnull is the constraint name and NOT NULL is the *default_value*.

Table constraint syntax: CONSTRAINT <constraintname> PRIMARY KEY <column_name>;
CONSTRAINT <constraintname> FOREIGN KEY <column_name> REFERENCES <table_name> [(<column_name>)];
CONSTRAINT <constraintname> UNIQUE <column_name>;
CONSTRAINT <constraintname> CHECK <search_condition>;

ILLUSTRATION 6.2 We consider that the registration number attribute REG_NUMBER in a STUDENTS table should be the primary key. Let REG_NO (registration number) be a foreign key in another table MARKS. These can be specified in the table definition as:

```
CONSTRAINT Pkey PRIMARY KEY REG_NO;
CONSTRAINT Fkey FOREIGN KEY REG_NO REFERENCES STUDENTS (REG_NO);
```

Also, if we want to specify that the ROLL_ NUMBER field should have UNIQUE values, then we can write the constraint as:

```
CONSTRAINT Unik UNIQUE ROLL_NUMBER;
```

A table constraint can also be defined as a column constraint. Generally, the table constraints are written at the end of table definition, and the column constraints are written along with the definition of the concerned column. Let us consider the example STUDENTS relation as shown below.

REG_NUMBER	NAME	ROLL_NUMBER	DISCIPLINE	DATE_ADMITTED

This table can be created by using the following statement.

```
CREATE TABLE STUDENTS
    (REG_NUMBER CHAR(10) CONSTRAINT Pkey PRIMARY KEY,
    NAME VARCHAR2(20),
    ROLL_NUMBER NUMBER(2),
    DISCIPLINE CHAR(3),
    DATE_ADMITTED DATE);
```

Here, the primary key constraint is a column constraint. The same table can also be defined as

```
CREATE TABLE STUDENTS
    (REG_NUMBER CHAR(10),
    NAME VARCHAR2(20),
    ROLL_NUMBER NUMBER(2),
    DISCIPLINE CHAR(3),
    DATE_ADMITTED DATE,
    CONSTRAINT Pkey PRIMARY KEY (REG_NUMBER));
```

where, the primary key constraint is a table constraint.

The CHECK constraint is applied for checking the range or domain of some attribute over possible values. For example, if we consider that the roll number of students must vary from 0 to 50 and not beyond, we can use the following constraint while creating the STUDENTS table.

```
CREATE TABLE STUDENTS
   (REG_NUMBER CHAR(10)CONSTRAINT Pkey PRIMARY KEY,
   NAME VARCHAR2(20),
   ROLL_NUMBER NUMBER(2)CONSTRAINT Ccheck CHECK(ROLL_NUMBER BETWEEN 0 AND 50),
   DISCIPLINE CHAR(3),
   DATE_ADMITTED DATE);
```

Note that, we can apply multiple constraints over the same attribute by concatenating CONSTRAINTS clauses with spaces between them.

It is also important to note that, when a table is copied into another table, only the NOT NULL constraints are copied, and the other constraints are not copied. They must be specified again for the new table if necessary.

6.2.2 Data Control Language (DCL)

Data control language is generally used by the Database Administrator (or other empowered users) for different control operations and security purposes. Such operations include creating user accounts, dropping an existing user, granting any specific role/permission to a user etc. Some commands are used to control specific operations related to a transaction. Sometimes, DCL is termed TCL (Transaction Control Language). Examples of some DCL statements are:

- CREATE USER command is used to create a new user.
- DROP USER command is used to delete an existing user from the database.
- GRANT command may be used to allow a user with any specific permission.
- REVOKE command withdraws an already given permission using GRANT.
- COMMIT command is used to save transactions permanently.
- ROLLBACK command is used to recall transactions after the last commit.
- SAVEPOINT command allows us to create a save-point in the midway of some operation and to give it a suitable name.

Syntax of DCL statements

The following are the syntaxes of the commonly used data control statements.

- CREATE USER <username> IDENTIFIED BY <password>
- DROP USER <username>
- GRANT <resource or role> TO <username>
- REVOKE <resource or role> FROM <username>
- COMMIT
- ROLLBACK
- SAVEPOINT <savepointname>

Example of DCL statements

Some examples of the commonly used data control statements are given below.

- CREATE USER: creates a new user account.
  — `CREATE USER mkp IDENTIFIED BY mkp01;`

- DROP USER: deletes an existing user account.
  - `DROP USER mkp;`
- GRANT: grants specific permissions to specific user. The complete syntax for the GRANT statement is given below.
  - GRANT SELECT / INSERT / DELETE / UPDATE / ALL PRIVILEDGES ON <*table-name*> TO <*user-name*> / PUBLIC [WITH GRANT OPTION];
  - Examples are:

```
– GRANT SELECT, INSERT ON STUDENTS TO mkp;
– GRANT ALL PRIVILEDGES ON STUDENTS TO mkp;
– GRANT ALL ON STUDENTS TO PUBLIC;
```

  - 'ALL' and 'ALL PRIVILEDGES' behave similarly. 'PUBLIC' means granting to all users.
- REVOKE: withdraws specific permissions granted earlier to specific user. The complete syntax for the REVOKE statement is given below.
  - REVOKE SELECT / INSERT / DELETE / UPDATE / ALL PRIVILEDGES ON <*table-name*> FROM <*user-name*> / PUBLIC;
  - Examples are:

```
– REVOKE SELECT, INSERT ON STUDENTS FROM mkp;
– REVOKE ALL PRIVILEDGES ON STUDENTS FROM mkp;
– REVOKE ALL ON STUDENTS FROM PUBLIC;
```

- COMMIT: completes database updation by a transaction.

```
— INSERT INTO EMP VALUES (…, …, …);
— COMMIT;
```

  - Insertion is saved.
- ROLLBACK: rolls back up to a certain statement in a transaction.

```
— INSERT INTO EMP VALUES (…, …, …);
— ROLLBACK;
```

  - Earlier insertion operation is cancelled.
- SAVEPOINT: specifies a certain statement using a label.

```
— CREATE TABLE EMP_DETAILS (…, …, … );
  INSERT INTO EMP VALUES (…, …, …);
  SAVEPOINT A;
  INSERT INTO EMP VALUES (…, …, …);
```

  - By execution of the above statements, a table is created, two records are inserted, and a save-point is created after the first insertion. An important use of the SAVEPOINT command is that after a save-point is created and named, we can rollback up to that point during an operation. For example, if we execute the following statement after the second insertion, the effect of the second insertion will be eliminated.
  - ROLLBACK TO A;

6.2.3 Data Manipulation Language (DML)

After tables are created for the database, we must insert records in them, and manipulate data according to the need of the applications concerned. These can be done by using Data Manipulation Language (DML). Besides insertion, deletion and updation, there are data retrieval operations. These retrieval operations are generally performed by means of SQL SELECT statements. We shall use a separate chapter to show various kinds of retrieval operations from one or more associated tables. In the present chapter, we shall try to describe the basic roles of the DML statements.

Syntax and Examples

Syntax of the commonly used data manipulation statements and some examples are shown below.

- The SELECT command is used to retrieve and display the contents of a table. Example syntaxes are:
  - — SELECT * FROM table_name;
  - — SELECT column_name1, column_name2 FROM table_name;
  - — SELECT * FROM table_name WHERE column_name < value;
  - — SELECT * FROM table_name WHERE column_name = value;
  - — SELECT * FROM table_name WHERE column_name > value;
- We shall describe different kind of SELECT statements in the next chapter in detail.
- The INSERT INTO command is used to insert a new record in an existing table. Example syntaxes are:
  - — INSERT INTO table_name VALUES (value1, value2, ...);
  - — INSERT INTO table_name [(column_name(s))] VALUES (value1, value2, ...);
  - — Using the above syntaxes, we can insert a single row in the table at a time. In the first syntax only column values are specified, and in the second syntax both column names and values are specified. If the number of column name and number of values do not match, or if the data types of corresponding pairs do not match, an error message will be displayed during execution.
  - — Following are the examples of valid INSERT statements:
    - – `INSERT INTO EMP_DETAILS VALUES ('E1', 'RAM', 'KOLKATA', 'CLERK', '10-JAN-2010', 5000);`
    - – `INSERT INTO EMP_DETAILS (E_ID, E_NAME, E_ADD, E_DESIG, E_JOINDATE, E_SAL) VALUES ('E1', 'RAM', 'KOLKATA', 'CLERK', '10-JAN-2010', 5000);`
  - — Following are the examples of invalid INSERT statements:
    - – `INSERT INTO EMP_DETAILS VALUES ('E1', 'RAM', 'KOLKATA', 'CLERK', '10-JAN-2010');`
    - – `INSERT INTO EMP_DETAILS (E_ID, E_NAME, E_ADD, E_DESIG, E_JOINDATE, E_SAL) VALUES ('E1', 'RAM', 'KOLKATA', 'CLERK', '10-JAN-2010');`
    - – Here, number of values specified is one less than that specified in table definition.

— Following is an example of invalid INSERT statements:

```
– INSERT INTO EMP_DETAILS (E_NAME, E_ADD, E_DESIG, E_JOINDATE, E_SAL)
  VALUES ('RAM', 'KOLKATA', 'CLERK', '10-JAN-2010');
```

– Here, the key attribute E_ID is not specified in either the column list or the value list. Before insertion of a record, SQL automatically assigns a NULL value to any non-specified attribute. However, E-ID being the primary key of EMP_DETAILS table, during insertion of the above record an entity integrity violation will take place.

— During insertion of a record SQL automatically inserts a NULL value for any non-specified attribute(s). Or, it may be specified by the user explicitly. Check the following valid examples.

```
– INSERT INTO EMP_DETAILS (E_ID, E_NAME, E_ADD, E_DESIG, E_JOINDATE) VALUES
  ('E1', 'RAM', 'KOLKATA', 'CLERK', '10-JAN-2010');
– INSERT INTO EMP_DETAILS (E_ID, E_NAME, E_ADD, E_DESIG, E_JOINDATE, E_SAL)
  VALUES ('E1', 'RAM', 'KOLKATA', 'CLERK', '10-JAN-2010', NULL);
```

- The DELETE command is used to remove specific attributes or specific records from a table. Examples of syntaxes are:

— DELETE FROM table_name;
— DELETE FROM table_name WHERE column_name = value;
— The first kind of DELETE statements will remove all existing records from the table. For example, we can remove all records from EMP_DETAILS table by using

```
– DELETE FROM EMP_DETAILS;
```

— The second syntax can be used to delete records selectively based upon a condition. For example, the following statement removes records having salary values < 500. This is safer strategy for deletion of records.

```
– DELETE FROM EMP_DETAILS WHERE E_SAL < 500;
```

— The following DELETE statements are incorrect

```
– DELETE * FROM EMP_DETAILS;
– DELETE E_ID FROM EMP_DETAILS;
```

- The UPDATE command is used to modify specific attribute values or specific records of a table. Example syntaxes are:

— UPDATE table_name SET column_name = expression/value;
— UPDATE table_name SET column_name 1 = value 1 WHERE column_name 2 = value 2;
— The first statement will set/replace all values in the specified column by the computed value of the given *expression*. For example

```
– UPDATE EMP_DETAILS SET E_SAL = 5000;
– UPDATE EMP_DETAILS SET E_SAL = NULL;
```

— The second type of UPDATE statements performs conditional updation of specific rows or columns. Examples are

```
– UPDATE EMP_DETAILS SET E_SAL = 5000 WHERE E_DESIG = 'CLERK';
– UPDATE EMP_DETAILS SET E_ADD = 'KOLKATA', E_SAL = E_SAL + 5000 WHERE
  E_DESIG = 'CLERK';
```

— In the last example, multiple columns and selective rows are updates conditionally.

6.3 Single Row Functions Used in SQL

These functions are stored in SQL library, and are used to simplify programming effort. Also, the use of these single row functions maintains the non-procedural nature of the basic SQL. These functions can be broadly categorized as:

- **Arithmetic functions:** Simplify using arithmetic/numeric operations.
- **Group functions:** Aggregate and statistical operations are facilitated.
- **String/Character functions:** String or character manipulations are done.
- **Date functions:** Facilitates different forms of representing a date.

6.3.1 Arithmetic Operations in SQL

Table 6.2 summarizes the use of some commonly used arithmetic operations. These operations can be applied over numeric fields only.

Table 6.2 Arithmetic Functions

Function	Result
ABS (column_name)	Returns absolute value
GREATEST (column_name1, column_name2)	Returns greatest of column_name1 and column_name2
LEAST (column_name1, column_name2)	Returns greatest of column_name1 and column_name2
TRUNC (column_name, no.)	Truncates column values to specified number of decimals
ROUND (column_name, no.)	Rounds column values to specified number of decimals

6.3.2 Group Operations in SQL

Table 6.3 summarizes the use of some commonly used group/statistical operations. These operations can be applied over numeric fields only.

6.3.3 String Functions in SQL

Table 6.4 summarizes the use of some commonly used string operations. These operations can be applied over character type attributes or fields only.

Table 6.3 Group Functions

Function	Result
AVG (column_name)	Returns average value of column, ignoring NULL values
COUNT (*)	Returns count of records/rows, where a conditional expression evaluates to some non-NULL value.
MAX(column_name)	Returns maximum value of a column, ignoring NULL values
MIN(column_name)	Returns minimum value of a column, ignoring NULL values
SUM(column_name)	Returns sum of a column, ignoring NULL values
STDDEV(column_name)	Returns standard deviation of a column, ignoring NULL values
VARIANCE (column_name)	Returns variance of a column, ignoring NULL values

Table 6.4 Character Functions

Function	Result
INITCAP (column/string)	Converts first letter of word to uppercase
LENGTH (column/string)	Returns the count of characters in the specified string
LOWER (column/string)	Converts to lower case
UPPER (column/string)	Converts to upper case
SUBSTR (column/string, n_1, n_2)	Displays substring from position n_1 up to n_2 characters
DECODE ()	Translates results
DECODE (code, 'X', 1, 'Y', 2, 100)	Converts X's into 1, Y's into 2 and other characters, if any, into 100
TO_NUMBER (char, [fmt])	Converts a character string containing a number into a format specified by the optional format (fmt).

6.3.4 Date Functions in SQL

Table 6.5 summarizes the use of some commonly used date operations. These operations can be applied over date type attributes or fields only.

Table 6.5 Date Functions

Built-in-function	Result
ADD_MONTHS (date, number)	Returns date plus number
MONTHS_BETWEEN (d_1, d_2)	Returns months between two dates d_1 and d_2
NEXT_DATE (d, 'Sunday')	Returns date first Sunday after the date (d)
TO_CHAR (d, format)	Converts d to character, the format specified Example: TO_CHAR (d, 'MM/DD/YY')
TO_DATE (cd, format)	Converts a character value to date according to format specified

The use of the above functions in association with different data retrieval operations will be discussed in a later chapter concerned with query handling.

Some examples of the use of single row functions are given below. Only SQL statements are presented here. The reader may assume any suitable set of tables for understanding.

```
1. SELECT AVG (SALARY) FROM EMPLOYEE GROUP BY DEPARTMENT;
2. SELECT MIN (SALARY), MAX(SALARY) FROM EMPLOYEE;
3. SELECT COUNT(*) FROM EMPLOYEE;
4. SELECT ROUND(COST) FROM PRODUCTS WHERE ITEM = 'PEN';
5. SELECT SUM(SALES) FROM SALE_DETAILS GROUP BY SALE_DATE WHERE SALE_DATE >
   '01-JAN-12';
6. SELECT SYSDATE, TRUNC(SALE_DATE, 'MONTH') FROM SALE_DETAILS;
7. SELECT SUBSTR(ENAME, 1, 3) FROM EMPLOYEE;
8. SELECT ITEM, LPAD(COST, 5, '#') FROM PRODUCTS;
9. SELECT ITEM, RPAD(COST, 5, '#') FROM PRODUCTS;
10. SELECT TO_CHAR(SALE_DATE, 'DD-Month YYYY HH:MI') FROM SALE_DETAILS;
11. SELECT INITCAP(TO_CHAR(SALE_DATE, 'MONTH YEAR')) DT_DESC FROM SALE_DETAILS;
12. SELECT ROWNUM, ENAME, SALARY FROM EMPLOYEE;
```

6.4 SQL*PLUS

SQL*PLUS is a command line SQL interpreter in Oracle. It comes with both the Oracle server and client software, and commands can be used either interactively from the command line prompt or as a part of the SQL script. Interaction with the Oracle database and system are made easy by the use of this SQL*PLUS. Although almost all the SQL statements can be executed from the command line of SQL*PLUS, it is better to use as some system oriented service provider.

6.4.1 Features of SQL*PLUS

SQL*PLUS is treated as an interactive user interface to the Oracle DBMS. SQL queries or commands can be typed using an inbuilt editor and query results can be displayed on the screen. Several features of the SQL*PLUS are listed below:

- A built command-line editor can be used for editing SQL queries. Although queries can be typed using any other editor available in the system, it is always better to use an integrated platform.
- Query outputs can be formatted using SQL*PLUS commands.
- SQL*PLUS provides a detailed online help.
- Query results can be stored in files which can be displayed later or can be printed. Frequently used queries can be saved in a file and invoked later. Queries can be parameterized so that a query can be invoked with different parameter values.

6.4.2 Editing Commands for SQL*PLUS

It is already mentioned that queries or commands can be typed using the SQL editor. The most recently used command is stored in the SQL buffer, and this command can be modified and re-executed. Some important editing commands used for this purpose are:

- l[ist]: lists all lines in the SQL buffer and sets the current line (marked with a ".") to the last line in the buffer.
- l<number>: sets the actual line to <number>.
- c[hange]/<old-string>/<new-string>: replaces first occurrence of <old-string> by <new-string> (for the actual line).
- a[ppend]<string>: appends <string> to the current line.
- .del: deletes the current line from the buffer.
- r[un]: executes the current buffer contents.
- get<file>: reads data from the file <file> into the buffer.
- save<file>: writes the current buffer contents into a file <file>.
- edit: invokes an editor and loads the current buffer into the editor. After exiting the editor, the modified SQL command is stored in the buffer again and can be executed.

The editor can be defined in the SQL*PLUS shell by typing the command ***define editor*** = *<name>*, where *<name>* can be any existing editor like *vi*, *emacs*, *jove* etc.

6.4.3 Help System in SQL*PLUS

- SQL*PLUS can provide online help to the users. By simply typing **help** *<command>* or just **help**, we can get information regarding how to use the desired *<command>* correctly.
- User passwords can be changed using the **passw***<user>* command.
- Host machine commands can be executed using the **host** *<UNIX command>* command.
- A complete database file can be copied using the command **copy from** command. Example is: **copy from** scott/tiger **create** EMPL **using select** * **from** EMP;
- SQL commands saved in a file *<filename>*.sql can be loaded into SQL*PLUS and executed using the command: @*<filename>*.

6.5 Data Dictionary

Data Dictionary (DD) is the storage of metadata (data regarding data). System level descriptions of data records, tables, indexes, views, triggers, comments etc. are maintained in Data Dictionary. Generally DD contents are accessed and used by the database administrator (DBA). However, many views of data may be provided by the DD to the common users. These views can be used in SQL queries just like normal tables. The DD has two parts: internal and external. Internal level data are used by the DBMS itself and are not available to common users. The external level data are related to user defined tables and objects, and they can be easily accessed.

6.5.1 Database Users and Data Dictionary

The Oracle database creates three different categories of users during installation. These are:

- **SYS:** This user has the highest degree of privileges to access and manage different objects and structures of the Oracle database, and can create other users.
- **SYSTEM:** This user is the owner of internal tables generated by different tools, such as SQL*Forms, SQL*Reports etc. This user has less privileges than SYS.
- **PUBLIC:** This is a dummy user in an Oracle database. All privileges assigned user are automatically assigned to all other users of the database.

The DD provides the following information to the database users:

- Users and their access privileges
- Tables, columns, data types and indexes used by the user
- Privileges granted on database objects
- Storage structures of the database.

Three different categories of views are provided by Oracle DD. These are USER view, ALL view, and DBA view. Some of the views under different categories are listed in Tables 6.6 to 6.8.

Table 6.6 USER Views of DD

ITEM	Description
USER_TABLES	Tables with their contents, number of columns, storage information, statistical information etc. (TABS)
USER_CATALOG	Tables, views and synonyms (CAT)
USER_COL_COMMENTS	Comments on columns
USER_CONSTRAINTS	Constraints defined on tables
USER_INDEXES	Information regarding indexes created on user tables
USER_OBJECTS	All database objects owned by the user (OBJ)
USER_TAB_COLUMNS	Columns of tables and views owned by the user
USER_TAB_COMMENTS	Comments on tables and views
USER_TRIGGERS	User defined triggers
USER_USERS	Current user information
USER_VIEWS	User defined views

Table 6.7 ALL Views of the DD

ITEM	Description
ALL_TABLES	Owners and names of all accessible tables
ALL_CATALOG	Owners, names and types of all accessible tables, views and synonyms
ALL_OBJECTS	Owners, names and types of all accessible objects
ALL_TRIGGERS	All defined triggers
ALL_USERS	All user information
ALL_VIEWS	All defined views

Table 6.8 DBA Views of the DD

ITEM	Description
DBA_TABLES	Tables of all users
DBA_CATALOG	Tables, views and synonyms in the database
DBA_OBJECTS	All accessible objects
DBA_DATA_FILES	Information about data files
ALL_USERS	All user information

6.5.2 SQL Commands to Access DD

Some SQL commands are given below which can show the contents of the DD.

```
SELECT * FROM DICT[IONARY];
```

This command lists all tables and views of the DD that are accessible to the user. The selected information includes the name and short description of each table and view. Before generating any query the user may check the structure and column definitions of tables and views (of the DD) by using the following command:

```
DESC DICT[IONARY];
```

The following command retrieves names of all accessible tables (owned by the user):

```
SELECT * FROM TAB;
```

Similarly, the command

```
SELECT * FROM COL;
```

returns all the information regarding columns of one's own tables.

Exercises

6.1 What are different components of SQL? Give example statements of different types.

6.2 Discuss common data types supported by SQL.

6.3 Specify differences between VARCHAR and VARCHAR2 declarations.

6.4 What operator is used in SQL for string manipulation? Show examples.

6.5 What is the purpose of using CREATE and DESCRIBE statements?

6.6 What are the differences between data definition language and data manipulation language

6.7 Write down example statements of different kinds of DCL.

6.8 Give a description of different kinds of variables used in SQL.

6.9 What are single line functions in SQL? List different types of such functions.

6.10 In what different formats a DATE can be specified in SQL? How to convert them from one format to another? Give examples.

6.11 What are constraints in SQL? How PRIMARY KEY can be declared as a row constraint or a table constraint? Explain with examples.

6.12 List all different kinds of constraints that are used in SQL with examples.

6.13 What are roles of checking constraints? How can you remove a constraint?

6.14 How NULL values are handled in SQL queries?

6.15 Discuss how set operations be implemented in SQL.

6.16 What are Data Control Statements? List all DCL statements and give examples for each of them.

6.17 Write down the roles of SQL*PLUS in query processing.

6.18 How SQL commands can be used to access data dictionary contents? Give examples.

CHAPTER 7

Information Retrieval and Data Manipulation

The most general approach for extracting information from a database is by generation of queries. In RDBMS, a query is nothing but an SQL statement. SQL (Structured Query Language) is a query language that allows access to data residing in the database. SQL is not only a command level language but a comprehensive language for processing, controlling and interacting with data in a database.

7.1 Features of SQL

SQL is standardized by ANSI and ISO with universal rules. SQL supports the following operations in relation to processing of a database.

- Acts as a command level language to support end-user queries.
- Acts as a comprehensive programming language by virtue of the property that it can be easily embedded into other high level programming languages.
- Acts as a comprehensive tool for the database administrator in controlling database structures, database transaction and granting authorisation for using resources.
- In Client-Server mode SQL allows remote execution of queries.
- SQL is platform independent and can be executed without regard to operating systems.

7.1.1 Query Handling in SQL

In this section, we shall illustrate query processing with some examples. For the purpose of generating queries we shall use example relations. Two such relations are shown in Tables 7.1 and 7.3. One of these relations is the STUDENTS relation and the other is an EMP_DETAILS (employee details) relation. The attributes of Tables 7.1 and 7.3, described in Tables 7.2 and 7.4, are self explanatory. The STUDENTS table contains information regarding marks and grade obtained by a student in an examination. The Institute computes grades as follows: Grade A means 80 or more, B grade means 60 to 79, C grade means 50 to 59, and below 50 is considered to be D grade.

Table 7.1 STUDENTS Table

NAME	ROLL-NO	DISCIPLINE	MARKS	GRADE
ANIL	1	CSE	86	A
RATHIN	2	CSE	67	B
SIKHA	3	ECE	54	C
SHYAMAL	4	ECE	45	D
PARESH	5	ME	49	D
TRISHA	6	ME	64	B
RINA	7	CSE	54	C
ANIK	8	ECE	54	C

In the STUDENTS table, we maintain the following attributes and specific data types.

Table 7.2 Data Types in STUDENTS Table

ATTRIBUTE	TYPE	SPECIFICATION
NAME	Alphanumeric	Char(10)
ROLL-NO	Numeric	Number(3)
DISCIPLINE	Alphanumeric	Char(5)
MARKS	Numeric	Number(3)
GRADE	Alphanumeric	Char(1)

Table 7.3 EMP_DETAILS Table

E_ID	E_NAME	E_DEPT	E_DESIGNATION	E_JOINDATE	E_SALARY
5	SAJAL	PRODUCTION	MANAGER	24-FEB-78	50000
12	RAMA	MARKETING	CLERK	12-JUL-85	16000
7	BHOLA	MARKETING	SALESMAN	11-JUN-99	12000
13	KRISHNA	MARKETING	ANALYST	22-MAR-87	35000
15	RIA	PRODUCTION	CLERK	30-AUG-89	15000
16	SUHEL	ACCOUNTS	ACCOUNTANT	23-DEC-88	36000
18	BHOLA	ACCOUNTS	CLERK	04-NOV-95	14500

In the EMP_DETAILS table, we maintain the following attributes and specific data types.

Table 7.4 Data Types in EMP_DETAILS

ATTRIBUTE	TYPE	SPECIFICATION
E_ID	Numeric	Number(3)
E_NAME	Alphanumeric	Char(10)
E_DEPT	Alphanumeric	Char(10)
E_DESIGNATION	Alphanumeric	Char(10)
E_JOINDATE	Date	Date
E_SALARY	Numeric	Number(5)

SELECT with WHERE clause

The WHERE clause is used in SELECT statement to specify a search condition that limits the number of rows or tuples retrieved. Complete rows or records are retrieved by this operation.

Syntax:

- SELECT * FROM table_name
  WHERE condition;
- SELECT column_name(s) FROM table_name
  WHERE condition;

ILLUSTRATION 7.1 Find a list of those students who have acquired more than 50 marks.

Solution

```
- SELECT * FROM STUDENTS
WHERE MARKS > 50;
```

Result:

NAME	ROLL_NO	DISCIPLINE	MARKS	GRADE
ANIL	1	CSE	86	A
RATHIN	2	CSE	67	B
SIKHA	3	ECE	54	C
TRISHA	6	ME	64	B
RINA	7	CSE	54	C
ANIK	8	ECE	54	C

ILLUSTRATION 7.2 Find name and roll number of those students who have acquired more than 50 marks.

Solution

```
- SELECT NAME, ROLL-NO FROM STUDENTS
  WHERE MARKS > 50;
```

Result:

NAME	ROLL_NO
ANIL	1
RATHIN	2
SIKHA	3
TRISHA	6
RINA	7
ANIK	8

ILLUSTRATION 7.3 Find name and designation of those employees who are working in production department.

Solution

```
- SELECT E_NAME, E_DESIGNATION FROM EMP_DETAILS
  WHERE E_DEPT = 'PRODUCTION';
```

Result:

E_NAME	E_DESIGNATION
SAJAL	MANAGER
RIA	CLERK

SELECT with DISTINCT clause

DISTINCT clause eliminates the possibility of producing duplicate rows for an entity, if any, in the output.

Syntax:

```
- SELECT DISTINCT column_name FROM table_name
```

ILLUSTRATION 7.4 Find a list of distinct names of employees.

Solution

```
- SELECT DISTINCT E_NAME FROM EMP_DETAILS
```

Result:

E_NAME
SAJAL
RAMA
BHOLA
KRISHNA
RIA
SUHEL

This query displays the names of distinct employees in the enterprise. Note that, only the first occurrence of the name 'BHOLA' is present in the output.

ILLUSTRATION 7.5 Find a list of distinct names of employees.

Solution

```
- SELECT DISTINCT E_DEPT FROM EMP_DETAILS
```

Result:

E_DEPT
PRODUCTION
MARKETING
ACCOUNTS

This query displays the names of distinct departments in the enterprise. Note that only the first occurrence of a department name is present in the output.

SELECT with BETWEEN clause

Using the BETWEEN operator we can specify the range of search attribute values for which outputs will be generated.

Syntax:

```
- SELECT column_name1 FROM table_name
    WHERE
    Column_name2 BETWEEN value1 AND value2;
```

ILLUSTRATION 7.6 Consider the STUDENTS database where marks for students are maintained. List names of students whose marks lie between 60 and 70 (including).

Solution

```
- SELECT NAME FROM STUDENTS
    WHERE
    PERCENTAGE BETWEEN 60 AND 70;
```

Result:

NAME
RATHIN
TRISHA

SELECT with IN clause

The IN operator checks whether values of the search attribute are taken from the specified set of values. While the BETWEEN operator checks for range of values, the IN operator checks for set membership.

Syntax:

```
- SELECT * FROM table_name
    WHERE
    column_name IN (value1, value2, value3, … );
```

ILLUSTRATION 7.7 Consider the EMP_DETAILS database. Find out the details of employees whose departments are MARKETING and PRODUCTION.

Solution

```
- SELECT * FROM EMP_DETAILS
    WHERE
    E_DEPT IN ('MARKETING', 'PRODUCTION');
```

Result:

E_NO	E_NAME	E_DEPT	E_DESIGNATION	E_JOINDATE	E_SALARY
5	SAJAL	PRODUCTION	MANAGER	24-FEB-78	50000
12	RAMA	MARKETING	CLERK	12-JUL-85	16000
7	BHOLA	MARKETING	SALESMAN	11-JUN-99	12000
13	KRISHNA	MARKETING	ANALYST	22-MAR-87	35000
15	RIA	PRODUCTION	CLERK	30-AUG-89	15000

SELECT with ORDER BY clause

The retrieved records will be produced, in ascending or descending order of values of the specified attribute, in the output.

Syntax:

```
- SELECT * FROM table_name
  ORDER BY
  column_name ASC / DESC;
```

ILLUSTRATION 7.8 Consider the STUDENTS database where marks for students are maintained. List name, and roll number of students in descending order of marks.

Solution

```
- SELECT NAME, ROLL-NO FROM STUDENTS
  ORDER BY
  MARKS DSC;
```

Result:

NAME	ROLL-NO
ANIL	1
TRISHA	6
RATHIN	2
SIKHA	3
RINA	7
ANIK	8
PARESH	5
SHYAMAL	4

SELECT with NULL clause

The NULL clause is used to indicate the presence or absence of a value in the specified attribute or column. Note that, the word "IS" is used (instead of equals to symbol) before the word NULL, this is due to the fact that NULL is not a value (of any specific data type) but an indicator of absence of value.

Syntax:

```
- SELECT * FROM table_name
  WHERE
  column_name IS NULL;
```

ILLUSTRATION 7.9 Consider the STUDENTS database where marks for students are maintained. Find a list of students' name and roll number whose marks are NULL.

Solution

```
- SELECT NAME, ROLL_NO FROM STUDENTS
  WHERE
  MARKS IS NULL;
```

Result:

NAME	ROLL-NO

This query displays the names and roll numbers of students having a 'NULL' value for marks. No such record is found in the table.

SELECT with NOT NULL clause

Its use is similar to that of the NULL clause, but in the opposite sense.

Syntax:

```
- SELECT * FROM table_name
  WHERE
  column_name IS NOT NULL;
```

ILLUSTRATION 7.10 List name and roll number of students where marks is not 'NULL'.

Solution

```
- SELECT NAME, ROLL-NO FROM STUDENTS
  WHERE
  MARKS IS NOT NULL;
```

Result:

NAME	ROLL-NO
ANIL	1
RATHIN	2
SIKHA	3
SHYAMAL	4
PARESH	5
TRISHA	6
RINA	7
ANIK	8

SELECT with AS clause

By using the AS clause we can get output values with different column headings (titles), other than those that are specified in the base table.

Syntax:

```
- SELECT column_name1 AS [newcolumn_name1], column_name2 AS [newcolumn_name2]
  FROM table_name;
```

ILLUSTRATION 7.11 Find a list of names and total marks from the STUDENTS database renaming of the above attributes as "Student's name" and "Marks obtained" respectively.

Solution

```
- SELECT NAME AS [Student's name], MARKS AS [Marks obtained] FROM STUDENTS;
```

Result:

Students' name	Marks obtained
ANIL	86
RATHIN	67
SIKHA	54
SHYAMAL	45
PARESH	49
TRISHA	64
RINA	54
ANIK	54

SELECT with expression

Expressions can be evaluated by SQL, using column names as variables, and output can be under the same column-name heading.

Syntax:

```
- SELECT expression using column_name
  FROM table_name;
```

ILLUSTRATION 7.12 Consider a STUDENTS database where name and marks obtained by each student are maintained. Suppose it is decided that 10% of the marks obtained will be given to each student as grace marks. Find a list of names and new marks.

Solution

```
- SELECT NAME, MARKS + MARKS * 10/100 USING MARKS FROM STUDENTS;
```

Result:

NAME	MARKS
ANIL	94.6
RATHIN	73.7
SIKHA	59.4
SHYAMAL	49.5
PARESH	53.9
TRISHA	70.4
RINA	59.4
ANIK	59.4

SELECT with LIKE clause

The LIKE operator is used to check similarity of strings. The character '_' indicates similarity with exactly one unknown character at the specified position, and the character '%' indicates similarity with any number of unknown characters.

Syntax:

```
- SELECT * FROM table_name WHERE column_name LIKE 'A%' ;
- SELECT * FROM table_name WHERE column_name LIKE 'A_' ;
```

ILLUSTRATION 7.13 Let us consider the STUDENTS database. Find all students' names and roll numbers whose name starts with 'S'.

Solution

```
- SELECT NAME, ROLL-NO FROM STUDENTS
  WHERE
  NAME LIKE 'S%';
```

Result:

NAME	ROLL-NO
SIKHA	3
SHYAMAL	4

ILLUSTRATION 7.14 Let us consider the STUDENTS database. Find all students' names and roll numbers whose name matches with 'ANI_'.

Solution

```
- SELECT NAME, ROLL-NO FROM STUDENTS
  WHERE
  NAME LIKE 'ANI_';
```

Result:

NAME	ROLL-NO
ANIL	1
ANIK	8

Select statements with set operations

Some set theoretic operations can be applied while retrieving data from tables. These operations are UNION and INTERSECTION.

The Union operation combines outputs from two different SELECT statements. Of course, the outcome from the SELECT statements must be of the same data types. As an example, we show

```
- SELECT E_ID FROM EMP_DETAILS WHERE E_DEPT = 'PRODUCTION'
  UNION
  SELECT E_ID FROM EMP_DETAILS WHERE E_DEPT = 'ACCOUNTS';
```

The output of the above query will be a list if employee identification numbers who are working either in the production or the accounts departments. Note that, here the two individual SELECT statements are applied over the same table; but they could be applied over different tables also.

The INTERSECT operator selects common rows from the output of two different SELECT statements. This operation can be defined in a similar way as that of the UNION operation. We may consider the following example:

```
- SELECT E_DESIGNATION FROM EMP_DETAILS WHERE E_DEPT = 'PRODUCTION'
  INTERSECT
  SELECT E_DESIGNATION FROM EMP_DETAILS WHERE E_DEPT = 'ACCOUNTS';
```

Here also, the two individual SELECT statements are applied over the same table; but they could be applied over different tables as well.

SELECT with aggregate (SUM) function

Syntax:

```
- SELECT SUM (column_name1) FROM table_name
  WHERE
  column_name2 IS NOT NULL;
```

ILLUSTRATION 7.15 Let us consider a STUDENTS database where total marks for each student are maintained. Find out total marks summed over all students.

```
- SELECT SUM(MARKS)FROM STUDENTS
  WHERE
  MARKS IS NOT NULL;
```

Result: 473

SELECT with aggregate (AVG) function

Syntax:

```
- SELECT AVG (column_name1) FROM table_name
  WHERE
  column_name2 IS NOT NULL;
```

ILLUSTRATION 7.16 Let us consider STUDENTS database where marks for students are maintained. Find out average total marks obtained by a student.

Solution

```
- SELECT AVG(MARKS)FROM STUDENTS
  WHERE
  MARKS IS NOT NULL;
```

Result: 59.125

Note: Since a NULL value cannot be used for the above operations, the NOT NULL clause is used in above query statements. Only records with non-NULL values will be considered in such computations.

SELECT with aggregate (MAX, MIN) functions

Syntax:

```
- SELECT MAX (column_name) FROM table_name;
- SELECT MIN (column_name) FROM table_name;
```

ILLUSTRATION 7.17 We consider the STUDENTS database where marks for students are maintained. Find out the maximum marks obtained by a student.

Solution

```
- SELECT MAX(MARKS) FROM STUDENTS;
```

Result: 86

ILLUSTRATION 7.18 Find out the minimum marks obtained by a student.

Solution

```
- SELECT MIN (MARKS) FROM STUDENTS;
```

Result: 45

ILLUSTRATION 7.19 Consider the EMP_DETAILS database where salary values for employees are maintained. Find out the minimum salary obtained by a clerk.

Solution

```
- SELECT MIN (SALARY) FROM EMP_DETAILS
  WHERE DESIGNATION = 'CLERK';
```

Result: 14500

SELECT with aggregate (COUNT) function

Syntax:

```
- SELECT COUNT (*) FROM table_name;
- SELECT COUNT (column_name1) FROM table_name
  WHERE
  Column_name2 IS NOT NULL;
```

ILLUSTRATION 7.20 Consider the STUDENTS database where marks for student are maintained. Find out the number of students who have got 50 marks or more.

Solution

```
- SELECT COUNT (*) FROM STUDENTS
  WHERE
  MARKS >= 50;
```

Result: 6

SELECT using GROUP BY clause

We can group a number of rows by using this clause. Generally, GROUP BY is associated with an aggregate function.

Syntax:

```
- SELECT column_name1, column_name2, …
  FROM table_name
  GROUP BY column_name
```

ILLUSTRATION 7.21 Consider the STUDENTS database where marks for student are maintained. Find NAME and ROLL-NO of students grouped by MARKS.

Solution

```
- SELECT ROLL-NO, MARKS
  FROM STUDENTS
  GROUP BY MARKS;
```

Result:

ROLL-NO	MARKS
1	86
2	67
3	54
7	54
8	54
4	45
5	49
6	64

Here, rows with all identical values in the MARKS column are grouped together. SIKHA, RINA and ANIK obtained 54, hence their records are listed together.

SELECT using HAVING clause

We can apply specific condition over the SELECT command with GROUP BY clause.

Syntax:

```
- SELECT column_name1, column_name2,…
  FROM table_name GROUP BY column_name2
  HAVING column_name2 >= value
```

ILLUSTRATION 7.22 Consider the STUDENTS database where marks for student are maintained. Find NAME and ROLL-NO of students whose marks is more than 50 grouped by MARKS.

Solution

```
- SELECT ROLL-NO, MARKS
  FROM STUDENTS GROUP BY ROLL-NO
  HAVING MARKS >= 50;
```

Result:

ROLL-NO	MARKS
1	86
2	67
3	54
7	54
8	54
6	64

Here, rows with all identical values (>= 50) in the MARKS column are grouped.

7.1.2 Query Using Joined Relations

In earlier examples, we have shown simple queries where only one table is used for information extraction. When it is necessary to extract information from two or more related tables, we need to JOIN these tables beforehand.

Let the employee information be represented in three tables EMP_DETAILS, EMPDATA and DEPARTMENT as shown below in Table 7.5.

Table 7.5 EMP_DETAILS Table

E_ID	E_DEPT	E_DESIGNATION	E_JOINDATE	E_SALARY
5	1	MANAGER	24-FEB-78	50000
12	2	CLERK	12-JUL-85	16000
7	2	SALESMAN	11-JUN-99	12000
13	2	ANALYST	22-MAR-87	35000
15	1	CLERK	30-AUG-89	15000
16	3	ACCOUNTANT	23-DEC-88	36000
18	3	CLERK	04-NOV-95	14500

Table 7.6 EMPDATA Table

E_ID	E_NAME	E_ADD
5	SAJAL	KOLKATA
12	RAMA	KOLKATA
7	BHOLA	DELHI
13	KRISHNA	DELHI
15	RIA	PUNE
16	SUHEL	MUMBAI
18	BHOLA	KOLKATA

Table 7.7 DEPARTMENT Table

DEPT_NO	DEPT_NAME
1	PRODUCTION
2	MARKETING
3	ACCOUNTS

ILLUSTRATION 7.23 Consider the above employee database with three tables EMP_DETAILS, DEPARTMENT and EMPDATA. Find name, employee number and department name of employees whose designation is 'CLERK'.

Solution

```
-   SELECT E_ID, E_NAME, DEPT-NAME
    FROM EMP_DETAILS E, DEPARTMENT D, EMPDATA ED
    WHERE E.E_ID = ED.E_ID
        AND D.DEPT-NO = ED.E_DEPT
        AND E_DESIGNATION = 'CLERK';
```

Result:

E_NO	E_NAME	DEPT-NAME
12	RAMA	PRODUCTION
15	RIA	MRKETING
18	BHOLA	ACCOUNTS

Here E, D, ED are aliases for EMPLOYEE, DEPARTMENT and EMP-DATA respectively. Since all required information are not in a single table, we need to join relations for extraction of information. The query is solved using the following steps:

- Cartesian product between tables EMP-DATA and EMPLOYEE
- Selection of records where E.EMP-NO = ED.EMP-NO
- Cartesian product between the resultant table and DEPARTMENT
- Selection of records where D.DEPT-NO = ED.DEPT-NO
- Selection of records where DESIGNATION = 'CLERK'
- Projection on EMP-NO, EMP-NAME, DEPT-NAME.

7.2 Sub-query Handling

So far we have dealt with very simple queries that are based on simple comparison conditions using a single WHERE clause. The comparison was limited to matching (or un-matching) an attribute variable with some constant. A more complicated situation arises when the R.H.S. of a comparison expression is generated as a result of execution of another SELECT statement. Here, one SELECT statement is nested within another SELECT statement. For such nested queries, the inner query is called a sub-query. The outer query (or parent query) can be solved only after the results of the inner query (sub-query) are available. A sub-query is associated with a WHERE or a HAVING clause, in general.

Sub-queries are of two types:

- **Independent sub-queries:** Here, the inner query is independent of the outer query. The inner query is executed at first, and its results are stored for use by the outer query. The outer query is executed on the results of the inner query only.
- **Co-related sub-queries:** In this case, the inner query is executed many times, once for each row of the outer query. The resultant rows arising out of the outer query are referred in the inner query.

The following are some examples of the above said two types of sub-queries.

ILLUSTRATION 7.24 Find id number, designation and salary of employees who works in the PRODUCTION department.

Solution

```
-   SELECT E_ID, E_DESIGNATION, E_SALARY
    FROM EMP_DETAILS
    WHERE E_DEPT IN
        (SELECT DEPT_NO
        FROM DEPARTMENT
        WHERE DEPT-NAME = 'PRODUCTION');
```

Result:

E_ID	E_DESIGNATION	E_SALARY
5	MANAGER	50000
15	CLERK	15000

ILLUSTRATION 7.25 Find id number, designation and salary of employees who lives in KOLKATA.

Solution The above query can be executed using the EXISTS clause. EXISTS represents an existential quantifier.

```
- SELECT E_ID, E_DESIGNATION, E_SALARY
  FROM EMP_DETAILS
  WHERE EXISTS
      (SELECT *
      FROM EMPDATA
      WHERE E_ADD = 'KOLKATA');
```

Result:

E_ID	E_DESIGNATION	E_SALARY
5	MANAGER	50000
12	CLERK	16000
18	CLERK	14500

ILLUSTRATION 7.26 Find id number, designation and salary of employees who does not live in KOLKATA.

Solution The above query can be executed using the NOT EXISTS clause. NOT EXISTS represents an existential quantifier.

```
- SELECT E_ID, E_DESIGNATION, E_SALARY
  FROM EMP_DETAILS
  WHERE NOT EXISTS
      (SELECT * FROM EMPDATA
      WHERE E_ADD = 'KOLKATA');
```

Result:

E_ID	E_DESIGNATION	E_SALARY
7	SALESMAN	12000
13	ANALYST	35000
15	CLERK	15000
16	ACCOUNTANT	36000

The EXISTS clause is used to check whether the associated sub-query has produced any row of results. If the result set of the sub-query is empty, no action will be taken by the outer query or parent query.

The EXISTS clause is beneficial when most of the selective filters are used in the parent query and the sub-query results are presented without much filtering. On the other hand, IN clause will be beneficial when most of the selective filters appear within the sub-query, and indexes are available on the join columns.

ILLUSTRATION 7.27 Find id number, designation and salary of employees who works in the PRODUCTION department.

Solution

```
- SELECT E_ID, E_DESIGNATION, E_SALARY
  FROM EMP_DETAILS E
  WHERE E_DEPT IN
     (SELECT DEPT_NO
     FROM DEPARTMENT D
     WHERE D.DEPT_NO = E.E_DEPT AND
     D.DEPT_NAME='PRODUCTION');
```

The last query is an example of co-related sub-query. Note that, here the department number from the outer query is referred in the inner query for every record in the EMP_DETAILS table.

7.3 Join Operations

The Join operation takes two relations as inputs and produces a new combined relation. The fundamental combination of two relations is performed by the *Cartesian Product* operation. This operation is sometimes referred to as the *Cross-Join* operation. Here, columns of the resultant tables are all columns of the first table, followed by all columns of the second table. Join operations can be of different types, mentioned below.

- Self join: Joining a relation with itself.
- Inner join: Join between two tables to satisfy a condition.
- Equijoin: A special case of Inner join where an equality condition is satisfied.
- Outer join: Join between two tables to dissatisfy a condition.
  - Full outer join
  - Left outer join
  - Right outer join

7.3.1 Self Join

To perform join with itself, a relation is aliased twice for resolving references to the same attributes. Let us consider an example using the EMPLOYEE table given in Table 7.8. In this table, instances for ordinary employees of each department contain manager identification number as M_ID.

Table 7.8 EMPLOYEE Table

E_ID	E_NAME	E_DEPT	E_DESIGNATION	M_ID
5	SAJAL	PRODUCTION	PROGRAMMER	NULL
12	RAMA	MARKETING	CLERK	13
7	BHOLA	MARKETING	SALESMAN	13
13	KRISHNA	MARKETING	ANALYST	NULL
15	RIA	PRODUCTION	CLERK	5
16	SUHEL	ACCOUNTS	ACCOUNTANT	NULL
18	BHOLA	ACCOUNTS	CLERK	16

The query is to list the names of all employees along with those of their managers. For this purpose, we use two aliases for the EMPLOYEE table. These are, say, EMP and MNG. The SQL query is given below which implements a join operation between EMP and MGR.

```
SELECT EMP.E_ID, EMP.E_NAME, MGR.M_ID, MGR.E_NAME
FROM EMPLOYEE EMP, EMPLOYEE MGR
WHERE EMP.M_ID = MGR.E_ID;
```

The output of the above query is

E_ID	E_NAME	M_ID	M_NAME
12	RAMA	13	KRISHNA
7	BHOLA	13	KRISHNA
15	RIA	5	SAJAL
18	BHOLA	16	SUHEL

7.3.2 Inner Join

It is nothing but the Cartesian Product of two relations that satisfies the join condition specified by a WHERE clause in SQL. The join condition is represented by a comparison operator like "=" or "<>" for matching rows from two tables based on the values in common attributes from each relation. A special class of inner join is the EquiJoin for which the join condition is represented by the equality operator.

Consider following two relations EMPRECORD and DEPARTMENT given in Tables 7.9 and 7.10 respectively.

Table 7.9 EMPRECORD Table

E_ID	E_DEPT	E_DESIGNATION
5	1	PROGRAMMER
12	2	CLERK
7	2	SALESMAN
13	2	ANALYST
15	1	CLERK
16	3	ACCOUNTANT
18	3	CLERK

Table 7.10 DEPARTMENT Table

DEPT_NO	DEPT_NAME
1	PRODUCTION
2	MARKETING
3	ACCOUNTS

Let the query is to list the E_ID, DEPT_NAME and E_DESIGNATION from Tables 7.9 and 7.10. The SQL query is given below.

```
SELECT EMPRECORD.E_ID, DEPARTMENT.DEPT_NAME, EMPRECORD.E_DESIGNATION
FROM EMPRECORD, DEPARTMENT
WHERE EMPRECORD.DEPT_NO = DEPARTMENT.DEPT_NO;
```

The output of the above query is obtained by applying EquiJoin operation and then selecting the desired attributes. Output is shown in Table 7.11.

Table 7.11 Output Table

E_ID	DEPT_NAME	E_DESIGNATION
5	PRODUCTION	PROGRAMMER
12	MARKETING	CLERK
7	MARKETING	SALESMAN
13	MARKETING	ANALYST
15	PRODUCTION	CLERK
16	ACCOUNTS	ACCOUNTANT
18	ACCOUNTS	CLERK

7.3.3 Outer Join

Inner join provides only those results that satisfy the specified condition. Sometimes, it may be necessary to find out all the results that match the condition, as well as those results that do not match in values of the joining attribute. The outer join operation yields the unmatched results.

Suppose a new employee has joined and he has not yet been allocated a department and a new department in created named STORE having department number 4. The modified tables (Tables 7.12 and 7.13) EMPRECORD and DEPARTMENT are as follows:

Table 7.12 EMPRECORD Table

E_ID	E_DEPT	E_DESIGNATION
5	1	PROGRAMMER
12	2	CLERK
7	2	SALESMAN
13	2	ANALYST
15	1	CLERK
16	3	ACCOUNTANT
18	3	CLERK
19	NULL	CLERK

Table 7.13 DEPARTMENT Table

DEPT_NO	DEPT_NAME
1	PRODUCTION
2	MARKETING
3	ACCOUNTS
4	STORE

Full outer join

The full outer join is computed as follows:

- Compute the inner join of two tables using the matching attribute.
- For each row of the left table that has no matching value in a row of the right table, add one row in the results, using values of the matching attribute in the left table, and assuming NULL values for all attributes in the right table.
- For each row of the right table that has no matching value in a row of the left table, add one row in the results, using values of the matching attribute in the right table, and assuming NULL values for all attributes in the left table.

The output of our earlier query as obtained by applying full outer join operation is shown in Table 7.14.

Table 7.14 Output Table

E_ID	DEPT_NAME	E_DESIGNATION
5	PRODUCTION	PROGRAMMER
12	MARKETING	CLERK
7	MARKETING	SALESMAN
13	MARKETING	ANALYST
15	PRODUCTION	CLERK
16	ACCOUNTS	ACCOUNTANT
18	ACCOUNTS	CLERK
19	NULL	CLERK
NULL	STORE	NULL

Note that, the final two results in Table 7.14 are representing unmatched rows in the cases of left and right outer joins respectively.

Left outer join

This is done as follows:

- Compute the inner join of two tables using the matching attribute.
- For each row of the left table that has no matching value in a row of the right table, add one row in the results, using values of the matching attribute in the left table, and assuming NULL values for all attributes in the right table.

Right outer join

This is done as follows:

- Compute the inner join of two tables using the matching attribute.
- For each row of the right table that has no matching value in a row of the left table, add one row in the results, using values of the matching attribute in the right table, and assuming NULL values for all attributes in the left table.

7.4 Data Consistency and Integrity Constraints

Data manipulation Language allows users to insert, delete, and update data or records in a database, and also to store and retrieve records from the database. Besides the above tasks, these statements also perform a very important task of maintaining data integrity. In a database, tables are interconnected, and integrity restrictions are applied over them to maintain database consistency and integrity. An integrity constraint restricts or prevents insertion of invalid data into a table.

7.4.1 INSERT Statement

The INSERT statement can be used, to insert new data record, with or without mentioning column names. When column names are not mentioned, data values must be in actual order of columns.

ILLUSTRATION *7.28* Insert a new record into the EMP_DETAILS with or without specifying column names.

Solution Suppose, we want to insert a new record with E_ID = 30, E_DEPT = 2, E_ DESIGNATION = ANALYST, E_JOINDATE = 23.08.2011 and E_SALARY = 16000. This can be done in the following ways:

1. ```
   INSERT INTO EMP_DETAILS VALUES (30, 2, 'ANALYST', '23-AUG-11', 16000);
   ```
   or,
2. ```
   INSERT INTO EMP_DETAILS (E_ID, E_NAME, E_ DESIGNATION, E_JOINDATE, E_SALARY)
   VALUES (30, 'BIRBAL', 2, '23-AUG-11', 16000);
   ```

What are the differences between the above two forms of the INSERT statements?

In the first statement, column names are not used, and hence data values must be in the pre-specified order (as in the table description). This restriction does not apply for the second statement form. Since, in the second statement, all columns are specified explicitly, we do not bother about the order of column names. That is, we can rewrite the second statement as

```
INSERT INTO EMP_DETAILS (E_ID, E_DEPT, E_DESIGNATION, E_SALARY, E_JOINDATE)
VALUES (30, 2, 'ANALYST', 16000, '23-AUG-11');
```

Note that, order in the column name sequence and value sequence must be the same.

NULL values for a column can be inserted only if it is not a key attribute. NULL values can be inserted either implicitly or explicitly.

ILLUSTRATION 7.29 Insert a new record into the EMP_DETAILS having NULL value for E_NAME attribute.

Solution Let us try to insert the above record used in Illustration 7.28. This can be done in the following ways:

```
1. INSERT INTO EMP_DETAILS VALUES(30, 2, ' ', '23-AUG-11', 16000);
   or,
2. INSERT INTO EMP_DETAILS (E_ID, E_DEPT, E_JOINDATE, E_SALARY) VALUES (30, 'ANALYST',
   '23-AUG-11', 16000);
```

Note that, in the first case, we used an explicit blank (as NULL) for the E_DESIGNATION attribute; but this attribute is omitted in the second statement. Here, the omitted value is automatically treated as NULL.

The above, however, is not true for a key attribute. If some column name represents a primary key or a foreign key, we cannot insert a NULL value as this violates the Entity Integrity restriction, and for such attempts the system will generate an error message.

New rows or records can be inserted using substitution variables. Substitution variables are column names themselves with '&' symbol preceding them. When such substitution variables are used in the INSERT statements, values can be inserted from an input screen supplied by SQL*PLUS environment.

ILLUSTRATION 7.30 Insert a new record into EMP_DETAILS using substitution variables.

Solution Let us try to insert the record used in Illustration 7.28. Substitution variables can be done in the following way:

```
INSERT INTO EMP_DETAILS(&E_ID, &E_NAME,&E_DEPT,&E_DESIGNATION, &E_JOINDATE,
&E_SALARY)
```

During execution of the above statement, the following prompts will appear on the input screen for user inputs for values of variables, one after another.

Enter value for e_id: 30
Enter value for e_name: 'BIRBAL'
Enter value for e_dept: 'PRODUCTION'
Enter value for e_designation: 'ANALYST'
Enter value for e_joindate: '23-AUG-11'
Enter value for e_salary: 16000

The right hand values are supplied by the user against displayed input request (prompt).

The current date information can be inserted into a record using the SYSDATE system function. If today is the join date of employee BIRBAL, we can use the following statement:

```
1. INSERT INTO EMP_DETAILS (E_ID, E_NNAME, E_DEPT, E_JOINDATE, E_SALARY) VALUES
   (30, 2, 'BIRBAL', 'ANALYST', SYSDATE, 16000);
   or
2. INSERT INTO EMP_DETAILS VALUES (30, 'BIRBAL', 2, 'PRODUCTION', 'ANALYST',
   SYSDATE, 16000);
```

We can insert a number of rows into a table by copying them from another existing table selectively. Suppose, we want to copy the employee records for employees who have joined on or after 01. 01. 2000 from EMP_DETAILS into a new table NEW_EMP_RECORDS, then we can use:

```
INSERT INTO NEW_ EMP_DETAILS (E_ID, E_NNAME, E_DEPT, E_DESIGNATION, E_JOINDATE,
E_SALARY) ;
SELECT E_ID, E_NNAME, E_DEPT, E_DESIGNATION, E_JOINDATE, E_SALARY
FROM EMP_DETAILS
WHERE E_JOINDATE >= '01-JAN-2000';
```

7.4.2 Update Statement

The UPDATE statement is used to modify the existing content of a table. Syntax of the UPDATE statement is

```
UPDATE <table_name>
SET <column_name = value> [,<column_name = value>, . . .]
[WHERE <condition>];
```

Using a single UPDATE statement, it is possible to modify single or multiple rows, single or multiple columns of a table.

***ILLUSTRATION** 7.31* Update the record of EMP_DETAILS for employee BIRBAL as he got a promotion from ANALYST to SENIOR ANALYST position.

Solution The updation required can be done in the following way:

```
UPDATE EMP_DETAILS
SET E_DESIGNATION = 'SR-ANALYST'
WHERE E_NAME = 'BIRBAL';
```

***ILLUSTRATION** 7.32* Update the record of EMP_DETAILS for employee BIRBAL as he got a promotion from ANALYST to SENIOR ANALYST position, and his salary increased to 20000.

Solution The updation required can be done in the following way:

```
UPDATE EMP_DETAILS
SET E_DESIGNATION = 'SR-ANALYST', E_SALARY = 20000
WHERE E_NAME = 'BIRBAL';
```

The effect of updation may be verified by displaying the contents of table EMP_DETAILS. As in the case of INSERT statements, the UPDATE operation also imposes integrity restrictions during updation. That is, if we try to update a record with a value that is tied to an integrity constraint, it will generate an error message. For example, we cannot update a record containing a foreign key value, if the parent table does not contain a record with the same value as primary key.

7.4.3 Delete Statement

The DELETE statement is used to remove a record or a set of records from a table. Syntax of the DELETE statement is

```
DELETE FROM <table_name>
[WHERE <condition>];
```

Using a single DELETE statement, it is possible to remove single or multiple rows of a table.

ILLUSTRATION *7.33* Delete the record of EMP_DETAILS for employee BIRBAL as he resigned from ANALYST position.

Solution The deletion required can be done in the following way:

```
DELETE FROM EMP_DETAILS
WHERE E_NAME = 'BIRBAL';
```

ILLUSTRATION *7.34* Delete all records from EMP_DETAILS.

Solution The deletion required can be done without mentioning any condition:

```
DELETE FROM EMP_DETAILS;
```

The second example for DELETE operation is generally undesirable. If inadvertently all records are deleted in this way, execution of an immediate ROLLBACK statement will recover all deleted records. This ROLLBACK must be done before execution of any subsequent COMMIT operation.

The effect of deletion may be verified by displaying the contents of table EMP_DETAILS. As in the case of INSERT and UPDATE, DELETE operation also imposes integrity restrictions. That is, if we try to delete a record with a value that is tied to an integrity constraint, it will generate an error message. For example, we cannot delete a record containing a primary key value, if another table contains a record with the same value as foreign key.

7.5 Transaction Control Statements

In database applications transactions are identified as a group of DDL, DML and DCL statements that together make a consistent change in the database. The effects of transactions are atomic in nature. That is, either the task specified by the group of statements will be done completely, or nothing will be done. In order to ensure this atomic behaviour of transactions, it is necessary to use some Transaction Control Statements (also called Transaction Control Language, TCL). Common statements are: COMMIT, SAVEPOINT and ROLLBACK.

Either a COMMIT or a ROLLBACK statement is used at the end of a transaction to ensure a permanent effect in the database or to nullify the effect respectively. By the use of such statements, we can ensure database consistency. COMMIT statement completes a transaction by making all pending changes permanent, and ROLLBACK statement completes a transaction by discarding all pending changes. The SAVEPOINT statement allows a subsequent ROLLBACK statement to roll back the current transaction up to the specified save-point only. If within a transaction body the SAVEPOINT statement is omitted, the ROLLBACK statement rolls back the entire transaction.

7.6 Views of Tables

Views of an existing table may be created by database users for convenience of work and in order to avoid chances of undesired data loss. A view is nothing but a virtual table. However, it is not maintained in the database. It can be created in the main memory for temporal usage. Important features of a view are listed below.

- Views are derived Tables or virtual Tables.
- Views are created based on some Tables.
- To a user, a view appears to be another Table.
- Using views instead of original Tables is a safer practice for security and convenience purposes.
- Most of the operations on Tables are also applicable on Views as well.
- Views generally contain a portion of a Table.
- A view is like a window through which we can see a limited region of an actual Table.
- The base Table from which data are extracted for a view is called the source Table.
- A view is never a part of the database, it is created in the user workspace temporarily.

Syntax for creating a view:

CREATE VIEW *viewname* AS *query*

– Here *viewname* is the suggested name for the view and *query* is a subquery that species the structure of the view.

ILLUSTRATION *7.35* Create a view of EMP_DETAILS using E_ID and E_NAME.

Solution

```
- CREATE VIEW VIEW1 AS SELECT EID, ENAME
  FROM EMP_DETAILS WHERE SALARY<20000;
```

Using Views:

– SELECT * FROM VIEW1
– SELECT * FROM VIEW1 WHERE DEPT = 'PURCHASE';
– DROP VIEW *viewname*

7.6.1 Types of Views

Depending on how a view is created, we can categorize a view as:

- Horizontal views
- Vertical views
- Row/Column subset views
- Grouped views
- Joined views

Horizontal views

- A horizontal subset of the base table is used to create the view.
- Very useful for categorize different types of records present in a table.
- Separate views for each category can be created for separate users.

Vertical views

- Here a subset of the attributes is used to define the view.
- Informations (attributes) sensitive to specific applications are extracted only.
- Enhances speed of operation and reduces chance of errors.

7.7 Embedded SQL

SQL statements can be executed by embedding them within a host language program like C, Pascal, COBOL, Fortran etc. By doing this, we can overcome the deficit of SQL for being a non-procedural language. In this section, we discuss a procedural language for SQL. Here, we describe how SQL statements can be blended with other procedural languages and executed. Embedding of SQL can be done using the following techniques:

- SQL statements are intermixed with the statements of a host language program. The embedded program is then fed to a SQL pre-compiler (pre-processor), which processes the SQL statements separately.
- Variables of the host language can be referenced in the embedded SQL statements, allowing values calculated by the program to be used by the SQL statements.
- Programming language variables are also used by the embedded SQL statements to receive the results of SQL queries, allowing the program to use and process the retrieved values.
- Special program variables are used to assign NULL values to database columns and to support the retrieval of NULL values from the database.

7.7.1 How SQL Statements are Embedded?

Within the host program, the SQL statements are introduced by an EXEC SQL introducer. This introducer flags it as a SQL statement.

A Data structure called SQLCA (SQL Communication Area) is defined in memory which stores error variables and status indicators. By examining this memory area, the host language program determines the success or failure of the embedded SQL statements. This area is defined by using the following statement:

EXEC SQL include SQLCA;

This statement tells the SQL pre-compiler to reserve the area SQLCA in the program.

As the RDBMS executes each embedded SQL statement, it sets the value of the variable SQLCODE in the SQLCA to indicate the completion status of the statement. Following execution results are possible:

- SQLCODE = 0 means successful execution of the SQL statement.
- SQLCODE < 0 means a serious error has occurred which prevented correct execution of the SQL statement.
- SQLCODE > 0 means a warning has been generated. The most common warning, that comes with the value SQLCODE = 100, is the out-of-data warning. Here, the program tries to retrieve the next row of the table but none are available in the database.

Host variables: A host variable is a host language program variable. If the host language is the 'C' language, then all the variables declared in the host C-program are host variables. Host variables can also be used in embedded SQL statements to store data values and to retrieve data values to or from the database. To differentiate a host variable from others, it is prefixed with a colon (:) when it appears in the embedded SQL statement.

There are two embedded SQL statements: BEGIN DECLARATION SECTION and END DECLARATION SECTION bracket the host variable declarations and these are non-executable statements.

Use of host variables to store data values into the database

- Host language routines are used to read user supplied data (scanf() in C).
- User supplied data values are temporarily stored in the host variables.
- Host variable contents are then written to the database by use of SQL statements (INSERT).

Use of host variables to retrieve data values from the database

- Data values retrieved by retrieval statements (SELECT) are held in the host variables.
- Contents of the host variables are then transferred to host language routines.
- Host language routines are used to display retrieved data (printf() in C).

Indicator variables: To store NULL values in the database, or to retrieve NULL values from the database, embedded SQL allows each host variable to have a companion host indicator variable. In an embedded SQL statement, the host variable and the indicator variable together specify a single SQL-style value. SQL-style values can be as follows:

- SQL-style value = 0 means host variable contains a valid data.
- SQL-style value < 0 means host variable may be assumed to hold a NULL value. Actual content of the indicator variable is irrelevant and should be ignored.
- SQL-style value > 0 means host variable contains a valid data; which may be rounded off or truncated.

A host variable is immediately followed by the name of the corresponding indicator variable. Both the variable names are preceded by a colon (:).

7.7.2 Example of Embedded SQL Program

Let us write down a program in C language using embedded SQL to retrieve records for those students who acquired 500 or more aggregate marks.

In the following program, it is assumed that student's roll number is input by the user and the corresponding record will be displayed on the monitor.

Note that the SQL statements started with the prefix EXEC SQL prefix.

Host variable combination `:stud_roll_no :srn` is used to denote that `:srn` is an indicator variable along with the variable `:stud_roll_no` for checking non-existent students.

SQLCODE is used to check out of data warning and other kinds of errors.

```
int main()
{
   EXEC SQL INCLUDE SQLCA;

   EXEC SQL BEGIN DECLARE SECTION
      char stud_name[20];
      int stud_roll_no;
      char stud_discipline[3];
      int stud_tot_marks;
      char stud_grade[1];
      short srn;

   EXEC SQL END DECLARE SECTION

   Printf("Input student's roll number:");
   scanf("%d", &stud_roll_no);
   EXEC SQL SELECT NAME, ROLL-NO, DISCIPLINE, MARKS, GRADE
      FROM STUDENTS
      WHERE MARKS > 500 INTO
      :stud_name, :stud_roll_no :srn, :stud_discipline,
      :stud_tot_marks, :stud_grade;
   if (SQLCA.SQLCODE == 0)
   {
      printf(" NAME: %s\n", stud_name);
      if (srn < 0) printf("Roll Number is NULL\n");
         else printf(" NAME: %s\n", stud_roll_no);
      printf(" NAME: %s\n", stud_discipline);
      printf(" NAME: %s\n", stud_tot_marks);
      printf(" NAME: %s\n", stud_grade);
   }
   else if (SQLCA.SQLCODE == 100)
      printf("No Student Found With Roll Number %d\n", stud_roll_no);
   else printf("SQL ERROR: %ld\n", SQLCA.SQLCODE);

      return 0;
}
```

Exercises

7.1 What do you mean by information retrieval? How is it done in SQL?

7.2 Give suitable examples of data retrieval from databases using the following clauses: WHERE, GROUP BY, ORDER BY, IN, HAVING, DISTINCT, EXISTS.

7.3 Show how data consistency and database integrity are maintained in DML statements using suitable examples.

7.4 Show different ways that you can use to modify an attribute name and its specification.

7.5 Specify the differences between UPDATE and MODIFY statements with examples.

7.6 What do you mean by sub-query? Classify different categories of sub-queries with suitable examples.

7.7 Mention different uses of the DROP statements. What is its difference with the DELETE statement?

7.8 How join operation is performed in SQL? Give an example.

7.9 What do you mean by inner and outer joins? Give examples for left and right outer join operations.

7.10 How can you express queries involving JOIN operation in SQL?

7.11 What are assertions and what are their utilities?

7.12 Define a view in SQL. Why do we require a view at all? What are the differences between a view and an assertion?

7.13 Explain differences between updation of views and updation of tables.

7.14 Consider the following schema of a database.

```
SUPPLIER(S#, SNAME, SADDRESS)
PARTS(P#, PNAME, PCOLOR)
CATALOG(S#, P#, COST)
```

Express the following queries in relational algebra and SQL:

(i) Find names of suppliers who supply yellow parts.
(ii) Find names of suppliers who supply both blue and green parts.
(iii) Find names of suppliers who supply all the parts.

7.15 Write down the SQL syntax for statements that may be used for INSERT, DELETE and UPDATION of records in a database.

7.16 Consider the following database, where the primary keys are underlined:

```
PERSON(DRIVER_ID, NAME, ADDRESS)
CAR(LICENCE, MODEL, YEAR)
ACCIDENT(REPORT_NUMBER, INFORMATION, LOCATION)
OWNER(DRIVER_ID, LICENCE)
DAMAGE(DRIVER_ID, REPORT_NUMBER, DAMAGE_AMOUNT)
```

Write the following SQL queries:

(i) Find the total number of persons that owned cars were involved in accidents in the year 2000.

(ii) Find the number of accidents in which one of the cars belonged to Mr. X.

(iii) Insert a new accident record in the database. Assume arbitrary values for attributes.

(iv) Delete the record that a SANTRO car belonged to Mr. Y.

(v) Update the damage amount for the car with licence number "AB2001" in an accident with report number "AR2197" to ₹ 25000.

7.17 Consider the following database, where the primary keys are underlined:

```
PROJECT(PROJ#, PROJ_NAME, PROJ_MANAGER)
EMPLOYEE(EMP#, EMP_NAME)
ASSIGNEDTO(EMP#, PROJ#)
```

Write the following SQL queries:

(i) Write down SQL-DDL statements to implement the database by clearly indicating primary and foreign keys.

(ii) Find the name of employees working on project P_1.

(iii) Find the name of employees who work on project P_1 but not on P_2.

(iv) Find the name of employees who work on project where employee E_1 is manager.

7.18 Consider a SALES database consisting of tables:

```
CUSTOMER(CUST_ID, CUST_NAME, CUST_ADD),
PRODUCT(PROD_ID, PROD_NAME, PROD_RATE),
SALE-DETAILS(CUST_ID, PROD_RATE, ITEM_COUNT, SALE_DATE).
```

Answer the following queries. Specific attributes for the SALE-DETAILS are SALE-NO and SALE-DATE. Create three tables corresponding to a set of data records. (Keep at least five records in each table. Answer the following queries by writing SQL statements. Show tabular outputs.

(i) List all product names in ascending order of name.

(ii) lıst all customer name and customer city sorted by city in descending order.

(iii) Find customers who live in 'Kolkata'.

(iv) Find customer name, product name, sale date for all customers.

(v) Find customer names who purchased 'Soap'.

(vi) Find customer names who purchased 'Soap' on or before 01-Oct-2011.

(vii) List all customers name and customers city sorted by city in descending order where in the output column headings should be CN and CC respectively.

(viii) Find customer names who purchased 'Soap' after 01-Jan-2011 and before 01-Oct-2011.

(ix) Find customer names who purchased any of 'Soap,' 'Shampoo,' or 'Conditioner'.

(x) Find customer names whose name starts with 'S'.

(xi) Find customer names the third character of whose name is 'S'.

(xii) Find customer names whose name includes the character 'S'.

(xiii) Find the number of 'Soap' procured by customer 'Sudha'.

(xiv) List all product names using only lower case.

(xv) List all product names using only upper case.

(xvi) Print rounded cost for each product.

(xvii) Find out the number of different products.

(xviii) Find total cost of all different items (sum of rates).

7.19 Consider the following relations for a database that keeps track of business trips of salespersons in a sales office:

```
SALESPERSON(SSN, NAME, START_YEAR, DEPT_NO)
TRIP(SSN, FROM_CITY, TO_CITY, DEPARTURE_DATE, RETURN_DATE, TRIP_ID)
EXPENSE(TRIP_ID, ACCOUNT_NO, AMOUNT)
```

Specify the following queries in either relationl algebra or in SQL.

(i) Give details (all attributes of trip relation) for trip that exceeded ₹ 2,000 in expenses.

(ii) Print SSN of salespersons who took trip to Andaman.

7.20 Consider the following tables:

```
DEPT(DCODE, DNAME)
EMP(ECODE, ENAME, BASIC, DCODE, DATE_JOINED)
```

Write SQL statements for the following:

(i) For each department, show DNAME and total basic of the employees.

(ii) Find out the name of the departments where no person in working.

(iii) Find out names of employees who are working in 'ABC' department.

(iv) Find out the maximum basic pay among the employees who has joined after year 2000.

7.21 What do you mean by embedded SQL? How variables are declared in embedded SQL? Explain with examples.

7.22 What are the potential problems of using embedded SQL and what are its advantages?

CHAPTER 8

Programming with PL/SQL

SQL is known to be a high level non-procedural language. In general, SQL contains a set of command line instructions, each of which is interpreted as a query (with proper arguments). These commands specify "What To Do?" rather than "How To Do?" Therefore, SQL instructions (commands) are different from those of the third generation languages like C, COBOL etc. These third generation languages are procedural languages, i.e., any algorithm can be implemented using these languages in detailed step-by-step fashion. Third generation languages powerful control constructs for sequence execution, conditional execution and repetitive execution. Use of these control constructs enables us to write a solution procedure of a complicated problem. Such a problem cannot be solved simply as a sequence of command level instructions, in general. PL/SQL is an augmentation of the basic SQL with suitable constructs that make it a powerful programming language while maintaining all desired properties of SQL commands.

8.1 Basics of PL/SQL Programming

PL/SQL stands for Procedural Language/Structured Query Language. As PL/SQL is a programming language, it supports writing procedural codes. It enables developers with the conditional execution and loop execution features. It also supports a richer set of variable types. A PL/SQL program can be edited with any general purpose editor and can be stored as a program file for future use. Oracle Database systems considers PL/SQL as its native programming language and it is portable across a number of Oracle development platforms.

PL/SQL is, therefore, a procedural language extension of the database query language SQL. Here SQL is augmented with features of a block structured programming language. We can pronunciate it as *procedural language* (PL) for *structured query language* (SQL). It is developed for efficient processing of relational databases. We shall describe some of the programming features of the PL/SQL in the following subsections.

8.1.1 PL/SQL Programming Environment

A PL/SQL Engine is used in association with the Oracle Server for execution of PL/SQL programs. Blocks of PL/SQL are fed to the PL/SQL Engine for the execution of the procedural components of the program. Basic SQL statements are executed by the Oracle Server. The PL/SQL Engine is generally treated as a part of the Oracle Server. The Server Manager, i.e., the *i*SQL*Plus processes the block. It separates the SQL statements from the control structures and sends them individually to the SQL statement executor. Therefore, the PL/SQL Engine acts as a control program executor and the Oracle Server acts as an SQL statement executor.

We can, therefore, visualize a PL/SQL program as embedding of SQL Blocks within a Block Structured control program as shown below:

```
BEGIN
   SQL statement block
   IF <condition> THEN
      SQL statement block
   ELSE
      SQL statement block
   ENDIF
   SQL statement block
END
```

In the above structure, each SQL Block may represent either a single SQL statement or a sequence of SQL statements.

8.1.2 PL/SQL Block Structure

PL/SQL is a block structured programming language. A program in PL/SQL should have a declaration section, executable section and an exception handling section. The second out of these three sections is an essential component of a program. Declaration and exception handling may be treated as optional; they may be used by the programmer as per requirement. A PL/SQL program consists of the following three parts:

- The Declaration section (optional).
- The Execution section (mandatory).
- The Exception (or Error) Handling section (optional).

Functions of individual sections are described below.

Declaration section: The declaration section is optional and is used to declare identifiers like variables, constants, records and cursors, which are used to manipulate data in the execution section. The declaration section of a PL/SQL Block starts with the reserved word DECLARE. Identifiers to be declared may be variables, constants and/or records, which store data temporarily. One can also declare a cursor in this section.

Execution section: The Execution section is a mandatory section and is the one where the program logic is written to perform any task. In a PL/SQL Block, execution section starts with the reserved word BEGIN and ends with reserved word END. Structured programming constructs like loops, conditional statement and sequential SQL statements that constitute the execution section part.

Exception section: This section deals with any error that may be generated during execution of a PL/SQL program so that the program terminates normally. The exception section starts with the reserved word EXCEPTION. This section is optional. While incorporating an exception declaration, we must ensure that the corresponding exception handler routine is present. Otherwise, execution of the exception block terminates abruptly with errors.

Individual statements in all the above sections must end with a semicolon. Any of these PL/SQL blocks can be nested within other PL/SQL blocks as mentioned earlier.

A general program structure is shown below:

```
DECLARE
    variables, constants, cursors etc.
    . . .
BEGIN
    Executable statements in SQL
    Executable statements in PL/SQL

EXCEPTION routines
    Error handling instructions and functions.
END
```

Roles of different parts are described in Table 8.1.

Table 8.1 Roles of Different Section in a PL/SQL Program

Part	Description	Nature
Declaration	All variables, constants, cursors and user defined routines that can be referenced during execution	Optional
Execution	SQL statements for manipulation of data in the database and PL/SQL instructions	Mandatory
Exception handling	Routines to deal with abnormal conditions or errors during execution	Optional

We can call named subprograms within the PL/SQL program. A subprogram may a procedure or a function. The prototypes of procedure and function are shown below.

```
PROCEDURE <proc_name>
IS
BEGIN
    PL/SQL statements
EXCEPTION
END;
```

```
FUNCTION <func_name>
RETURN <datatype>
IS
BEGIN
    PL/SQL statements
    RETURN <value>;
EXCEPTION
END;
```

8.1.3 PL/SQL Programming Features

PL/SQL is a programming language and it has all the features like a general purpose programming language. We shall provide descriptions of different programming features in the following.

Characters in PL/SQL

Common alphanumeric characters that are generally used in other high level programming languages are also supported by PL/SQL. A list of such characters is displayed in Table 8.2.

Table 8.2 Characters in PL/SQL

Type of characters	Characters
Uppercase/Lowercase letters	A-Z, a-z
Numeric digits	0-9
Mathematical operators and punctuation marks and other symbols	+, -, *, /, =, >, <, ~, !, @, #, $, %, &, (,), {, }, [,], |, :, ;, , ,‘, “, ?
Blank or white space	Space, tab, carriage return/new line

Operators in PL/SQL

Operators in PL/SQL are the same as those in SQL. Operators have their precedence of operations (Table 8.3).

Table 8.3 Operators in PL/SQL

Operation	Operator
Exponentiation, multiplication, division, addition, subtraction	**, *, /, +, –
Assignment, negation, concatenation	:=, –, | |
Comparison	>, <, >=, <=, <>, !=, ~=, =, IS NULL, LIKE, BETWEEN, IN
Logical negation	NOT
Logical conjunction	AND
Logical inclusion	OR

Data types in PL/SQL

Data types in PL/SQL specify storage formats, constraints, and valid range of values. Following are the different categories of data types supported by PL/SQL—scalar, composite, reference, and LOB (Large Object). Variables, constants and pointer data can be declared using these types of data.

- Scalar data types are corresponding to individual column types in database tables. PL/SQL supports Boolean variables also.
- Composite data types represent combination of attributes (columns) or records, i.e., a group of fields at a time.

- Reference data types are called pointers and they designate different program items.
- LOB (Large Binary Object) data types hold locators, i.e., location of large objects like files or images etc. It can hold up to 4 GB of data.

Variables declared in PL/SQL can be used anywhere in SQL and procedural statements. A variable can be used for:

- **Temporary storage of data:** Temporary values of data are stored in variables.
- **Manipulation of stored data:** Variables are used for data manipulation and expression evaluation etc.
- **Reuse of data:** After declaration, a variable can be used for holding a value throughout the program.
- **Ease of maintenance:** Variables are declared after the column data types. Whenever an underlying data definition changes, the variable declaration changes accordingly at run time. This reduces maintenance cost and allows programs to adapt as database changes for new applications.

As already mentioned, PL/SQL supports scalar, composite, reference and LOB data types and corresponding variables. Besides, some Non-PL/SQL variables that are supported by the host language *i*SQL*Plus are also supported by PL/SQL.

Examples of PL/SQL data types and variables

Type BOOLEAN : Example is TRUE
Type NUMBER : Example is 345.68
Type VARCHAR2 : Example is 'KOLKATA'
Type LONG : Example is "This is an example of long type value which is long string."
Type DATE : Example is 20-JUL-11
Type BLOB : Example is an image, book, etc.
Type BFILE : Example is a video sequence file, a movie file.

PL/SQL constants

In a PL/SQL Block, we can define a constant whose value remains unchanged during program execution. Constants are user-defined literal values. The following example illustrate the use of constants. If within a program that creates students' mark-sheets, we want to provide grace marks of value 10 to students, we can do this by declaring a constant at the beginning and use it all over the program globally. During another execution, if we want to provide a different grace mark, we can redefine the constant with another value in the declaration section again. Use of constants, therefore, helps us changing the value of a literal throughout the program.

General syntax for declaring a constant is:

```
constant_name CONSTANT datatype := VALUE;
```

- constant_name is the name of the constant or literal.
- CONSTANT is a reserved word used to define (and name) a value that does not change.
- VALUE is assigned to a constant during declaration phase only.

An example code for declaring the constant grace_marks (of value 10) is presented below:

```
DECLARE
grace_marks CONSTANT number (2) := 10;
```

A value can be assigned to a constant only during initial declaration. Any attempt to assign a value to a constant in the execution section will generate an error. For example, during execution, the following PL/SQL block will generate error:

```
DECLARE
   grace_marks CONSTANT number(2);
BEGIN
   grace_marks:= 10;
   dbms_output.put_line (grace_marks);
END;
```

PL/SQL variables

Variables are memory locations that store the values that can change through the PL/SQL Block. Following is the syntax for the declaration of a variable in PL/SQL. Terms within square bracket are optional.

Syntax:

```
DECLARE
      identifier [CONSTANT] datatype [NOT NULL] [:= | DEFAULT expression];
```

Here, `identifier` is the name of the variable, `datatype` is a valid PL/SQL datatype. NOT NULL is an optional specification to indicate that this constant cannot assume NULL value. `Default_value / DEFAULT expression` is also an optional specification, by which one can define a variable. Variable declaration statements must be terminated by semicolon. For example, to store the pay of an employee, we can use a variable `salary` as shown below.

```
DECLARE
   pay number (5);
```

Here, `pay` is a variable of datatype number and of length 5.

ILLUSTRATION 8.1

```
DECLARE
   deptno NUMBER (2) NOT NULL := 5;
   address VARCHAR2 (10) := 'KOLKATA';
   joindate DATE;
   dutyhours CONSTANT NUMBER NOT NULL := 10;
```

A non-null variable must be initialized during declaration. Let us show examples of declaring variables of null and non-null types.

```
DECLARE
   pay number(5);
   dept varchar2(10) NOT NULL := "CSE";
```

Values of variables can change within execution or exception sections of a PL/SQL Block. Values can be assigned to variables in the following two ways:

1. Direct assignment of values from input device to variables. General syntax is:

```
variable_name:= value;
```

2. Assignment from database columns by using a SELECT … INTO statement. General syntax is:

```
SELECT column_name INTO variable_name
FROM table_name
```

[WHERE condition];

ILLUSTRATION 8.2 Using the following code, we can get the pay of an employee with identification number '100' and display it on the output device.

```
DECLARE
    pay number(5);
    empid number(5) = 100;
BEGIN
    SELECT salary INTO salary
    FROM employee
    WHERE emp_id = empid;
    dbms_output.put_line(var_salary);
    dbms_output.put_line('Salary of emp'||empid||'is'||salary);
END;
```

Declaring variables with the %TYPE attribute

We can declare a PL/SQL variable to hold values of a variable, column or table which are declared previously. This is a safe way to declare variables, so that, type mismatch would not occur. Using the %TYPE declaration is also called anchoring.

ILLUSTRATION 8.3

```
DECLARE
    var_name EMPLOYEE.NAME%TYPE;
```

In the above declaration of variable `var_name`, type and precision will be automatically set as that of the column name `EMPLOYEE.NAME` where the attribute NAME for table EMPLOYEE is already declared.

Scope of variables

In PL/SQL, we can define a Block of codes within another Block, i.e., nesting of blocks is allowed. Here, the execution section of an outer block can contain inner blocks. Therefore, a variable which is accessible to an outer Block is also accessible to all nested inner Blocks. The reverse, however, is not true, i.e., variables declared in an inner blocks are not accessible to an outer block. This type of nested declaration allows us to classify variables into two types.

- **Local variables:** Declared in an inner block and cannot be referenced by outside Blocks.
- **Global variable:** Declared in an outer block and can be referenced by itself as well as its inner blocks.

ILLUSTRATION 8.4 Let us consider the following example where two variables 'val1' and 'val2', are declared in the outer block and their product is assigned to a third variable 'prod' declared in the inner block. Variable 'prod', declared in the inner block, cannot be accessed from the outer block, but the other variables 'val1' and 'val2' can be accessed from anywhere within the nested block as their declaration is global.

```
DECLARE
   val1 NUMBER;
   val2 NUMBER;
BEGIN
   val1 := 20;
   val2 := 30;

   DECLARE
         prod NUMBER;
   BEGIN
         prod := val1 * val2;
   END;
END;
```

PL/SQL records

Records are known as composite datatypes in PL/SQL. This means records are the combination of different scalar datatypes like char, varchar, number, etc. A record may be considered as a row of data where each entry is a scalar value. In a database perspective, it can contain a complete row from a database table.

Declaring a record: In order to declare a record, we need to form a composite datatype at first and then we can declare a record for that type. General syntax to declare and define such a composite datatype is:

```
TYPE record_type_name IS RECORD
   (col_name_1 column_datatype,
   col_name_2 column_datatype, ...);
```

Here, record_type_name is the name of the composite datatype. col_name_1, col_name_2, etc., are the names of the fields/columns within this composite type and column_datatype defines the scalar datatype that represent individual fields of the composite type.

We can declare the datatype of the fields in there different ways.

1. We can declare the field in the same way as we declare the fields while creating the table.
2. If a field represents a column from a database table, the field_type can be defined as:

```
col_name table_name.column_name%type;
```

If we declare field datatype in this manner, datatype of the column is automatically applied to the field. This is very useful when we need to alter column specification of the table as this does not require any other change in the code. We can also use the *%type* to declare variables and constants.

The General syntax to declare a record as a user-defined datatype is:

```
record_name record_type_name;
```

We can use the following code segment to declare an employee record called emp_rec based on a user-defined type.

```
DECLARE
TYPE employee_type IS RECORD
   (emp_id number(5),
   emp_first_name varchar2(25),
   emp_last_name emp.last_name%type,
   emp_dept emp.dept%type);
   emp_salary emp.salary%type;
   emp_rec employee_type;
```

If all the fields of a record are based on the columns of a table, we can declare the record as follows:

```
record_name table_name%ROWTYPE;
```

For example, the above declaration of emp_rec can as follows:

```
DECLARE
   emp_rec employee%ROWTYPE;
```

There are several advantages of declaring the record as a ROWTYPE as mentioned below:

- It is not necessary to explicitly declare variables for all the columns present in a table.
- Any alter operation over the column specification in the database table does not require a modification of the code.

Declaring the record as a ROWTYPE involves some disadvantages also.

- If we create a record as a ROWTYPE, fields will be created for all the columns in the table and memory will be used to create datatypes for all the fields. So, we use ROWTYPE only when all the columns of the table are used.
- By creating a record, we just create a new datatype which is similar to create a variable. We need to assign values to variables of the record to use them. Table 8.4 consolidates different ways in which one can define and declare a PL/SQL record.

Passing values to and from a record

During assigning values to a record, we actually assign values to its individual fields. The General Syntax for direct assignment of a value to a column within a record is:

```
rec_name.col_name := value;
```

Table 8.4 Declaring Records in PL/SQL

Syntax	Usage
TYPE record_type_name IS RECORD (col_name1 datatype, col_name2 datatype, ...);	Define a composite datatype, where each field is scalar.
col_name table_name.column_name%type;	Dynamically defining the datatype of a column based on a database column.
rec_name record_type_name;	Declaring a record based on a user-defined type.
rec_name table_name%ROWTYPE;	Dynamically declaring a record based on an entire row of a table. Each column in the table corresponds to a field in the record.

If we use %ROWTYPE to declare a record, we can assign values as:

```
rec_name.col_name := value;
```

We can also use SELECT Statements to assign values to records:

```
SELECT column1, column2
INTO rec_name.col_name1, record_name.col_name2
FROM table_name
[WHERE clause];
```

When %ROWTYPE is used to declare a record, we can directly assign values to the fields of the record at a time, without considering individual columns separately. For doing this, we must SELECT all the columns from the table into the record using a single SELECT statement:

```
SELECT * INTO rec_name
FROM table_name
[WHERE clause];
```

We can read/retrieve values from a record by simple assignment statements. The General syntax to retrieve a specific field value from a record into a variable is:

```
var_name := rec_name.col_name;
```

Table 8.5 shows the different ways we can assign values to and from a record:

Table 8.5 Value Assignment in PL/SQL

Syntax	Usage
rec_name.col_name := value;	Directly assigning a value to a specific column of a record
rec_name.column_name := value;	Directly assigning a value to a specific column of a record, when record is declared using %ROWTYPE
SELECT col1, col2 INTO rec_name. col_name1, rec_name.col_name2 FROM table_name [WHERE clause];	Assigning values to individual fields of a record from a database table
SELECT * INTO rec_name FROM table_name [WHERE clause];	Assigning a value to all fields in the record from a database table
variable_name := rec_name.col_name;	Reading a value from a record column and assigning it to a variable

Use of delimiters in PL/SQL

Different delimiters are used in PL/SQL with specific meaning. Table 8.6 summarizes use of such delimiters.

Table 8.6 Delimiters in PL/SQL

Delimiters	Functionality
--	Single line comments, placed at the beginning of a line
/*	Initiator for multi line comment
*/	Terminator for multi line comment
(	Initial parenthesis for expression
)	Closing parenthesis for expression
<<	Begin label delimiter
>>	End label delimiter
,	Item separator
'	Literal delimiter
“	Starting quote for literal
”	Finishing quote for literal
:	Host variable indicator
%	Attribute indicator
.	Component selector
@	Remote database indicator
. .	Range indicator
;	Statement terminator

8.1.4 Control Flow Instructions in PL/SQL

As with conventional programming languages, PL/SQL supports conditional execution of instructions or statements. Both the conditional statements and loop control statements are available.

Conditional flow control

For conditional statements the following syntaxes are available:

- Simple IF statement

```
IF <condition>
THEN
    <statement>
END IF;
```

- IF-THEN-ELSE statement

```
IF <condition>
THEN
```

```
    <statement>
    ELSE
    <statement>
END IF;
```

- Nested IF-THEN-ELSE statement

```
IF <condition>
THEN
    <statement>
ELSE IF <condition>
    THEN
       <statement>
    ELSE
       <statement>
    END IF;
    END IF;
```

ILLUSTRATION 8.5 Let us write a very simple program in PL/SQL. The program takes two integer inputs and subtracts the smaller number from the larger and prints the result. The program code is given below.

```
SET SERVEROUTPUT ON
SET VERIFY OFF
DECLARE
   A NUMBER := &A;
   B NUMBER := &B;
   C NUMBER;

BEGIN
   IF A >= B THEN DBMS_OUTPUT.PUT_LINE ('Difference is ' || (A-B));
      ELSE DBMS_OUTPUT.PUT_LINE ('Difference is ' || (B-A));
   END IF;
END;
```

ILLUSTRATION 8.6 Now, let us consider three input numbers and the program has to print the largest difference between any two of them. The program code is given below.

```
SET SERVEROUTPUT ON
SET VERIFY OFF

DECLARE
 A NUMBER := &A;
 B NUMBER := &B;
 MAX NUMBER;
 MIN NUMBER;
BEGIN
 IF A >= B
THEN
    IF A >= C
    THEN
         MAX := A;
```

```
        ELSE
            MAX := C;
        END IF;
    ELSE
        IF B >= C
        THEN
            MAX := B;
        ELSE
            MAX := C;
        END IF;
    END IF

    IF A >= B
    THEN
        IF A <= C
        THEN
            MIN := A;
        ELSE
            MIN := C;
        END IF;
    ELSE
        IF B <= C
        THEN
            MIN := B;
        ELSE
            MIN := C;
        END IF;
    END IF
    DBMS_OUTPUT.PUT_LINE ('Difference is'||(MAX - MIN));
  END;
```

Iterative flow control

Iterative program flow control is possible using FOR loop and WHILE loop statements. There are three types of loop structures.

Basic Loop: It is the simplest type of loops. This encloses a sequence of statements between keywords LOOP and END LOOP.

Syntax:

```
LOOP
    <statement 1>;
        .
        .
    <statement n>;
    EXIT [WHEN <condition>];
END LOOP;
```

The basic loop will be executed at least once even if the condition is met before entering the loop. Without the EXIT statement, a loop will be infinite.

FOR Loop: It has a similar function as that of basic loops. A conditional control statement is executed before execution of the sequence of loop statements. A LOOP keyword indicates the start of the sequence. EXIT statement is not needed in this case.

Syntax:

```
FOR <counter> IN [REVERSE] <lower_bound> . . <upper_bound>
LOOP
   <statement 1>;
     .
     .
   <statement n>;

END LOOP;
```

ILLUSTRATION 8.7 The following program displays the cumulative sums of a series of *n* numbers from 1 to *n,* such that the *i*th output is the cumulative sum of the first *i* numbers.

```
SET SERVEROUTPUT ON
SET VERIFY OFF

DECLARE
    N NUMBER;
    SUM_NUM NUMBER;

BEGIN
    N := &N;
    FOR COUNT1 IN 1 . . N LOOP
       SUM_NUM := 0;
       FOR COUNT2 IN 1 . . COUNT1 LOOP
          SUM_NUM := SUM_NUM + COUNT2;
       END LOOP;
       DBMS_OUTPUT.PUT_LINE ('Sum From 1 TO' ||COUNT2|| 'is' ||
       SUM_NUM);
    END LOOP;
END;
```

WHILE Loop: To repeat a sequence of statements conditionally, the WHILE statement is used.

Syntax:

```
WHILE <condition>
LOOP
    <statement 1>;
      .
      .
    <statement n>;

END LOOP;
```

ILLUSTRATION 8.8 The preceding illustration is repeated below with the WHILE LOOP.

```
SET SERVEROUTPUT ON
SET VERIFY OFF

DECLARE
        N               NUMBER;
        SUM_NUM         NUMBER;

BEGIN
        N := &N;
        COUNT1 := 1;
        WHILE COUNT1 < N LOOP
                SUM_NUM := 0;
                COUNT2 := 1;
                WHILE COUNT2 < COUNT1 LOOP
                        SUM_NUM := SUM_NUM + COUNT2;
                        COUNT2 := COUNT2 + 1;
                END LOOP;
                DBMS_OUTPUT.PUT_LINE ('Sum From 1 TO' ||COUNT2|| 'is' ||
                SUM_NUM);
                COUNT1 := COUNT1 + 1;
        END LOOP;
END;
```

ILLUSTRATION 8.9 Let us consider the EMPLOYEE table having attributes as

```
E_ID NUMBER(5)
E_NAME VARCHAR2(20)
E_CITY VARCHAR2(20)
E_JOIN_DATE DATE
E_SALARY NUMBER(5)
E_DEPT_ID NUMBER(2)
```

Our objective is to read selective columns of records from EMPLOYEE and insert into another table MANAGERS.

```
DECLARE
   eid          employee.e_id%TYPE;
   ename        employee.e_name%TYPE;
   ecity        employee.e_city%TYPE;
   edepartment  employee.e_dept_id%TYPE;
   counter      NUMBER(2) := 1;

BEGIN
   SELECT e_id, e_dept_no, e_name, e_city INTO eid, edepartment, ename, ecity
   FROM employee
   WHERE e_salary > 10000;
   LOOP
        INSERT INTO managers (m_id, m_dept_id, m_name, m_city)
```

```
        VALUES (eid, edepartment, ename, ecity);
        counter := counter + 1;
        EXIT WHEN counter > 5;
    END LOOP;
END;
```

8.2 PL/SQL Programming

For writing program codes in PL/SQL, it is very useful to maintain some standard and conventions. Generally, SQL statements and keywords are written uppercase letters, and variable names, parameter names, database table names or column names are written in lowercase letters. Also, while declaring variables, it is a good idea to use a type identifier, like "v_max" to declare "max" as a variable, "p_roll_no" to identify "roll_no" as a parameter etc. Table 8.7 summarizes some commonly used guidelines regarding this.

Table 8.7 Guidelines for Naming and Case Convention in PL/SQL

Code item	Case convention	Examples
SQL statement	Uppercase	SELECT, UPDATE
PL/ SQL statement	Uppercase	DECLARE, BEGIN, FOR
Data types	Uppercase	VARCHAR2, NUMBER
Variables and parameters	Lowercase	v_ stud_id, v_dept_no, p_roll_no
Tables and columns	Lowercase	students, student_id, department_id

Maintaining indentation of statements and control blocks is a very good idea and helps in understandability and debugging of the program.

Using SQL statements in PL/SQL

Generally, the SELECT statement in SQL has the following form:

```
SELECT <column_name>
FROM <table_name>
WHERE <condition>;
```

This can also be written as (for printing output under a different name):

```
SELECT <column_name>
INTO <variable_name>
FROM <table_name>
WHERE <condition>;
```

In the case of PL/SQL, the use of an output variable name (<variable_name>) in the INTO clause is mandatory. This means that the return value from the SELECT statement must be stored in some variable. In PL/SQL, the above code becomes:

```
DECLARE
   v_<variable_name>;
```

```
BEGIN
    SELECT <column_name>
    INTO <variable_name>
    FROM <table_name>
    WHERE <condition>;
END;
```

Note that we have shown a simple structural form only. Here, the local variable `<variable_name>` may have a specified type in the DECLARE block, `<column_name>` may be replaced by a list of column names, etc. According to the ANSI standard of embedded SQL the SELECT statement (the query) can return one and only one row. Attempt to return more than one row or no row at all will generate error.

Oracle and PL/SQL

PL/SQL is the default procedural language for Oracle. All the Data Manipulation statements of SQL can be used in PL/SQL, but Data Definition and Data Control statements cannot be used in PL/SQL program.

ILLUSTRATION 8.10 Let us consider the the following program to demonstrate the use of SQL DML statements in PL/SQL.

```
DECLARE
    v_count NUMBER(2);

BEGIN
    SELECT COUNT(*) INTO v_count FROM students;
    DBMS_OUTPUT.PUT_LINE ('Number of students before ='||v_count);
    DELETE FROM students WHERE roll_no = 5;
    DELETE FROM students WHERE roll_no = 15;
    COMMIT;
    DBMS_OUTPUT.PUT_LINE('Number of students after =’|| v_count);
END
```

If the number of records in the STUDENTS table was 15 before deleting records then output of the above program will be printed as:

Number of students before = 15
Number of students after = 13

8.2.1 Subprograms in PL/SQL

As with other high level programming languages, PL/SQL also supports subprograms, i.e., *functions* and *procedures*. This facility allows PL/SQL programmer to write modular programs whose components can be reused in other applications. This improves system productivity, consistency etc. Functions and procedures are the specific categories of subprograms used in a PL/SQL program. A group or collection of related subprograms may be used to form a *package*.

Each subprogram has a specific name that encapsulates a group of PL/SQL statements (i.e., a block of PL/SQL codes) along with declaration statements and exception handling statements. Functions return a single output parameter, while procedures perform several related tasks. Runtime error situations are handled by codes in the exception handling section.

Functions

A function contains a function specification and a function body. The specification part is generally a single line statement declaring function name, input parameters list, and return parameter with data type. Function body contains PL/SQL statements to perform the task the function is desired for. The syntax for defining a function is as follows:

```
CREATE [OR REPLACE] FUNCTION <function_name> [<argument_list>]
RETURN DATATYPE IS(VARIABLE DATATYPE)
BEGIN
   <function statements>
END
[EXCEPTION]
    <error handling statements>
END;
```

ILLUSTRATION 8.11 The following function takes two numbers as inputs and returns their sum.

```
CREATE OR REPLACE PROCEDURE fn_sum [x NUMBER, y NUMBER]
IS z NUMBER;
BEGIN
   z := x + y;
   RETURN z;
END fn_sum;
```

Procedures

A procedure contains a procedure specification and a procedure body. The specification part is generally a single line statement declaring procedure name and input parameters list. Procedure body contains PL/SQL statements to perform the tasks the procedure is desired for. The syntax for defining a procedure is as follows:

```
CREATE [OR REPLACE] PROCEDURE <procedure_name> [(<parameter_list>)]
IS (variable datatype)
BEGIN
   <procedure statements>
END

[EXCEPTION]
   <error handling statements>
END <procedure_name>;
```

In the <parameter_list> each parameter should be mentioned with the following syntax:

```
<variable_name> [IN | OUT | IN OUT] <datatype>
```

ILLUSTRATION 8.12 The following procedure takes two numbers as inputs and produces their sum.

```
CREATE OR REPLACE PROCEDURE pr_sum [x NUMBER, y NUMBER]
   IS z NUMBER;

BEGIN
   z := x + y;
   DBMS_OUTPUT.PUT_LINE('sum of'||x||'and'||y||'is'||z );
END pr_sum;

[EXCEPTION]
   <error handling statements>
END;
```

8.2.2 Passing Input and Output Parameters between Subprograms

Input parameters are passed to a subprogram by using the IN parameter. An input parameter is specified in subprogram definition as:

```
<parameter_name> IN <datatype>
```

Output parameters are used to return computed values to the caller program or subprogram. Procedures having OUT parameters cannot be executed from the SQL command line. It must be called from other PL/SQL programs. In a manner similar to the input parameters, output parameters are specified by

```
<parameter_name> OUT <datatype>
```

ILLUSTRATION 8.13 Our earlier function fn_sum can now be defined as:

```
CREATE OR REPLACE FUNCTION fn_sum (x IN NUMBER, y IN NUMBER)
IS z OUT NUMBER;
BEGIN
   z := x + y;
   RETURN z;
END fn_sum;
```

Besides IN and OUT parameters, PL/SQL supports another kind of parameters, called the IN OUT parameters. The same parameter is used here for both input and output purposes. Such parameters have an initial value set by the caller, and returns an updated value to the caller. Procedures having IN OUT parameters cannot be executed from the SQL command line. It must be called from other PL/SQL programs. An input output parameter is specified in subprogram definition as

```
<parameter_name> IN OUT <datatype>
```

ILLUSTRATION 8.14 In the following the procedure pr_sum takes two numbers as input output parameters and produces their sum as a output parameter only.

```
CREATE OR REPLACE PROCEDURE pr_sum (x IN OUT NUMBER, y IN OUT NUMBER)
IS z NUMBER;
BEGIN
   z := x + y;
   DBMS_OUTPUT.PUT_LINE('sum of' ||x||'and'||y||'is'|| z);
END pr_sum;
```

8.3 Exception Handling in PL/SQL

In a PL/SQL program structure, there is a section called EXCEPTION. This section contains (if present at all) specific statements or codes that takes necessary actions whenever runtime errors and exceptions occur during execution of the program. If an SQL program is written carefully enough, there are very little chances of occurrence of exceptions. However, some kinds of exceptions are out of control of the programmer and these cannot be anticipated. Oracle has some built-in exception handler routines that occur very frequently. However, the programmer can always define his own exception routine and include within the program body. While writing an exception, the programmer should check whether one is already supplied automatically by Oracle. A list of some commonly used built-in exception handler is given in Table 8.8.

Table 8.8 Common Errors in PL/SQL

Pre-defined exception names	Error No.	Description
INVALID_NUMBER	ORA-01722	Raised when a conversion from character to number fails.
INVALID_CURSOR	ORA-01001	Raised when an illegal cursor operation is performed.
CURSOR_ALREADY_OPEN	ORA-06511	Raised when attempt is made to open an already opened cursor.
NO_DATA_FOUND	ORA-01403	Raised when SELECT ... INTO statement returns no rows.
TOO_MANY_ROWS	ORA-01422	Raised when SELECT ... INTO statement returns multiple rows.
DUP_VAL_ON_INDEX	ORA-00001	Raised when duplicate value in the database is found affecting uniqueness of index values.
ZERO_DIVIDE	ORA-01476	Raised when attempt is made to divide a number by zero.
PROGRAM_ERROR	ORA-06501	Raised when PL/SQL detects any internal software problem.
VALUE_ERROR	ORA-06502	Raised when arithmetic conversion, truncation or size restriction rules are violated.
STORAGE_ERROR	ORA-06500	Raised when PL/SQL runs out of memory.
TIMEOUT_ON_RESOURCE	ORA-00051	Raised when a timeout occurs during waiting for a resource.

(*Contd.*)

Table 8.8 Common Errors in PL/SQL (*Contd.*)

Pre-defined exception names	Error No.	Description
LOGIN_DELIED	ORA-01017	Raised when an invalid login name or password is detected.
SUBSCRIPT_BEYOND_COUNT	ORA-06533	Raised when a subscripted data item beyond maximum number of elements is referenced.
SUBSCRIPT_OUTSIDE_LIMIT	ORA-06533	Raised when a subscripted data item beyond the logical limit is referenced (ex. subscript = –1).
ACCESS_INTO_NULL	ORA-06530	Raised when values are attempted to be assigned to attributes of an uninitialized object.
CASE_NOT_FOUND	ORA-06592	Raised when none of the choices in a CASE statement if matched and there is no ELSE statement.
COLLECTION_IS_NULL	ORA-06531	Raised when attempt is made to collect using other than EXISTS to an uninitialized nested table or array.
ROWTYPE_MATCH	ORA-06504	Raised when host computer variable and PL/SQL cursor variable involved in an assignment have incompatible return types.

The system defined exception handlers automatically raised and executed whenever any of the predefined error/situation occurs. For safety, it is suggested to use implicit exception handlers NO_DATA_FOUND and TOO_MANY_ROWS whenever possible.

In many situations, the developer/programmer can determine certain conditions that might execute abnormally. In such cases, the programmer should declare a user-defined exception routine and define it in EXCEPTION section. User defined exceptions, however, must be raised explicitly by using a statement like

```
RAISE <exception_name>
```

These exception handling statements have the following syntax:

```
WHEN <exception_name> THEN <SQL_statements>
```

Exception handling section starts with the keyword EXCEPTION. In this section, several exception handlers may be allowed, but only one exception will be processed before PL/SQL program control leaves this block of codes. After all the exception handling clauses, there should be one OTHERS clause. This has syntax as:

```
WHEN OTHERS
```

So, WHEN OTHERS is the last clause in the exception section. Actually, OTHERS is an optional exception handling clause that traps unspecified exceptions. The OTHERS handler traps all exceptions not already trapped. Trapping an exception means successful execution of the corresponding handler routine.

Syntax of the exception block of code is, therefore, given as:

```
BEGIN
. . .
```

```
EXCEPTION
   WHEN NO_DATA_FOUND THEN
      SQL statements;
   WHEN TOO_MANY_ROWS THEN
      SQL statements;
   WHEN OTHERS THEN
      SQL statements;
END;
```

ILLUSTRATION 8.15 Treat the situation that an employee residing in KOLKATA has salary > 5000 as an exception and print a line of output regarding this.

```
SET SERVEROUTPUT ON
SET VERIFY OFF

DECLARE
   v_emp_no  emp.id%TYPE;
   v_emp_sal  emp.salary%TYPE;
   TOO_HIGH_SAL  EXCEPTION;

BEGIN
   SELECT emp_id, salary INTO v_emp_no, v_emp_sal
      FROM emp WHERE emp_city = 'KOLKATA'
      IF v_emp_sal > 5000 THEN RAISE TOO_HIGH_SAL;
      END IF;
EXCEPTION
   WHEN NO_DATA_FOUND THEN ROLLBACK;
   WHEN TOO_HIGH_SAL THEN
   DBMS_OUTPUT.PUT_LINE('salary of employee'||v_emp_no||'is high');
END;
```

Note that, in the above example, both implicit and explicit exceptions are used.

User defined exception handlers

PL/SQL in ORACLE uses a built-in general exception handling procedure. This procedure RAISE_APPLICATION_ERROR is used to display the user-defined error messages along with an error number in the specified range between -20000 and -20999. Note that, the numbers are preceded by the hyphen sign and they are not negative numbers.

Whenever RAISE_APPLICATION_ERROR procedure displays an error message, all previous transactions which are not committed within the PL/SQL Block are rolled back automatically. This means, any change due to INSERT, UPDATE, or DELETE statements, within the present block, are nullified.

It is important to note that RAISE_APPLICATION_ERROR raises an exception but does not handle it. RAISE_APPLICATION_ERROR is used primarily for the following reasons:

1. In order to create a unique id for an user-defined exception.
2. In order to make the user-defined exception look like an Oracle error.

The General syntax to use this error displaying procedure is:

```
RAISE_APPLICATION_ERROR (error_number, error_message);
```

The `error_number` must be between –20000 and –20999. The `error_message` is the text message we want to display whenever the error occurs.

The following steps need to be followed to use RAISE_APPLICATION_ERROR procedure within a block:

- We need to declare a user-defined exception in the declaration section.
- We must raise the user-defined exception based on a specific predefined rule (required under the concerned application) in the execution section.
- It is required to detect the occurrence of the exception and to associate it to a user-defined error number in RAISE_APPLICATION_ERROR.

Let us consider an example of how and when we can display an error message using RAISE_APPLICATION_ERROR.

```
SET SERVEROUTPUT ON
SET VERIFY OFF
DECLARE
   huge_quantity EXCEPTION;

   CURSOR product_quantity is
      SELECT p.product_name as name, sum(o.total_units) as units
      FROM order_items o, product p
      WHERE o.product_id = p.product_id;

   quantity order_items.total_units%type;

   up_limit CONSTANT order_items.total_units%type := 20;

   message VARCHAR2(50);

BEGIN
   FOR product_rec in product_quantity LOOP
     quantity := product_rec.units;
      IF quantity > up_limit THEN
        RAISE huge_quantity;
      ELSEIF quantity < up_limit THEN
       message:= 'The number of unit is below the discount limit.';
       END IF;
       dbms_output.put_line (message);
   END LOOP;
   EXCEPTION
   WHEN huge_quantity THEN
         raise_application_error(-20001, 'The number of unit is above
         the discount limit.');
END;
```

8.4 SQL Cursor

A cursor is user defined work area in memory where all user defined commands within the cursor are executed. Whenever a SQL statement is executed, the Oracle server opens an area in memory where the statement is parsed and executed. This area is called the cursor. Cursors are of two types; implicit and explicit.

Implicit cursors are implied and supported by Oracle server. In other words, they are automatically created and handled by the Oracle server. These cursors contain DMLs and SELECT statements, that return only one row as output, are examples of implicit cursors. No explicit cursors need to be defined for such operations. When invoked (either implicitly or explicitly) Oracle reserves the required memory for processing data, and releases the memory immediately after processing. Explicit cursors are explicitly declared by the application programmer.

PL/SQL cursors can have four attributes. Using these attributes one can verify the outcome of execution of the concerned SQL statement. After execution of an SQL statement, these attributes are automatically (implicitly) set to specified values. These attributes and their functionality are shown in Table 8.9.

Table 8.9 Cursor Attributes in PL/SQL

Attribute	Functionality
SQL%ROWCOUNT	Returns the number of rows affected by the most recent SQL statement.
SQL%FOUND	Returns the Boolean value TRUE if the most recent SQL statement affects at least one row.
SQL%NOTFOUND	Returns the Boolean value TRUE if the most recent SQL statement does not affect at least one row.
SQL%ISOPEN	Always returns the Boolean value FALSE because the PL/SQL closes implicit cursors immediately after they are executed completely.

Cursors (explicit) are declared in the DECLARATION section after variable declaration and they are used in the EXCEPTION section. In general, cursors can be invoked within the scope of the PL/SQL program but not within the SQL DML section. PL/SQL does not return any error if a DML statement does not affect any row in the concerned table, but if any SELECT statement does not retrieve any rows it returns an exception.

The following illustration show the usage of implicit cursors. We will consider the STUDENTS table.

ILLUSTRATION 8.16 This illustration shows the use of %ROWCOUNT attribute.

```
SET SERVEROUTPUT ON
SET VERIFY OFF

DECLARE
   v_count NUMBER(2);
BEGIN
   SELECT COUNT(*) INTO v_count FROM students;
   DBMS_OUTPUT.PUT_LINE ('Number of students before ='||v_count||);
```

```
        DELETE FROM students WHERE roll_no = 5;
        DELETE FROM students WHERE roll_no = 15;
        COMMIT;
        DBMS_OUTPUT.PUT_LINE ('Number of students after ='||v_count||);
          DBMS_OUTPUT.PUT_LINE ('SQL%ROWCOUNT VALUE');
    END;
```

Here the output will be
Number of students before = 15
Number of students after = 13

```
  SQL%ROWCOUNT VALUE
  2
```

ILLUSTRATION 8.17 This illustration shows the use of %FOUND and %ROWCOUNT attributes.

```
    SET SERVEROUTPUT ON
    SET VERIFY OFF

    DECLARE
      v_count NUMBER(2);
    BEGIN
      SELECT COUNT(*) INTO v_count FROM students;
      -- check the value of %FOUND attribute
      DBMS_OUTPUT.PUT_LINE ('SQL%FOUND VALUE');
      IF SQL%FOUND THEN
        DBMS_OUTPUT.PUT_LINE ('TRUE');
      ELSE
        DBMS_OUTPUT.PUT_LINE ('FALSE');
      END IF;

      -- check the value of %ROWCOUNT attribute

      v_count := SQL%ROWCOUNT;
      IF SQL%FOUND THEN
        DBMS_OUTPUT.PUT_LINE('SQL%ROWCOUNT VALUE'||'Records Found');
      ELSE
        DBMS_OUTPUT.PUT_LINE ('No Records Found');
      END IF;
    END;
```

Here the output will be
SQL%FOUND VALUE
TRUE
5 Records Found

8.5 SQL Trigger

A SQL trigger is a PL/SQL block of codes that is executed automatically when the concerned *triggering event* occurs on a table. The triggering event may occur during `insert, delete` or `update` operations. A trigger is associated with a database table and is fired when the triggering event takes place on the relevant table. Triggers are created in Oracle using the `create trigger` statement. A trigger definition contains trigger statement, trigger restriction and trigger body. A trigger is commonly used to enforce error checking, security and safe backing-up of data. It must be carefully defined in order to avoid duplication or replacement of existing built-in-functions. The trigger statement specifies the DML statement executed over a certain table. Trigger body is a block of PL/SQL statements, and the restriction represents any checking condition expressed as WHEN statement. The syntax and structure of this statement is given below.

```
CREATE [or REPLCE] TRIGGER trigger_name
{BEFORE | AFTER}
{DELETE | INSERT |UPDATE [OF column_name[, column_name]...]}
]...
ON table_name
[[REFERENCING {OLD [AS] <old> [NEW [AS] <new>]
               | NEW [AS] <new> [OLD [AS] <old>]}]
FOR EACH ROW
[WHEN <condition>]]
```

There are two types of triggers mentioned below.

1. **Row level trigger:** An event is triggered for each row updated, inserted or deleted.
2. **Statement level trigger:** An event is triggered for each SQL statement executed.

The following time sequence is followed when a trigger is fired:

- BEFORE statement trigger fires before starting SQL statement execution
- BEFORE row level trigger fires once before each row is affected.
- AFTER row level trigger fires once after each row is affected.
- AFTER statement level trigger fires after completion of SQL statement execution.

OLD and NEW qualifiers

In the preceding syntax, we have used two qualifiers OLD and NEW. These qualifiers are related to row triggers and represent old and new values of a column before and after the operation. The functionality of the prefix qualifiers OLD and NEW are given in Table 8.10.

Table 8.10 Qualifiers in PL/SQL

DML statement	OLD value	NEW value
DELETE	Value before deleted	NULL
INSERT	NULL	Value inserted
UPDATE	Value before update	Value after update

LLUSTRATION 8.18 Let us define triggers for insert and update of employee records in order to check whether the salary value exceeds the pre-specified range.

```
CREATE OR REPLCE TRIGGER sal_lim_chk
BEFORE
INSERT OR UPDATE
ON emp
FOR EACH ROW
WHEN (NEW.salary > 50000) OR NEW.salary < 500)

BEGIN
    RAISE_APPLICATION_ERROR(-20000, 'Salary must be > 500 and <50000');
END;
```

The above trigger is saved in an SQL file and executed to enable the trigger. Now, whenever we try to insert a record in the EMP table (or update an existing record) using a statement like

```
INSERT INTO EMP VALUES(<name>,<address>,<joindate>,<sal>);
```

the trigger will be fired and following error report will be generated, if the new salary value is out of the specified limit.

```
INSERT INTO EMP VALUES(<name>,<address>,<joindate>,<sal>);
```

ERROR at line:
ORA-20000: Salary must be > 500 and <50000

The trigger definition can contain statements accessing data from database tables and use them in its body for programming purposes. Let us consider the following illustration.

ILLUSTRATION 8.19 Let the minimum and maximum salary are predefined and stored in table SALGRADE. Let us now define triggers for insert and update of employee records in order to check whether the salary value exceeds the pre-specified range. Three situations are considered; when a new salary value falls outside range, when an existing salary value is decreased, and when an increment in salary is beyond a limit.

```
CREATE OR REPLCE TRIGGER sal_lim_chk
BEFORE
INSERT OR UPDATE
ON emp
FOR EACH ROW

DECLARE
  mnsal, mxsal salgrade.maxsal%TYPE;

BEGIN
  SELECT minsal, maxsal AS mnsal, mxsal FROM salgrade;

  IF(NEW.sal < mnsal OR NEW.sal > mxsal) then
      RAISE_APPLICATION_ERROR(-20000, 'Salary range exceeded');
  ELSEIF (NEW.sal < OLD.sal) THEN
      RAISE_APPLICATION_ERROR(-20010, 'Salary is decreased');
  ELSEIF (NEW.sal < 1.5 * OLD.sal) THEN
```

```
        RAISE_APPLICATION_ERROR(-20010,'Salary increase beyond limit');

    END IF;
 END;
```

Some more features of triggers

If a trigger is specified within the SQL*Plus shell, the trigger definition must end with a period (.) symbol at the end of the last line. Execution of the trigger definition causes SQL*Plus to compile it. When a trigger definition is saved earlier in an SQL file (e.g., trig1.sql), it can be loaded from the file using @ command (e.g., @trig1). Such a saved trigger definition must have a slash (/) symbol at the end.

A trigger definition cannot be changed or modified, it can only be recreated using the `CREATE` or `REPLACE` statements. The `DROP <trigger_name>` statement removes the trigger `<trigger_name>`.

A trigger is automatically enabled after it is successfully compiled. It can, however, be enabled or disabled using the following syntax (statement) explicitly.

```
ALTER TRIGGER <trigger_name> ENABLE | DISABLE
```

All triggers defined over table <table_name> can be enabled or disabled using

```
ALTER TTABLE <table_name> ENABLE | DISABLE ALL TRIGGER;
```

The data dictionary stores all information about triggers in the table USER_TRIGGERS. This information includes trigger name, type, concerned table name, and the PL/SQL code block defining the trigger.

Packages

A PL/SQL package is a database object that contains functions, procedures, cursors, exceptions in a single unit. Structurally, a package has two components: package specification and package body. In the former, specifications of procedures, functions, cursors etc. used in the package are maintained; and in the later, detailed definitions of these items are provided. Both package specification and package body need to be compiled before they can be used (executed). Both package specification and package body are stored as .SQL files in the system. For example, syntax of package specification and package body is given below.

Specification

```
CREATE OR REPLACE PACKAGE <package_name> AS
<declarations>
BEGIN
      <object specifications>
END (<package_name>);
```

Body

```
CREATE OR REPLACE PACKAGE BODY <package_name> AS
<declarations>
BEGIN
     <executable statements>
END (<package_name>);
```

ILLUSTRATION 8.20 We shall show an example package for a simple calculator program. This program allows addition, subtraction, multiplication and division operations. Functions and procedures for these operations are provided.

```
CREATE OR REPLACE PACKAGE  calculator AS
<declarations>
BEGIN
     FUNCTION fsum(a NUMBER, b NUMBER) RETURNS NUMBER;
     FUNCTION fsubtract(a NUMBER, b NUMBER) RETURNS NUMBER;
     FUNCTION fmultiply(a NUMBER, b NUMBER) RETURNS NUMBER;
     FUNCTION fdivide(a NUMBER, b NUMBER) RETURNS NUMBER;
     PROCEDURE psum(a NUMBER, b NUMBER);
     PROCEDURE psubtract(a NUMBER, b NUMBER);
     PROCEDURE pmultiply (a NUMBER, b NUMBER);
     PROCEDURE pdivide (a NUMBER, b NUMBER);
END calculator;

CREATE OR REPLACE PACKAGE BODY calculator AS
<declarations>
BEGIN
     FUNCTION fsum(a NUMBER, b NUMBER) RETURNS NUMBER IS c NUMBER;
     BEGIN
          c:= a-b;
          RETURN c;
     END;

     FUNCTION fsubtract(a NUMBER, b NUMBER) RETURNS IS c NUMBER;
     BEGIN
          c:= a-b;
          RETURN c;
     END;

     FUNCTION fmultiply(a NUMBER, b NUMBER) RETURNS IS c NUMBER;
     BEGIN
          c:= a*b;
          RETURN c;
     END;

     FUNCTION fdivide(a NUMBER, b NUMBER) RETURNS IS c NUMBER;
     BEGIN
          IF b <> 0 THEN c:= a/b;
          ELSE RAISE_APPLICATION_ERROR(-20000, 'divide-by-zero');
          END IF;
     RETURN c;
     END ;

     PROCEDURE psum(a NUMBER, b NUMBER) IS c NUMBER;
     BEGIN
```

```
        c:= a+b;
        DBMS_OUTPUT.PUT_LINE (a||'+'|| b ||'is'|| c);
    END psum;

    PROCEDURE psubtract(a NUMBER, b NUMBER);
    BEGIN
        c:= a-b;
        DBMS_OUTPUT.PUT_LINE (a||'-'|| b ||'is'|| c);
    END psubtract;

    PROCEDURE pmultiply (a NUMBER, b NUMBER);
    BEGIN
        c:= a*b;
        DBMS_OUTPUT.PUT_LINE (a||'*'|| b ||'is'|| c);
    END pmultiply;

    PROCEDURE pdivide (a NUMBER, b NUMBER);
    BEGIN
        IF b <> 0
        THEN
        c:= a/b;DBMS_OUTPUT.PUT_LINE (a||'/'|| b ||'is'|| c);
        ELSE RAISE_APPLICATION_ERROR(-20000, 'divide-by-zero');
        END IF;
    END pdivide;

END calculator;
```

8.6 Benefits of PL/SQL

From the foregoing discussion, we may summarize the advantages of PL/SQL as follows:

- PL/SQL programs can be stored as functions, procedures, triggers, and packages.
- This library of sub-programs can be shared for development purposes.
- SQL data types are supported in PL/SQL. Hence, PL/SQL easily bridges the gap between database technology and procedural execution facilities.
- The procedural statement executor processes only local data in the client machine and not the database itself. Hence, procedural statements do not overburden the database server access procedure in any way.
- Procedural facilities are available in PL/SQL which are not available in SQL. For example, users can declare their own variables, constants etc., and desired control structures. Error handling is also possible using exception handler routines.
- Block structuring of codes in PL/SQL helps developer writing good codes easily. These are easy to debug being modular in nature.
- PL/SQL is portable, i.e., it is platform independent (provided a Oracle server is available).

Exercises

8.1 Why PL/SQL is treated as a block structured language?

8.2 How does PL/SQL facilitates database applications development?

8.3 Mention different types of subprograms that can be used in PL/SQL. Specify how can these subprograms be defined.

8.4 What are the different types of parameters that can be passed to PL/SQL subprograms? Show the use of such parameters along with suitable examples.

8.5 What is a SQL cursor? How does a cursor is defined and used in a PL/SQL program?

8.6 What is a SQL trigger? What is the importance of triggers in PL/SQL programming?

8.7 Write a PL/SQL program to output sum of first N integers using FOR loop.

8.8 Write a PL/SQL program to output factorial of an integer N using a WHILE loop.

8.9 Describe scopes of variables, in a PL/SQL program, declared in different nested blocks.

8.10 Explain the use of %TYPE and %ROWTYPE attributes using suitable examples.

CHAPTER 9

Query Processing and Optimization

A query language, such as SQL, is a non-procedural language. That is, the statements written in SQL (the query) only specify what to do, and not how to do. This is quite different from the specifications provided by a procedural language like C, COBOL, Java etc. In procedural languages instruction sequences clearly specify the details of the execution path, starting from the beginning and finishing at the end. The execution pattern can never be changed unless we explicitly rewrite the program in a different way. For such a program, the source code translation phase generates a unique object code which is used for execution. In SQL, the execution path is never explicitly specified. A query may be executed following a number of possible execution paths. That is, reordering of fundamental processing steps is possible in many cases. Since alternative execution strategies are available, we need to select the best possible option before code generation.

9.1 Query Processing

A database query is generally expressed in a very high-level language like the SQL. This query needs to be pre-processed before execution. An SQL query must pass through scanning, parsing, validation, optimization and code generation phases before actual execution. The scanning process checks for key words and other tokens (attribute names, relation names etc.), used in the SQL query statement. The parser checks for the language syntax and the validation process checks for semantic correctness. After a query is found to be grammatically and semantically correct, it is represented as an internal data structure, called the query tree (query graphs are also possible). Query trees contain, at its nodes, individual operations in relational algebraic form. This query tree may be re-organized, by changing order of execution, or splitting and merging, of different individual operations, in order to find out the best execution plan. A code generator generates executable codes for different operations and links them. After all these are done, the runtime database processor executes the code using suitable data access paths and methodologies. An SQL code may be either interpreted or compiled depending on the availability of the interpreter and/or compiler. If any error is detected during execution, the runtime database processor displays error messages on the user terminal; otherwise it displays results of operations.

The efficiency of query execution depends mainly on the data structure and data access methodologies. In a later Chapter, we shall discuss the different methodologies of organizing database data in physical storage. These data files may be unordered or ordered according to some key attribute. In many cases, extra index files are also available to help search processes. If an index is not available, it may be created using suitable techniques. The physical data can be made ordered by external sorting processes which may be very time costly. However, the indexes can provide a quick solution by creating a logically ordered data file. Generally, a data file is physically ordered according to its primary key, and other non-key attributes can be used for logical ordering as secondary indexes.

In Figure 9.1, we shall illustrate the steps of query processing along with inputs and outputs to each step.

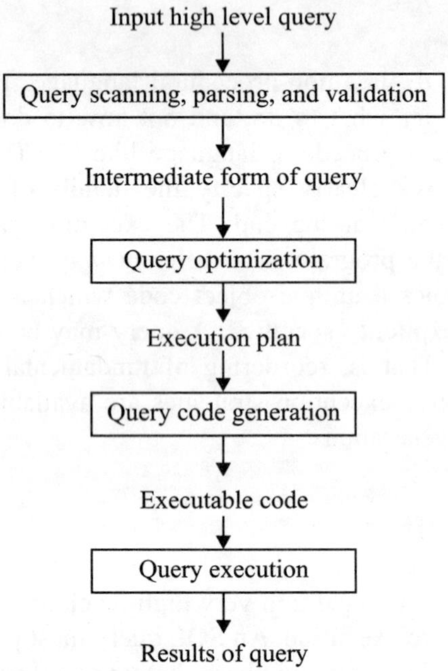

Figure 9.1 Steps of query processing.

Query processing involves the operations of parsing of query statements, reordering of computational steps to produce equivalent parse trees, selection of the best parse tree, code generation and execution.

Let us consider an example query to illustrate the processing technique. Suppose a library database contains the following tables:

```
BOOKS (TITLE, AUTHOR, PUB_NAME, LC_NO)
PUBLISHERS (PNAME, PADDR, PCITY)
BORROWERS (BNAME, BADDR, BCITY, CARD_NO)
LOANS (CARD_NO, LC_NO, DATE_ISSUE)
```

In the above database, LC_NO indicates the Library-of-Congress number of a book. Other attributes has usual meaning and are easily understandable. The input query is to find out the titles of books that were borrowed before 01. 01. 2011. We can express this query in SQL as:

```
SELECT TITLE FROM BOOKS, BORROWERS, LOANS
WHERE BORROWERS.CARD_NO = LOANS.CARD_NO
AND BOOKS.LC_NO = LOANS.LC_NO
AND LOANS.DATE_ISSUE < '01-JAN-2011';
```

This query involves two join operations among BOOK, BORROWER, and LOAN. The same query may also be expressed as:

```
SELECT TITLE FROM BOOKS
WHERE LC_NO IN
   (SELECT LC_NO FROM LOANS, BORROWERS
   WHERE BORROWERS.CARD_NO = LOANS.CARD_NO
   AND DATE_ISSUE < '01-JAN-2011');
```

Again, we can express the same query as follows:

```
SELECT TITLE FROM BOOKS
WHERE LC_NO IN
   (SELECT LC_NO FROM LOANS
   WHERE DATE_ISSUE < '01-JAN-2011')
   AND CARD_NO IN
      (SELECT CARD_NO FROM BORROWERS);
```

We can describe the execution plans for the above three possible query statements in following three different ways:

(a) In the first approach, let the join of the three relations produces a relation called X, such that

$$X = \Pi_S (\sigma_F(\text{LOANS} \times \text{BORROWERS} \times \text{BOOKS}))$$

where

F = BORROWERS.CARD_NO = LOANS.CARD_NO AND BOOKS.LC_NO = LOANS.LC_NO

S = TITLE, AUTHOR, PNAME, LC_NO, NAME, ADDR, CITY, CARD_NO, DATE

Then we may apply the date restriction over the results, and the desired titles may be found as

$$Z = \Pi_{\text{TITLE}}(\sigma_{\text{DATE}<1/1/11}(X))$$

The query tree can now be drawn in Figure 9.2 as follows.

(b) In the second approach, we perform a join between BORROWERS and LOANS relations, and select tuples where BORROWERS.CARD_NO = LOANS.CARD_NO is satisfied. The result (say X) is then joined with the BOOKS relation and tuples are selected where BOOKS.LC_NO = LOANS.LC_NO to produce relation Y. Now the date restriction may be applied over Y, and the desired titles may be found as:

$$Z = \Pi_{\text{TITLE}}(\sigma_{\text{DATE}<1/1/11}(Y))$$

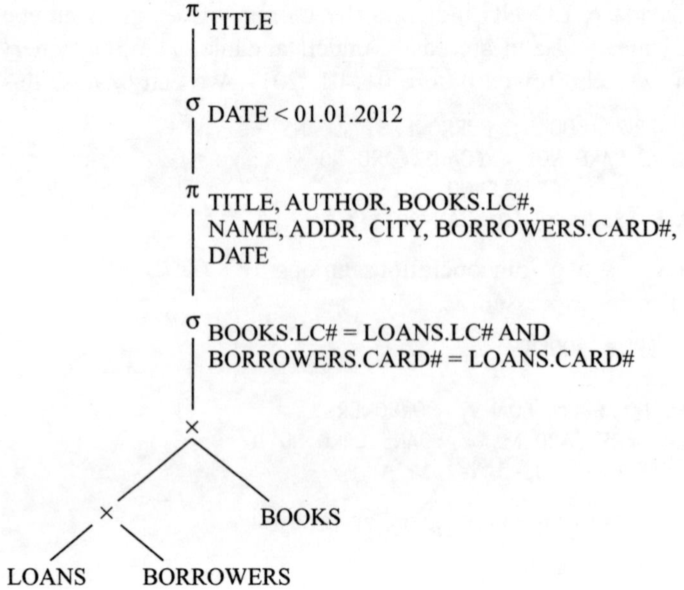

Figure 9.2 Query tree for execution plan (a).

The query tree is shown below in Figure 9.3.

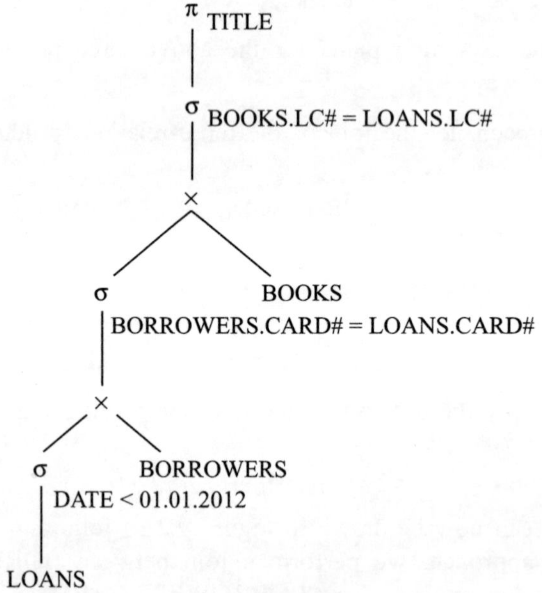

Figure 9.3 Query tree for execution plan (b).

(c) In the third approach, we shall apply the date restriction over the LOANS relations initially to get relation X. Then we get Y as a result of joining X with BORROWERS where the condition is BORROWERS.CARD_NO = LOANS.CARD_NO.

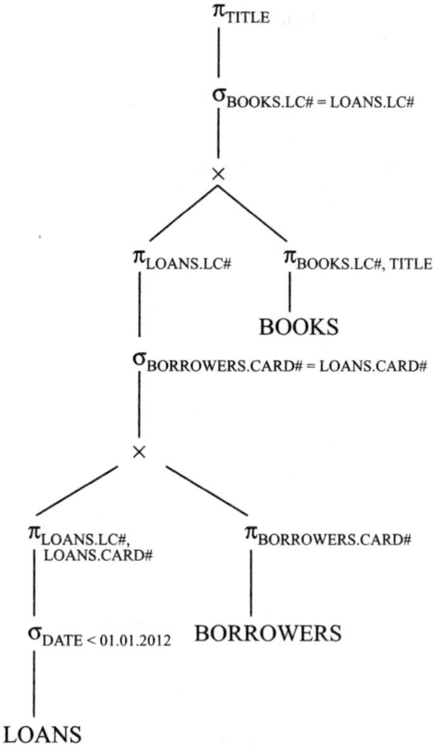

Figure 9.4 Query tree for execution plan (c).

Finally, Y is joined with BOOKS and titles are selected from tuples where BOOKS.LC_NO = Y.LC_NO.

9.2 Query Optimization

When queries are expressed in a declarative language, such as a relational query language, it is easy for the DBMS to execute queries. However, an extensive optimization phase must select, among the many possible ways to implement a given query, one of the few efficient implementations. Ideally, the best implementation must be selected.

There are various query optimization techniques. One such technique is called algebraic optimization. Here relational algebraic expressions are manipulated (pre-processed) to produce equivalent expressions that are very efficiently executed. Another technique deals with queries written in relational calculus and is called the hyper-graph elimination technique. There is also a tabular technique, called the tableaux method, which can be implemented as software.

It seems that the query optimization process will always output the best possible execution scheme, for an input query, in terms of execution efficiency. However, in practice, the optimizer rarely does so. Generation of an absolute optimal query is hardly possible. The optimizer, generally, tries to select an execution plan which is reasonably efficient and a near optimal one. In doing so, the optimizer tries to reformulate a query in a number of different possible forms, using available heuristic rules, computes possible execution times for each of them, and then selects the most promising one. Therefore, the process of optimization involves the following:

- Logical transformation of the input query into some mathematical form.
- Generation of alternative execution plans using heuristics.
- Evaluation of each alternative plan separately.
- Selection of the best alternative.

9.2.1 Logical Transformation of Query

A query, generally in SQL, can be decomposed as a sequence of relational algebraic operations, performed one after another. The query optimizer represents each individual operation in its own specific mathematical notation that depends on actual implementation. Complex queries may involve a number of join, selection and projections operations. It is observed that generally, there exist a number of alternative sequences of operations that produce the same final results. In other words, all these execution sequences are equivalent. Each alternative execution plan can be represented as a parse tree, called a query tree.

9.2.2 Heuristic Alternative Generation

An algebraic expression can be put forward in different ways without changing its meaning or effect. However, difference in the form of expression also incurs a difference in the sequence of sub-operations and execution time of different expressions may be very different. In order to design an efficient DBMS, we need to select a query expression representation technique that ensures faster execution.

Let us consider the following algebraic expression defined over relations R and S.

$$\Pi_{A_2A_3}(R(A_1A_2A_3) \bowtie S(A_3A_4)) \tag{9.1}$$

An equivalent algebraic expression is given by

$$\Pi_{A_2A_3}(R(A_1A_2A_3)) \bowtie \Pi_{A_3}(S(A_3A_4)) \tag{9.2}$$

Equations (9.1) and (9.2) are equivalent, i.e., on the same input, they produce the same output. But they are not equivalent computationally. In the second case, the join operation is less costly as the earlier projections yielded smaller sized relations.

The selection of best equivalent expressions is not supported by any mathematical proof, but heuristic methods may be applied based upon some pragmatic condition.

Equivalent algebraic expressions

There are some well established equivalence between algebraic expressions. These standard forms may assist in finding out equivalent expressions for any arbitrary query. The standard equivalences are given below.

1. Commutative law of Cartesian product and join operations:

$$E_1 \times E_2 \equiv E_2 \times E_1$$

$$E_1 \bowtie E_2 \equiv E_2 \bowtie E_1$$
$$E_1 \underset{F}{\bowtie} E_2 \equiv E_2 \underset{F}{\bowtie} E_1$$

where F is a formula.

2. Associative law:

$$(E_1 \times E_2) \times E_3 \equiv E_1 \times (E_2 \times E_3)$$
$$(E_1 \bowtie E_2) \bowtie E_3 \equiv E_1 \bowtie (E_2 \bowtie E_3)$$
$$(E_1 \underset{F_1}{\bowtie} E_2) \underset{F_2}{\bowtie} E_3 \equiv E_1 \underset{F_1}{\bowtie} (E_2 \underset{F_2}{\bowtie} E_3)$$

where F_1 and F_2 are formulae.

3. Cascade of projections:

$$\Pi_{A_1A_2...A_n}(\Pi_{B_1B_2...B_m}(E)) \equiv \Pi_{A_1A_2...A_n}(E)$$

Where $(A_1A_2 \ldots A_n) \subseteq (B_1B_2 \ldots B_m)$

4. Cascade of selections:

$$\sigma_{F_1}(\sigma_{F_2}(E)) \equiv \sigma_{F_1 \wedge F_2}(E)$$

5. Commutation of selection and projection:

$$\Pi_{A_1A_2...A_n}(\sigma_F(E)) \equiv \sigma_F(\Pi_{A_1A_2...A_n}(E))$$

or, more generally

$$\Pi_{A_1A_2...A_n}(\sigma_F(E)) \equiv \Pi_{A_1A_2...A_n}(\sigma_F(\Pi_{B_1B_2...B_m}(E))$$

6. Commutation of selection and Cartesian product:

$$\sigma_{F_1}(E_1 \times E_2) \equiv \sigma_{F_1}(E_1) \times E_2$$
$$\sigma_F(E_1 \times E_2) \equiv \sigma_{F_1}(E_1) \times \sigma_{F_2}(E_2)$$
$$\sigma_F(E_1 \times E_2) \equiv \sigma_{F_2}(\sigma_{F_1}(E_1) \times E_2)$$

where, F_1 and F_2 involve attributes of E_1 and E_2 respectively.

7. Commutation of selection and union:

$$\sigma_F(E_1 \cup E_2) \equiv \sigma_F(E_1) \cup \sigma_F(E_2)$$

8. Commutation of selection and set difference:

$$\sigma_F(E_1 - E_2) \equiv \sigma_F(E_1) - \sigma_F(E_2)$$

9. Commutation of selection and natural join:

$$\sigma_F(E_1 \bowtie E_2) \equiv \sigma_F(E_1) \bowtie \sigma_F(E_2)$$

10. Commutation of projection and Cartesian product:

$$\Pi_{A_1A_2...A_n}(E_1 \times E_2) \equiv \Pi_{B_1B_2...B_m}(E_1) \times \Pi_{C_1C_2...C_k}(E_2)$$

where $(B_1B_2 \ldots B_m) \subseteq (A_1A_2 \ldots A_n)$ and $(C_1C_2 \ldots C_k) \subseteq (A_1A_2 \ldots A_n)$

11. Commutation of projection and union:

$$\Pi_{A_1A_2...A_n}(E_1 \cup E_2) \equiv \Pi_{A_1A_2...A_n}(E_1) \cup \Pi_{A_1A_2...A_n}(E_2)$$

9.2.3 Evaluation Alternative Plans

After alternative query trees are developed using the above heuristics, each of them are evaluated for computational efficiency. Computational efficiency depends on many things including table size (that determines the number of disk block accesses needed), number of operations of a particular type (one operation may be costlier than the other), number of indexes to be created etc.

9.3 Common Rules of Algebraic Manipulation

To optimize an algebraic expression we must have some rules as the steps of the optimization algorithm. Actually, there is no algorithm that is guaranteed to produce the optimal expression for any given expression, but the following rules are generally useful:

1. **Move selections down the tree as far as possible:** Instead of using a complete table, if we extract the necessary part of it at the beginning, a high degree of computational efficiency can be attained.
2. **Perform projections as early as possible:** This is responsible for saving order of magnitude in execution time, because it tends to make the intermediate results of multistep evaluation small.
3. **Combine certain selections with a prior Cartesian product to make a join:** In case of a join, the product $R \times S$ is the argument of a selection which involves comparison between attributes of R and S. If a comparison involves no attributes of R or S, then it can be moved ahead of the product and can be applied to R or S separately.
4. **Combine sequence of unary operations:** A cascade of unary operations; selection or projection can be combined to form a single operation, in a group, as we scan each tuple.
5. **Pre-compute the common sub-expressions in an expression:** If the result of a common sub-expression is not a large relation and can be read from secondary storage in much less time than it takes to compute it, then it is advantageous to pre-compute the common sub-expression once.
6. **Defer sorting as much as possible:** Initially operand tables are generally larger, and hence performing sorting may consume much time. In the later stages, as we approach toward the final result, this operation becomes less costly.

Most of these rules of thumbs are obvious and straightforward. One of the major objectives behind using them is to reduce the size of intermediate results, because computation cost of some operation depends directly on the size of its operands.

9.4 Algorithms for Relational Algebraic Operations

For the purpose of efficient processing of database queries, we need to develop efficient algorithms for the relational algebraic operations. These operations are the constituents of any high level query. These algorithms can be implemented in many different ways having varying complexities. However, all such algorithms have their relative advantages and disadvantages.

Since all algebraic operations accept inputs from database tables, efficiency of the concerned algorithm depends on the data access efficiencies also. A database table may be accessed in various ways depending on its organization, index structure, etc.

9.4.1 Computing Selection

The selection operation retrieves a number of tuples from a relation based on certain condition (defined over a subset of its attributes). The condition has several specific syntaxes (based on the query language used). The efficiency of any database operation mainly depends on the access path and access strategy for reading data from the database. Generally, data files are stored in any of the following structures: sequential, sorted according primary index, sorted according to a secondary index, hash organized. Therefore, the efficiency of selection operations depends on the relative efficiencies of the data access techniques of these underlying storage structures.

9.4.2 Computing Projection

In projection, we select a subset of columns from a table. Thus, we need to scan a data file (a relation), and then keeping the desired columns and discarding other columns we get the result. In SQL, if the user query does not specify a DISTINCT clause, all possible attribute values for each selected column are maintained. In case a DISTINCT clause is present, we need to sort the result of projection (according to the specified column) and to eliminate the duplicates.

9.4.3 Computing Cartesian Product and Join

Various strategies exist for computing the Cartesian Product and the Join of two relations, and an optimizer has to consider which one is the best in a given situation. Generally, these two operations are the most expensive compared to the other operations, i.e., Selection and Projection. So, a query optimizer must try to minimize the cost of product or join operations whenever possible.

The join operation is one of the most time consuming operation in relational algebra, and most of the relational queries involve a number of join operations, in general. Although join can be of many different types, natural join and equijoin are the two types which are used most frequently. We shall discuss implementations of these join operations in the following.

Methods of implementation

Join operation can be performed in many different ways depending on the availability of sufficient memory buffers, indexes on joining attributes and the algorithms used. Some of the common techniques are discussed as follows:

- **Nested loop join:** This is a brute-force approach, and the easiest technique to implement. The records or tuples from two concerned relations R and S are read, one by one, using a nested loop structure and the join condition is checked.

- **Single loop join:** This method is applied only when at least one of the relations, say S, has an index over its joining attribute. In this case, tuples from R are read one by one; one at a time, and then the index structure is used to retrieve all matching tuples from S.
- **Sort-merge join:** When R and S are both physically sorted according to their joining attributes, both the files can be scanned in order of the joining attributes, and joined whenever a match is found. This is the most efficient algorithm. This algorithm is very similar for that of merging two sorted files. When only secondary indexes are available on the joining attributes of both the files, then the indexes help only to identify the matching records or blocks. However, since the physical records are scattered, in the worst case, the efficiency may reduce to that of the nested loop join algorithm.
- **Hash join:** Here records from both files R and S are hashed into the same file using the same hash function over their hashing attributes. In the first pass, called the partitioning phase, the file with fewer records is partitioned into hash blocks. In the second pass, called the probing phase, records from the other file are hashed to probe the appropriate hash blocks, and the record is combined with all matching records in that block. This algorithm assumes that the smaller of the two files fits entirely in main memory after the first pass.

Some analysis for nested loop, single loop and sort join strategies are presented below. We shall use the following notations for the purpose of analysis and explanation. Let U be the number of blocks needed to store the result of computation. So, to output the U blocks to the secondary storage requires U block accesses. Also, M be the number of available blocks in main memory.

Let R and S are the two relations to be joined, and B_R and B_S are the required number of blocks to maintain R and S respectively. Also, let T_R and T_S are the number of tuples in R and S respectively. We shall consider input and output costs separately and finally, we merge them to compute the final cost of computation.

The algorithm for computing nested Natural Join is outlined below.

```
begin
   get relation R; get relation S;
      for every tuple t1 in R do
         for every tuple t2 in S do
           for every common attribute Ai do
                If (t1[Ai] ≠ t2[Ai]) then break;
           end for;
           include (t1 ⋈ t2) in the output;
      end for;
   end for;
end;
```

Nested loop join

(a) If the main memory has a single input buffer block (M = 1) which is available for the relations, one at a time, then we must read tuples from the two relations in the same buffer, one at a time. That is, for each tuple in R, we must access relation S for B_S times. So, the total number of disk accesses for both the files becomes $T_R \times B_S$.

(b) If one of the relations fits in the main memory completely, then the following situation may arise. Let us consider that $B_S \leq B_R$. Now, if $(M > B_S)$, so that all tuples of relation S fit in the main memory with at least one block left over, then we can read all of S in B_S block accesses. Then we read each block of R, in turn. So, the total cost of reading input relations becomes $B_R + B_S$. Now, we must compute the output cost U. Let, a tuple in R and S are of length l_R and l_S bytes respectively. Let b be the number of bytes in a block. In an output tuple there are approximately $(l_R + l_S)$ bytes. Further, there will be $T_R \times T_S$ tuples in the output. Therefore, the number of blocks needed to store the output becomes

$$U = \frac{T_R \times T_S(I_R + I_S)}{b}$$

Now, BR is approximately $T_R\ l_R/b$ and B_S is approximately $T_S\ l_S/b$. Thus, we can write

$$U = \frac{(T_R \times T_S \times I_R + T_R \times T_S \times I_S)}{b} = B_R \times T_S + T_R \times B_S$$

So, the total cost of computation, i.e., the total input-output cost will be

$$C = B_R + B_S + B_R \times T_S + T_R \times B_S = B_R(T_S + 1) + B_S(T_R + 1)$$

(c) If none of the relations fits in main memory, then the following situation will arise. Let, $(B_S \leq B_R)$ and $(M \leq B_S)$. In this case, we divide the relation S into segments of $(M - 1)$ blocks each, for optimal performance. We read a segment of S and in the remaining block of memory, a block of R is read, in turn, producing the product. We repeat this for each segment. Formally, the algorithm can then be written as:

```
begin
 for each segment S' of relation S do
   for every tuple t2 in segment S' do
      for every block B of relation R do
      for every tuple t2 of block B do
            if (t1 and t2 are joinable) then
            include (t1 ⋈ t2) in the output;
            end for;
      end for;
   end for;
 end for;
end;
```

In this case, we read $(M - 1)$ blocks of S at a time. Since total number of blocks in S is B_S, the number of segments in S is $B_S/(M - 1)$. For each segment of S, the relation R is accessed B_R number of times. Therefore, the input cost is $B_R \times B_S/(M - 1) + B_S$. We know that the output cost is

$$U = B_R \times T_S + T_R \times B_S$$

Thus, total input-output cost is

$$C = B_R\left(\frac{T_S + B_S}{(M-1)}\right) + B_S(T_R + 1)$$

Join using index

In this case, we assume that S has an index structure, and records in S are sorted physically according to the indexing attribute which is also the joining attribute. The obvious way to compute R ⋈ S is to first compute R × S. However, instead of emitting every tuple pair $t_1 - t_2$ (t_1 in R and t_2 in S), it is better to emit those tuples that agree on the common attributes of R and S. If A is the common attribute then the algorithm looks like

```
begin
  for each segment S' of relation S do
    for every tuple t2 in segment S' do
      get tuples t1 of R which agree on attribute A
        and include (t1 ⋈ t2) in the output;

    end for;
  end for;
end;
```

In this case, the input cost is: $B_R B_S/(M - 1) + B_S$, and the output cost is $(B_R T_S + T_R B_S)/I$, where I is the domain size of the attribute A in either R or S, whichever is a superset of the other. Therefore, the total cost is

$$C = C = B_R\left(\frac{T_S}{I} + \frac{B_S}{M-1}\right) + B_S\left(\frac{T_R}{I+1}\right)$$

Sort-Merge join

Here, we need to sort the two relations R and S before joining them. Let, R (A, B) and S (B, C) are the two relations. B is the common attribute in both the relations, and hence, we start by sorting R and S with respect to attribute B. Then we set up cursors to scan tuples from R and S, starting with the lowest B-value first.

Let, we are scanning the tuples ab_1 from R and b_2c from S at any moment. If one of b_1 or b_2 is smaller than the other, we move the cursor down, past the smaller one, and we leave the other cursor fixed. Here, the smaller one cannot match with the B-value in the other relation. If $b_1 = b_2$, we find all the following tuples in R and S with the same B-value. We pair and join each of the tuples accordingly. Then we move the cursors, in both relations, just below the last tuple in sequence with this B-value.

Analysis: The above join process has input cost $B_R + B_S$, since we need only to read each block of the sorted relations once, as we move cursors down through them. The output cost is $(B_R T_S + B_S T_R)/I$, where I is the domain size of attribute B.

Along with the above process, we must compute the cost of sorting. If we use multiway merge sort, then this sorting cost becomes $2\ B_R \log M\ B_R + 2\ B_S \log M\ B_S$. Hence total cost is the sum of above two cost factors.

Output cost for joins

Let, R (A, B) and S (B, C) are the two relations to be joined. The output size of the join result depends on the number of tuples of R with a certain B-value are joined with a tuple of S having the same B-value.

Now, let us consider a set of potential tuples of a given relation R as the Cartesian product of the domains of all its attributes. Let R has T tuples and the product has N tuples. Then we can assume that the current instance of R is a randomly chosen set of T tuples out of the N possible tuples. Thus, each potential tuple occurs with probability T/N (for being chosen).

Now, we are computing R join S, i.e., AB $\bowtie$ BC, so, every B-value of AB also appears in B-attribute of at least one tuple of BC but not vice-versa. Let, D_A, D_B and D_C be the domains of A in AB, B in BC and C in BC. Also, let E_B be the domain of B in AB. I_A, I_B, I_C and J_B are domain sizes of D_A, D_B, D_C and E_B respectively. T_{AB} and T_{BC} are the number of tuples in AB and BC respectively.

Let, *abc* be an arbitrary tuple in $D_A \times D_B \times D_C$. The possible number of all such tuples will be $I_A\ I_B\ I_C$. We have to compute the probability of occurrence of *abc* in the join. For abc to be in the join, *ab* must be in AB and *bc* must be in BC. The probability of *bc* in BC is $T_{BC}/(I_B\ I_C)$. Now, we have to find out the probability of occurrence of *ab* in AB. If *b* does not occur in E_B but occurs in D_B, then this probability is zero. This case occurs for the fraction $(I_B - J_B)/I_B$ times. However, for fraction J_B/I_B of the times *b* will be in E_B. Then the probability that *ab* will occur in AB is T_{AB} divided by the product of the sizes of domains of A and B in relation AB, i.e., $I_A\ J_B$, i.e., the probability is $(J_B/I_B) \times (T_{AB}/I_A J_B)$, i.e., $(T_{AB}/I_A I_B)$. So, the probability that *abc* will appear in AB join BC is $(T_{AB}\ T_{BC})/(I_A\ I_B^2\ I_C)$.

Finally, we must multiply, this with the number of possible tuples i.e., $I_A\ I_B\ I_C$, to get the size of AB $\bowtie$ BC as $T_{AB}\ T_{BC}/I_B$. That is, the size of the join output is the size of the Cartesian product divided by the domain size of the common attribute. If there are *k* number of attributes between relations R and S having domain sizes $I_1, I_2, I_3, \ldots, I_k$ in either R or S whichever is a superset of the other, we have this output size as $T_R \times T_S/(I_1 \times I_2 \times \cdots \times I_k)$, i.e., $T_R \times T_S/I$, where $I = I_1 \times I_2 \times \cdots \times I_k$. So, the number of blocks output, as the result of join operation, is given by $(B_R T_S + T_R B_S)/I$.

Exercises

9.1 What is meant by query optimization? Why is it needed?

9.2 Mention different steps of query processing phases. Describe roles of each step with the help of a clear block diagram.

9.3 In computing efficiency of a database operation, what may be considered as the most significant contributor? Explain.

9.4 How can you compute the efficiencies of different types of selection and projection operations?

9.5 Compute the efficiency of Cartesian product of two relations that uses a nested loop algorithm, assuming the main memory to have a single input buffer block.

9.6 Consider two relations R(A, B) and S(B, C) with primary keys A and B respectively. Cardinality of the relations are 1000 and 2000 respectively. Estimate the cost of natural join of these two relations.

9.7 What do you mean by heuristic query optimization? What heuristics may be applied for this purpose?

9.8 Consider the following query: $\sigma_{A='v'}(AB \bowtie BC)$. Show examples of tables where the join operation should be performed before the selection operation and vice versa.

9.9 Consider an employee database of a company and the following SQL query.

```
SELECT EMP_NAME
FROM EMPLOYEE, WORKS_ON, PROJECT
WHERE PRJ_NAME = 'ASSEMBLY' AND PRJ_NO = 'P1' AND JOIN_DATE > 31.12.11;
```

Construct a query tree for the above query.

9.10 Optimize your query tree obtained as result of Exercise 9.9 using heuristic optimization technique.

CHAPTER 10

Concurrent Transaction Processing

A database is commonly used by a number of users simultaneously in relation to a certain specific application. As an example, we may consider the railway reservation system where hundreds of booking clerks are working for issuing or cancelling passenger tickets. It may be the case that at an instant, more than one clerk is trying to get access to a single relation (or even the same record) concurrently. Although their objectives may be quite different, such kind of concurrent access of data from a database may result in conflict and ambiguity in maintaining data consistency. To solve such conflicting data requests, application programs are designed as a set of logical units having atomicity property. Atomicity implies that any such logical unit will either be completely executed or they will do nothing. Such logical program units are called transactions.

Again, since a number of transactions (same or different) are running simultaneously and each of them needs to function in real-time (fast and uniform response time), they must be executed in instruction-interleaved fashion. This interleaving requires arranging the instructions in any instance of a transaction (one copy of a number of concurrent transactions) in suitable sub-sequences so that after completion of all concurrent transactions the database remains consistent. Such kind of sequencing of transaction instructions is called transaction scheduling.

10.1 Transaction and Concurrency Control

A transaction can be viewed as a logical program unit whose execution preserves the consistency of the database. Transactions are executed either in *do-all* or *do-nothing* fashion. Transactions perform operations like insertion, deletion, updation or simply retrieval of data. A transaction, designated for data retrieval operation only is called a "read" transaction, and a transaction that performs data updation is called a "write" transaction.

- **Read** operation: A data value or record (X) is read into a local variable (x).
  - — Read (X, x) or simply Read (X)

- **Write** operation: A data value or record from a local variable (x) is written back to a database item (X).
  - — Write (X, x) or simply Write (X)

If a number of concurrent transactions be executed on a database in an uncontrolled fashion they are found to produce erroneous or ambiguous results and make the database inconsistent. Therefore, for concurrent transaction processing, we must maintain some provision for concurrency control and recovery schemes.

10.1.1 Properties of a Transaction

There are four desirable characteristics of a transaction. These properties are jointly called ACID properties. These are mentioned below:

- **Atomicity (A)**: A transaction is an atomic unit. It must either be successfully completed or not executed at all.
- **Consistency (C)**: The database must remain in consistent states before and after a transaction.
- **Isolation (I)**: Operations performed by a transaction must be isolated from those of other transactions. That is, execution of a transaction should not interfere with other transactions being executed concurrently.
- **Durability (D)**: The modification made by a transaction must be persistently stored in the physical database.

Example transaction

- **Bank account access transaction:** We consider a banking transaction system where one of the frequent transactions are "account transfer". This transaction transfers money from one account to another. We have used here two global account variables X and Y which are permanent residents of the database, and two corresponding local variables x and y in the transaction for local processing. Consider an example:

  — Transaction T (account transfer)

  Read (X, x);
  $x \leftarrow x - 100$;
  Write (X, x);
  Read (Y, y);
  $y \leftarrow y + 100$;
  Write (Y, y);

  The transaction will produce consistent results and keeps the database integral only when the amount transferred from account X is exactly the same as the amount deposited in account Y.

It should be noted that we have used the "Read(X, x)" and "Write(X, x)" notations in this text. However, simpler notations may be possible. For example, "Read(X, x)" and "Write(X, x)" may be denoted as "r(X)" and "w(X)" respectively. When multiple transactions are considered, then "r_k(X)" and "w_k(X)" are used to denote operations of the kth transaction.

10.2 Serial and Concurrent Transaction Schedules

Transactions may be serial or concurrent. When a number of transactions are executed one after another, they are called serial transactions and the corresponding schedule is a serial schedule. When a number of transactions are executed parallely, in an interleaved fashion, they are called concurrent transactions and the corresponding schedule is a concurrent schedule.

10.2.1 Serializability

When execution of a schedule of concurrent transactions has the same effect as that of a serial schedule, using the same set of transactions, the concurrent schedule is called a serializable schedule.

The concept of serializability is essential in concurrent transaction execution. Let us consider two transaction T_1 and T_2 as shown below in Tables 10.1 and 10.2, in connection with bank accounts X and Y.

Table 10.1 Transaction

Time	Transaction: T_1
1	Read (X, *x*);
2	$x \leftarrow x - 100$;
3	Write (X, x);
4	Read (Y, *y*);
5	$y \leftarrow y + 100$;
6	Write (Y, *y*);

Table 10.2 Transaction

Time	Transaction: T_2
1	Read (X, *x*);
2	$x \leftarrow x - 500$;
3	Write (X, *x*);
4	Read (Y, *y*);
5	$y \leftarrow y + 500$;
6	Write (Y, *y*);

Let initial balance in both X and Y accounts be ₹ 1000/- each.

- For serial execution of transactions T_1 and T_2 (with T_2 after T_1, say), the final fund positions will be : X = 400 and Y = 1600.
- In concurrent execution, we can execute instruction from T_1 and T_2 in an overlapped fashion.
- What will be the result?

Consider the schedule given in Table 10.3.

Here we have scheduled the individual operations of T_1 and T_2 in an arbitrary order (keeping individual transactions unchanged). Final results for database items X and Y indicate that this schedule in erroneous.

10.2.2 Serial Schedule and Serializable Schedule

- A schedule is serial if all steps of each transaction occur consecutively.
- A schedule which is equivalent to a serial schedule, but not a serial schedule, is called a serializable concurrent schedule.
- A schedule is serializable if its effect is equivalent to that of some serial schedule.

Table 10.3 An arbitrary Schedule of Transactions T_1 and T_2

Time	Transaction: T_1	Transaction: T_2
1	Read (X, x);	
2	$x \leftarrow x - 100$;	
3		Read (X, x);
4		$x \leftarrow x - 500$;
5		Write (X, x);
6		Read (Y, y);
7	Write (X, x);	
8	Read (Y, y);	
9	$y \leftarrow y + 100$;	$y \leftarrow y + 500$;
10	Write (Y, y);	
11		Write (Y, y);

Results are: X = 900 and Y = 1500 → inconsistent result.

Let us consider the following example having transactions T_1 and T_2:

- T_1: Read (A, a); $a \leftarrow a - 10$; Write (A, a);
  Read (B, b); $b \leftarrow b + 10$; Write (B, b)
- T_2: Read (B, b); $b \leftarrow b - 20$; Write (B, b);
  Read (C, c); $c \leftarrow c + 20$; Write (C, c);
- Consistency check condition: A + B + C = constant (before and after execution).

A serial schedule in given in Table 10.4

Table 10.4 Serial Schedule of T_1 and T_2

Time	Transaction: T_1	Transaction: T_2
1	Read (A, a);	
2	$a \leftarrow a - 10$;	
3	Write (A, a);	
4	Read (B, b);	
5	$b \leftarrow b + 10$;	
6	Write (B, b);	
7		Read (B, b);
8		$b \leftarrow b - 20$;
9		Write (B, b);
10		Read (C, c);
11		$c \leftarrow c + 20$;
12		Write (C, c);

A non-serial schedule is shown in Table 10.5. In this interleaved schedule perfect order among read and write operations is maintained. Hence, the effect of execution of this schedule is equal to that of the serial schedule. However, we can rearrange interleaved instructions in different order to obtain an incorrect outcome.

Table 10.5 Non-serial Schedule of T_1 and T_2

Time	Transaction: T_1	Transaction: T_2
1	Read (A, *a*);	
2		Read (B, *b*);
3	$a \leftarrow a - 10$;	
4		$b \leftarrow b - 20$;
5	Write (A, *a*);	
6		Write (B, *b*);
7	Read (B, *b*);	
8		Read (C, *c*);
9	$b \leftarrow b + 10$;	
10		$c \leftarrow c + 20$;
11	Write (B, *b*);	
12		Write (C, *c*);

A serializable schedule is listed in Table 10.6. Here interleaved instructions are specifically ordered, whose execution displays equivalence with that of the original serial schedule.

Table 10.6 Serializable Schedule of T_1 and T_2

Time	Transaction: T_1	Transaction: T_2
1	Read (A, *a*);	
2	$a \leftarrow a - 10$;	
3		Read (B, *b*);
4	Write (A, *a*);	
5		$b \leftarrow b - 20$;
6	Read (B, *b*);	
7		Write (B, *b*);
8	$b \leftarrow b + 10$;	
9		Read (C, *c*);
10	Write (B, *b*);	
11		$c \leftarrow c + 20$;
12		Write (C, *c*);

From the above examples, we see that only a serializable schedule of a number of transactions is equivalent to a serial schedule. Thus, we need a mechanism to identity a serializable schedule, and if possible, to develop a method of generating them.

10.2.3 Concept of Lock and Unlock

In a concurrent schedule, any component transaction may try to access any secured item at any time as per requirements. However, this access should be restricted by the data consistency constraint. To ensure consistency even after execution of a concurrent schedule, we can make use of the following strategies:

- We may impose Lock and Unlock over data items.
- Within a Lock and Unlock pair (over a certain data item), all steps are executed consecutively without break.
- Steps within a Lock and Unlock pair are atomic in nature.
- We can place a Lock over an item any number of times (and Unlock eventually) within a transaction.

10.2.4 Serializability Test Algorithm

In order to determine whether a given schedule is serializable or not, we can perform a serializability test. This test depends on the order of placing a Lock by different transactions over a given item. This order should be equivalent to that of a corresponding serial schedule. The algorithm is described below. Here, it is assumed that every time a Lock is placed on an item, some modification of the item is made by the concerned transaction.

- Input: A schedule S for transactions T_1, T_2, T_3, …, T_k.
- Draw a directed graph G, called the precedence graph, with transactions as nodes.
- Draw an arc between T_i and T_j, if we encounter a "unlock A" in T_i followed by a "lock A" in T_j. Direction of arc is $T_i \rightarrow T_j$.
- If there is cycle in G, the schedule is not serializable.

ILLUSTRATION 10.1 Apply the preceding algorithm over the following schedule of three transactions T_1, T_2 and T_3. The schedule and the use of Locks over three items A, B and C are shown in Table 10.7.

Table 10.7 Table of Illustration 10.1

Time	Transaction: T_1	Transaction: T_2	Transaction: T_3
1	Lock A		
2		Lock B	
3		Lock C	
4		Unlock B	
5	Lock B		
6	Unlock A		
7		Lock A	
8		Unlock C	
9		Unlock A	
10			Lock A
11			Lock C
12	Unlock B		
13			Unlock C
14			Unlock A

Solution Here, there are three nodes corresponding to T_1, T_2 and T_3. We draw the following arcs for Locks and Unlocks on A, B and C between the three nodes of the directed graph. The directed arcs are:

1. $T_2 \rightarrow T_1$: "Unlock B" in T_2 is followed by "Lock B" in T_1.
2. $T_1 \rightarrow T_2$: "Unlock A" in T_1 is followed by "Lock A" in T_2.
3. $T_2 \rightarrow T_3$: "Unlock A" in T_2 is followed by "Lock A" in T_3.
4. $T_2 \rightarrow T_3$: "Unlock C" in T_2 is followed by "Lock C" in T_3.

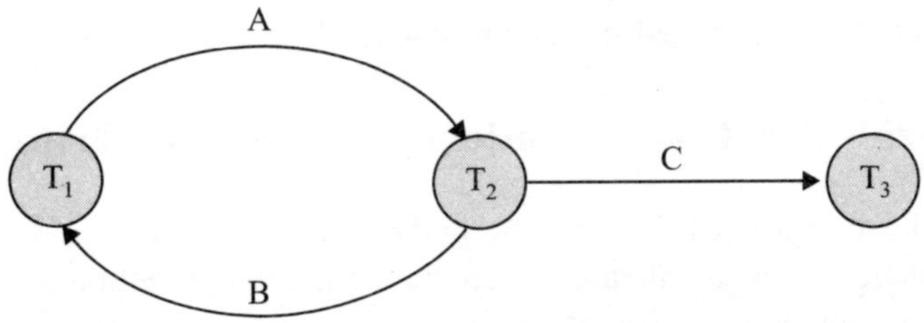

Figure 10.1 Precedence graph for Illustration 10.1.

From the above arcs, as shown in Figure 10.1, we see that there is a loop between T_1 and T_2. Hence, the schedule is not serializable.

Now, how can one ensure that the above algorithm guarantees to determine whether a schedule is serializable or not? The following is a proof.

Let we have the directed graph (also called precedence graph) G. The schedule S contains transactions T_{i1}, T_{i2},..., T_{ik} (among others) which place Locks and Unlocks on an item A in the same order of the transactions (as listed here). Then the graph G contains the arcs $T_{i1} \rightarrow T_{i2} \rightarrow \cdots \rightarrow T_{ik}$. Therefore, the transactions must appear in that order in a serial schedule. As no other transactions Locks A, we can say that the given schedule is equivalent to a serial schedule with respect to item A. This is true for any other items also. Therefore, S is serializable.

Conversely, let G has a cycle $T_{i1} \rightarrow T_{i2} \rightarrow \cdots \rightarrow T_{ij} \rightarrow T_{i1}$. Let there exists a serial schedule R equivalent to S, and that the transaction T_{ip} appears first among the transactions in the cycle. Let the arc $T_{i(p-1)} \rightarrow T_{ip}$ (consider $i(p-1) = ij$ if $p = 1$) be in G because of item A. Then in R, since T_{ip} appears before $T_{i(p-1)}$, the final operation for A applies a function f associated with some {Lock A, Unlock A} pair in T_{ip} before applying some operation g associated with a {Lock A, Unlock A} pair in $T_{i(p-1)}$. However in S, arc $T_{i(p-1)}$ precedes T_{ip}, since there is an arc $T_{i(p-1)} \rightarrow T_{ip}$. Therefore, in S, g is applied before f. Thus, the final value of A in S and R will be different (when f and g are not the same operation), and, therefore, S and R are not equivalent, and S is not serializable.

10.2.5 Different Types of Locks

In order to provide controlled access over a database item (called a resource), we use the locking facility. Whenever a resource is put under Lock by some transaction, generally, other transactions will have no access or only a restricted access for that resource. The nature of access allowed to the other transactions depends on the type of Lock applied. Locking is a very useful technique for preserving system consistency during concurrent transactions over a database.

Locks are of two types:

1. READ Lock or *Shared* Lock: A read locked resource, locked by a certain transaction, may be read accessed by other transactions also.
2. WRITE Lock or *Exclusive* Lock: A locked resource, locked by a certain transaction, cannot be accessed by other transactions until the above Lock is released or the resource is unlocked. This kind of Lock is applied during INSERT, DELETE or UPDATE operations.
   Therefore, depending on the database operation needed over an item/resource, it may be READ or WRITE locked by a transaction.

10.2.6 Serializability Test Considering Read and Write Locks

We have seen earlier that Read Locks can be placed over an item by a number of concurrent transactions. So, there is no serializability conflict among transactions requiring concurrent Read Locks over a shared item. Therefore, our earlier serializability test algorithm may be modified by considering this fact. For simplicity, in the transactions, we shall not explicitly mention the Locks and Unlocks. However, we assume their presence before and after every read and write operations.

If we remember that a Lock is used before reading or writing an item, and Unlock is used after each of these operations, we can rewrite our earlier algorithm, for drawing the precedence graph G, in the following form:

- Input: A schedule S for transactions T_1, T_2, T_3, …, T_k.
- Draw a directed graph G, called the precedence graph, with transactions as nodes.
- Draw an arc between T_i and T_j if we encounter a "Read(X)" in T_i followed by a "Write(X)" in T_j. Direction of arc is $T_i \rightarrow T_j$.
- Draw an arc between T_i and T_j if we encounter a "Write (X)" in T_i followed by a "Read(X)" in T_j. Direction of arc is $T_i \rightarrow T_j$.
- Draw an arc between T_i and T_j if we encounter a "Write (X)" in T_i followed by a "Write(X)" in T_j. Direction of arc is $T_i \rightarrow T_j$.
- If there is cycle in G, the schedule is not serializable, otherwise it is serializable.

ILLUSTRATION 10.2 Consider the following schedule of two transactions T_1 and T_2. Check whether the schedule is serializable (Table 10.8).

Solution In this case, the directed arcs are:

1. $T_1 \rightarrow T_2$: "Read A" in T_1 is followed by "Write A" in T_2.
2. $T_2 \rightarrow T_1$: "Write A" in T_2 is followed by "Write A" in T_1.
3. $T_2 \rightarrow T_1$: "Read B" in T_2 is followed by "Write B" in T_1.
4. $T_1 \rightarrow T_2$: "Write B" in T_1 is followed by "Write B" in T_2.

From the above arcs, as shown in Figure 10.2, we see that there is a loop between T_1 and T_2. Hence, the schedule is not serializable.

Table 10.8 Table of Illustration 10.2

Time	Transaction: T_1	Transaction: T_2
1	Read (A, *a*);	
2	$a \leftarrow a - 10$;	
3		Read (A, *a*);
4		$a \leftarrow a - 20$;
5		Write (A, *a*);
6		Read (B, *b*);
7	Write (A, *a*);	
8	Read (B, *b*);	
9	$b \leftarrow b + 10$;	
10	Write (B, *b*);	
11		$b \leftarrow b + 20$;
12		Write (B, *b*);

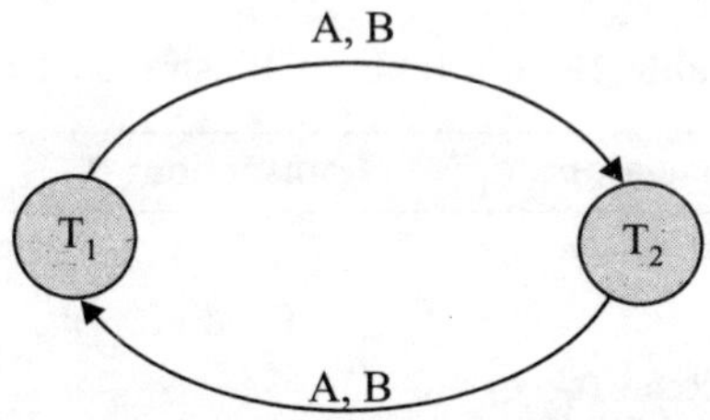

Figure 10.2 Precedence graph of Illustration 10.2.

ILLUSTRATION 10.3 Consider the following schedule of three transactions T_1, T_2 and T_3. Check whether the schedule is serializable (Table 10.9).

Table 10.9 Table of Illustration 10.3

Time	Transaction: T_1	Transaction: T_2	Transaction: T_3
1	Read (A, *a*);		
2	$a \leftarrow a - 10$;		
3			Read (A, *a*);
4			$a \leftarrow a + 10$;
5	Write (A, *a*);		
6		Read (A, *a*);	
7			Write (A, *a*);

Solution In this case, the directed arcs are:

1. $T_1 \rightarrow T_3$: "Read A" in T_1 is followed by "Write A" in T_3.
2. $T_1 \rightarrow T_2$: "Write A" in T_1 is followed by "Read A" in T_2.
3. $T_1 \rightarrow T_3$: "Write A" in T_1 is followed by "Write A" in T_3.

4. $T_2 \rightarrow T_3$: "Read A" in T_2 is followed by "Write A" in T_3.
5. $T_3 \rightarrow T_1$: "Read A" in T_3 is followed by "Write A" in T_1.

From the above arcs, as shown in Figure 10.3, we see that there are loops between T_1, T_3 and among nodes T_1, T_2 and T_3. Hence, the schedule is not serializable.

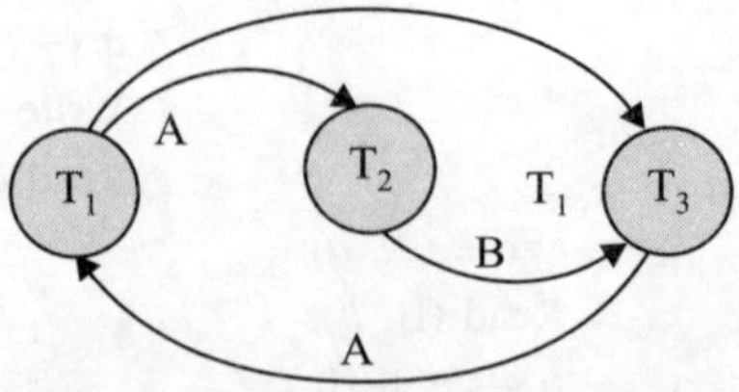

Figure 10.3 Precedence graph of Illustration 10.3.

ILLUSTRATION 10.4 Consider the following schedule of three transactions T_1, T_2 and T_3. Check whether the schedule is serializable (Table 10.10).

Table 10.10 Table of Illustration 10.4

Time	Transaction: T_1	Transaction: T_2	Transaction: T_3
1	Read (A, *a*);		
2		Read (C, *c*);	
3	Read (C, *c*)		
4			Read (A, *a*);
5		Read (B, *b*);	Read (B, *b*);
6		Write (C, *c*);	Write(A, *a*)
7		Write (B, *b*);	

Solution In this case, the directed arcs are:

1. $T_1 \rightarrow T_3$: "Read A" in T_1 is followed by "Write A" in T_3.
2. $T_1 \rightarrow T_2$: "Read C" in T_1 is followed by "Write C" in T_2.
3. $T_3 \rightarrow T_2$: "Read B" in T_3 is followed by "Write B" in T_2.

From the above arcs, as shown in Figure 10.4, we see that there is a loop among nodes T_1, T_2 and T_3. Hence, the schedule is not serializable.

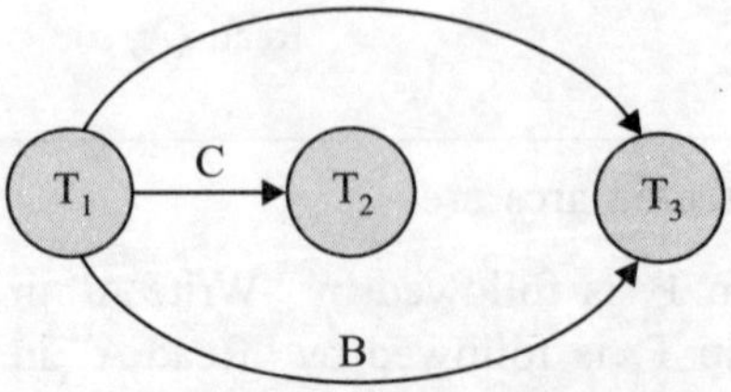

Figure 10.4 Precedence graph of Illustration 10.4.

ILLUSTRATION 10.5 Consider the following schedule of three transactions T_1, T_2 and T_3. Check whether the schedule is serializable (Table 10.11).

Table 10.11 Table of Illustration 10.5

Time	Transaction: T_1	Transaction: T_2	Transaction: T_3
1	Read (A, *a*);		
2		Write (A, *a*)	
3			Read (A, *a*);
4	Write (A, *a*);		
5			Write (A, *a*);

Solution In this case, the directed arcs are:

1. $T_1 \rightarrow T_2$: "Read A" in T_1 is followed by "Write A" in T_2.
2. $T_1 \rightarrow T_3$: "Write A" in T_1 is followed by "Write A" in T_3.
3. $T_2 \rightarrow T_3$: "Write A" in T_2 is followed by "Write A" in T_3.
4. $T_2 \rightarrow T_1$: "Write A" in T_2 is followed by "Write A" in T_1.
5. $T_3 \rightarrow T_1$: "Read A" in T_3 is followed by "Write A" in T_1.

From the above arcs, as shown in Figure 10.5, we see that there are loops between T_1, T_3 and T_1, T_2. Hence, the schedule is not serializable.

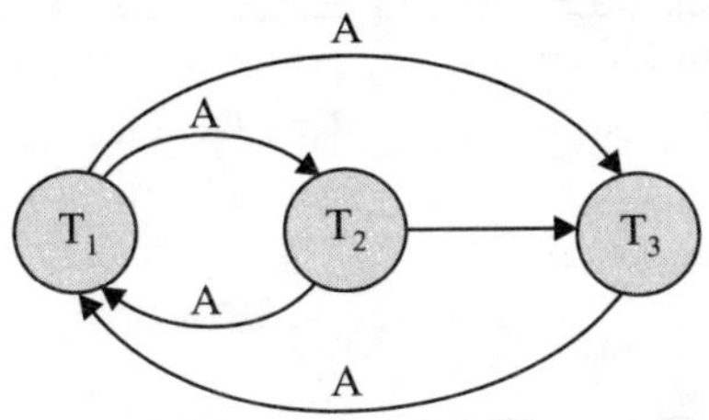

Figure 10.5 Precedence graph of Illustration 10.5.

ILLUSTRATION 10.6 Consider the following schedule of three transactions T_1, T_2 and T_3. Check whether the schedule is serializable (Table 10.12).

Table 10.12 Table of Illustration 10.6

Time	Transaction: T_1	Transaction: T_2	Transaction: T_3
1	Read (A, *a*);		
2		Read (A, *a*);	
3		Write (A, *a*);	
4			Read (A, *a*);
5			Write (A, *a*);

Solution In this case the directed arcs are:

1. $T_1 \rightarrow T_2$: "Read A" in T_1 is followed by "Write A" in T_2.
2. $T_1 \rightarrow T_3$: "Read A" in T_1 is followed by "Write A" in T_3.
3. $T_2 \rightarrow T_3$: "Read A" in T_2 is followed by "Write A" in T_3.
4. $T_2 \rightarrow T_3$: "Write A" in T_2 is followed by "Write A" in T_3.

From the above arcs, as shown in Figure 10.6, we see that there is no loop among nodes T_1, T_2 and T_3. Hence, the schedule is serializable. Note also that, the given schedule is actually a serial schedule.

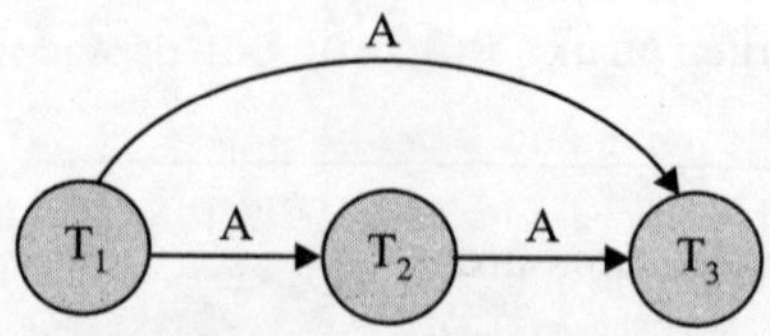

Figure 10.6 Precedence graph of Illustration 10.6.

ILLUSTRATION 10.7 Consider the following schedule of three transactions T_1, T_2 and T_3. Check whether the schedule is serializable (Table 10.13).

Table 10.13 Table of Illustration 10.7

Time	Transaction: T_1	Transaction: T_2	Transaction: T_3
1	Read (A, *a*);		
2		Read (A, *a*);	
3			
4	Write (A, *a*);		
5			Read (A, *a*); Write (A, *a*);

Solution In this case, the directed arcs are:

1. $T_1 \rightarrow T_3$: "Read A" in T_1 is followed by "Write A" in T_3.
2. $T_2 \rightarrow T_1$: "Read A" in T_2 is followed by "Write A" in T_1.
3. $T_2 \rightarrow T_3$: "Read A" in T_2 is followed by "Write A" in T_3.
4. $T_1 \rightarrow T_3$: "Write A" in T_1 is followed by "Write A" in T_3.

From the above arcs, as shown in Figure 10.7, we see that there is no loop among nodes T_1, T_2 and T_3. Hence, the schedule is serializable.

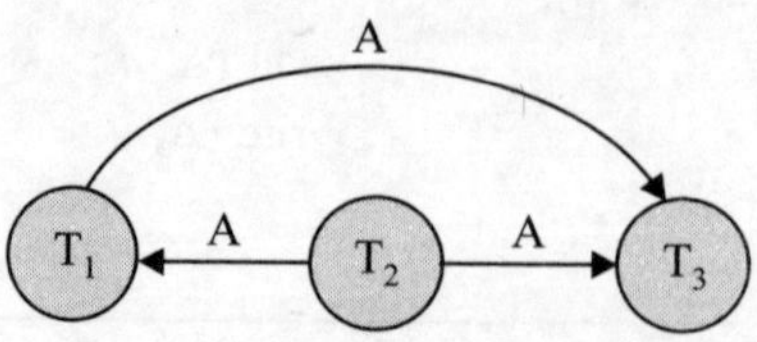

Figure 10.7 Precedence graph of Illustration 10.7.

Using the serializability test algorithm, we can test whether a given schedule is serializable or not. However, our objective is to develop a technique for obtaining serializable schedules for concurrent transactions directly. Fortunately, there are several such techniques.

10.3 Two Phase Lock-Unlock Protocol

The two phase Lock-Unlock protocol is the simplest technique for having a serializable schedule for a number of concurrent transactions. This protocol requires that, *in any transaction, all locks precede all unlocks*. Transactions obeying this protocol are termed two-phase transactions; one Locking phase and one Unlocking phase. Properties of protocol are:

- There are two phases: growing and shrinking.
- All locks are requested/granted in the growing phase.
- All locks are released during the shrinking phase.
- This guarantees serializability.
- It is very simple to implement.
- All Locks, in any transactions, precede all Unlocks".

Proof of serializability

That a two-phase protocol guarantees serializability can be proved as follows:

- Let a two-phase schedule S is not serializable.
- Then the precedence graph G (of schedule S) has a cycle. Suppose the cycle is $T_1 \rightarrow T_2 \rightarrow \cdots \rightarrow T_p \rightarrow T_1$.
- According to the principle of construction of G, a Lock by T_2 follows an Unlock by T_1, a Lock by T_3 follows an Unlock by T_2, and so on.
- Finally, a Lock by T_1 is followed by an Unlock by T_p.
- Thus, a Lock of T_1 follows an Unlock of T_1.
- This is a contradiction of the assumption that T_1 is two-phase.

Two-phase locking protocols can be of following different types:

- **Conservative two-phase protocol:** This requires that all locks be requested/granted prior to execution of a transaction. If any requested lock is not granted, the transaction waits until all requested items are locked. This locking protocol is free from deadlock but difficult to use in practice as interleaving among transactions can be hardly achieved.
- **Strict two-phase protocol:** In this case, none of the transactions releases its write locks until it is committed or aborted.
- **Rigorous two-phase protocol:** Here, none of the transactions releases its read or write locks until it is committed or aborted. It has the advantage that for a set of conflicting transactions, their commit order is the same as their serializability order. Such a behaviour is sometimes expected by the user.

Lock conversion

Transactions may change the mode of locks they hold into another mode (e.g., from read lock to write lock). A transaction may request a lock on a data item any number of times during execution of the transaction, but it can hold *only one lock* on the data item at any time. Lock conversion helps achieving more concurrency.

Suppose a transaction T_1 holds a shared (read) lock on item X, and it needs a "write X" operation at the end. Another transaction T_2, following two-phase locking scheme, requires exclusive locks (write) over items X, Y and Z. At the beginning, if T_1 places a shared lock over item X, and then T_2 placed all the exclusive locks, T_1 has to wait for attaining the desired exclusive lock over X until T_2 unlocks its exclusive locks altogether. Instead T_1 may hold its shared lock over X, and upgrade its lock to an exclusive one. This type of conversion of shared lock to exclusive lock is called upgradation of locks. Conversely, change of lock modes from exclusive to shared ones is called degradation of locks. Therefore, for the purpose of attaining more concurrency, two-phase locking may be extended to allow conversion of locks.

It should be noted that, an upgradation is possible only in the growing phase (of a two-phase protocol), and a degradation is possible only in the shrinking phase.

10.4 Deadlock

The above mentioned Locking and Unlocking strategy may give birth to an undesirable event called a deadlock. Deadlock is a situation when one transaction is waiting for another transaction to release the resource it needs, and vice versa. In such a situation, each transaction will be waiting forever and cannot proceed.

Let us consider that transactions T_1 and T_2 are currently acquiring resources A and B respectively. That is, A and B are now exclusively locked by T_1 and T_2 respectively. Now, if it happens that T_1 requires B for its completion before it can release A, and T_2 requires A for its completion before it can release B, then T_1 and T_2 will be waiting, for B and A respectively, forever. Table 10.7 may be considered as an example.

In this table, at time-unit 1, transaction T_1 requested a lock over A and granted. At time-unit 2, transaction T_2 requested a lock over B and granted. At time-unit 3, T_1 requested a lock over B and rejected (as B is occupied by T_2). At time-unit 4, T_2 requested a lock over A and rejected (as A is occupied by T_1). Therefore, none of the transactions is able to proceed further; and each will wait indefinitely for release of the desired item locked by the other.

Note that, the given schedule of transactions T_1 and T_2, as shown in Table 10.14 is a two-phase one and is serializable, yet a deadlock occurs here.

Table 10.14 Two-phase Deadlock Table

Time	Transaction: T_1	Transaction: T_2
1	Lock A	
2		Lock B
3	Lock B	
4		Lock A
5		Unlock A
6	Unlock B	
7	Unlock A	
8		Unlock B

10.4.1 Deadlock Handling

A deadlock among the members of a set of transactions occurs when two or more transactions from the set are waiting for release of locks held by others. The waiting may be due to direct or indirect locking effects. In the above example, T_1 and T_2 are directly waiting for T_2 and T_1 respectively.

Now, if we consider a deadlock among three transactions T_1, T_2 and T_3, where T_1 holds a lock over A and waiting for item C being held by T_3, T_2 holds a lock over B and waiting for item A being held by T_1, and T_3 holds a lock over C and waiting for item B being held by T_2, we see that each of the transactions are waiting over different items indirectly. Such a situation is also called *circular-waiting*.

Deadlock detection

The easiest way to detect a deadlock is to construct a *wait-for* graph and maintaining it in the system. In such a graph, a directed arc (like $T_1 \rightarrow T_2$) is drawn from a transaction requiring an item to the transaction holding it, with an annotation of the item being sought for over the arc. If, a cycle is found in the graph, there occurs a deadlock; and all the transactions over the cycle are deadlocked. If we draw the *wait-for* graph between transactions T_1 and T_2, it will look like Figure 10.8. For example with three transactions, the graph is shown in Figure 10.9.

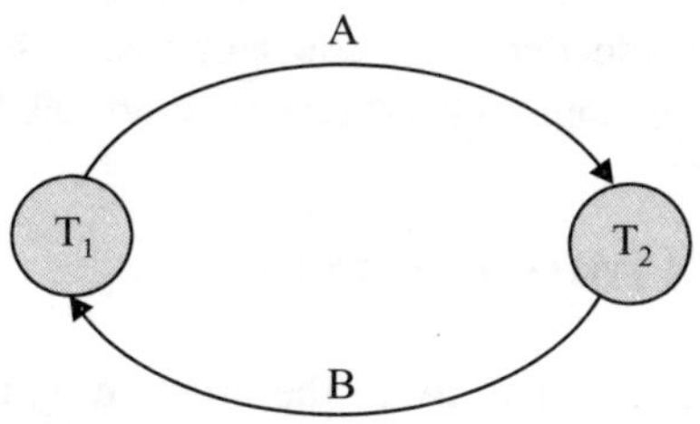

Figure 10.8 Wait-for graph for example with two transactions.

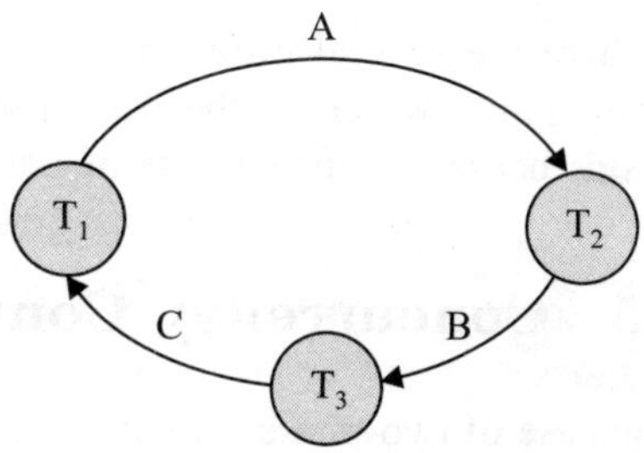

Figure 10.9 Wait-for graph for example with three transactions.

Recovery from deadlock

As soon as the system detects a deadlock, it tries to recover from this state. To break the deadlock, one or more of the deadlocked transactions are to be rolled back. The remedial steps may be considered:

- **Selection of victim:** We need to determine which of the transactions may be rolled back. There are various options to rollback transactions. Usually, a transaction may be rolled back based on
  - — How long the transaction have been running
  - — Amount of data already updated by the transaction
  - — Amount of data remains to be updated by the transaction.

- **Rollback:** Once a victim is selected, we have to decide how far the transaction needs to be rolled back. A total rollback, although is the safest, may not always be the best option. Such partial rollback, of course, needs additional information to be stored by the system. The aborted transaction may be restarted later on.
- **Starvation:** In a system where selection of transactions for rollback is based on the cost factor, it may happen that some of them are picked up and not restarted immediately.

Deadlock prevention

Although there exist techniques for deadlock prevention, most of the RDBMS products prefer allowing deadlocks to occur, and to resolve them when detected. Deadlock Prevention means ensuring that no deadlock may occur. Following measures may be considered for this purpose:

- **Conservative two-phase lock:** Here, each transaction locks all the data items it needs in advance.
- **Assigning orders to all required data items:** An ordering is assigned to all data items in the database. Each transaction acquires locks on an item in the sequence consistent with that order.
- **Timestamps along with locking:** Transactions are assigned with priorities using a unique timestamp which determines whether a transaction is allowed to wait over access permission or to be rolled back. Here, a lower timestamp means higher priority.

There are several problems in applying the first two methods. It is hard to determine, at the beginning, which of the data items will be actually needed by a transactions. Also, these methods cause significant loss of concurrency. The third approach is generally adopted.

10.5 Concurrency Control Using Timestamps

In the case of two-phase schedules, transactions are executed mainly in the order in which they acquire locks on data items. A transaction requesting a lock over a locked item is forced to wait until the data item is unlocked. In many cases, this will produce almost a serial schedule. We also noticed that in the case of a two-phase locking protocol, we cannot avoid deadlocks.

One alternative approach for executing concurrent schedules of transactions is to use timestamps. A *timestamp* is a unique identifier for a transaction assigned by the DBMS itself. Whenever a transaction is submitted to the system for execution, the DBMS assigns a unique number to it. This number may be generated by using a counter which is incremented as and when a new transaction is submitted to the system, or it may be the system time at that instance. Therefore, we may assume a timestamp as the starting time of a transaction. A timestamp (TS) for a transaction T is denoted as `TS(T)`.

If timestamps are generated by using counter then timestamp values for individual transactions will be 1, 2, 3 … etc. Since the system can generate only finite number of such integers this counter must be reset to zero periodically, whenever none of the transactions are in execution state. If the system time is used for this purpose, there is no requirement of such resetting. Since timestamp strategy does not use locks, deadlocks cannot occur in this scheme.

10.5.1 Timestamp Ordering

Suppose a new transaction T_j is submitted to the system after another transaction T_i. In this case, the timestamp value of T_i is less than that of T_j, i.e., TS(T_i) < TS(T_j). Timestamps place an order of execution of the transactions based on timestamp values. So, in our case, the system generates a serializable schedule in which transaction T_i appears before transaction T_j. This is called timestamp ordering (TO).

When timestamp ordering is enforced, data access during conflicting requests does not violate the serializability order of the transactions. To ensure this, the following two timestamp values are associated with each shared data item X.

- `read_TS(X)`: the read timestamp of X. This is the largest timestamp among all the timestamps of transactions that have successfully executed read(X) operation.
- `write_TS(X)`: the write timestamp of X. This is the largest timestamp among all the timestamps of transactions that have successfully executed write (X) operation.

  Whenever a new read(X) or a new write(X) operation is executed, earlier values of `read_TS(X)` and `write_TS(X)` are updated accordingly.

  Timestamp ordering ensures that all the conflicting operations are executed in timestamp orders. Several different implementations of timestamp ordering have been proposed. Some of them are discussed below.

Basic timestamp ordering

The basic timestamp ordering ensures that the transaction T_i is executed in the timestamp order whenever T_i requests read or write operation on X. This is done by comparing the timestamp values of T_i associated with `read_TS(X)` and `write_TS(X)`. Whenever a violation in the timestamp order occurs, the system rolls back the transaction T_i and restarts it with a new timestamp. Under such a situation, a transaction T_j, which may have used a value updated by T_i must also be rolled back. Similarly, any other transaction T_k, which may have used a value updated by T_j must also be rolled back, and so on. This situation is called *cascading of roll back*. This is one of the major problems of timestamp ordering.

Detailed steps of the basic timestamp ordering are as follows:

- Transaction T_i requests a read operation on X:
  - If TS(T_i) < `write_TS(X)`, the read operation is rejected and T_i is rolled back. This is because another transaction with higher timestamp (started later) has already written a new value for X. The transaction T_i is too late in performing the read operation, any other values it has accessed are expected to be inconsistent with the new value of X. Hence, it is suggested to rollback T_i, and to restart it with a new timestamp value.
  - If TS(T_i) ≥ `write_TS(X)`, the read operation is executed and `read_TS(X)` is set to the maximum of `read_TS(X)` and TS(T_i). This is because T_i follows (have a higher timestamp value) the transaction that has updated the value of X. If TS(T_i) is greater than the current value of `read_TS(X)`, the value of `TS(X)` is set to the new value of `read_TS(X)`.

- Transaction T_i requests a write operation on X:
  - — If `TS(`T_i`)` < `read_TS(X)`, the write operation is rejected and T_i is rolled back. This is because, another transaction having a higher timestamp value has already read the value of X. So, writing a new value of X by T_i would violate the timestamp ordering. Hence, it is suggested to rollback T_i, and to restart it with a new timestamp value.
  - — If `TS(`T_i`)` < `write_TS(X)`, the write operation is rejected and T_i is rolled back. This is because, another transaction having a higher timestamp value has already written the value of X. So, the value T_i is trying to write is obsolete. Hence, it is suggested to rollback T_i, and to restart it with a new timestamp value.
  - — If `TS(`T_i`)` ≥ `read_TS(X)` and `TS(`T_i`)` ≥ `write_TS(X)`, the write operation is executed and the value of `TS(`T_i`)` becomes the new value for `write_TS(X)`. This is because T_i is younger than both the transactions that have last written the value for X, and read the value of X.

Strict timestamp ordering

This is a variation of the basic timestamp ordering. One extra constraint applies here to ensure a strict schedule, and also to ensure recoverability. This constraint states that: whenever a transaction T_i requests a read or write operation for X, then if `TS(`T_i`)` > `write_TS(X)`, until the other transaction T_j, that wrote a value for X is committed or aborted.

Thus in strict timestamp ordering, the item X is locked by transaction T_j and maintains the lock until it is committed or aborted. Therefore, the strict timestamp ordering is free from deadlocks, because T_i waits for T_j only if `TS(`T_i`)` > `TS(`T_j`)`.

Thomas' write rule

This is yet another modification of the basic timestamp ordering rule. This rule is described below with reference to a transaction T_j requesting a write operation for item X.

- If `TS(`T_i`)` < `read_TS(X)`, the write operation is rejected and T_i is rolled back. This is because another transaction with higher timestamp has already read the value of X. So, the value of X generated by T_i is now obsolete.
- `TS(`T_i`)` < `write_TS(X)`, the write operation can be ignored. This is because another transaction with higher timestamp has immediately overwritten the value of X. So, none of the transactions can read the value written by T_i, as this value is now obsolete.
- If both the Conditions 1 and 2 above are false, the write operation of T_i is executed and value of `write_TS(X)` is set to that of `TS(`T_i`)`.

The difference between Thomas' rule and the basic time stamping lies in the 2nd rule. This rule says that, if T_i requests a wrire operation on X and `TS(`T_i`)` < `write_TS(X)`, the write operation can be ignored. While, the basic rule says that, if T_i requests a wrire operation on X and `TS(`T_i`)` < `write_TS(X)`, T_i is rolled back.

Exercises

10.1 Define a transaction. What are ACID properties of transaction? Explain.

10.2 Draw the state diagram of a transaction and explain different states. When may a transaction be called completed or failed? Explain with suitable examples.

10.3 Why is concurrent execution of transactions necessary? Explain with a real-life example.

10.4 What anomalies may arise in the database due to uncontrolled concurrent execution of transactions?

10.5 Define the following and cite suitable examples for each case.

(i) Transaction schedule (ii) Serial schedule
(iii) Non-serial schedule (iv) Serializable schedule

10.6 In concurrent schedules, when do two instructions conflict? Explain with an example.

10.7 What is a precedence graph? Analyze its capacity to detect serializability of a transaction.

10.8 Consider a set of three transactions T_1, T_2, and T_3. If schedules S_1 and S_2 are executed for these three transactions concurrently, will the database remain consistent?

T_1: r_1(P); r_1(R); w_1(P);
T_2: r_2(R); r_2(Q); w_2(R); w_2(Q);
T_3: r_3(P); r_3(Q); w_3(Q);
S_1: r_1(P); r_2(R); r_1(R); r_3(P), r_3(Q); w_1(P); w_3(Q); r_2(Q); w_2(R); w_2(Q);
S_2: r_1(P); r_2(R); r_1(R); r_3(P), r_1(R); r_2(Q); r_3(Q); w_1(P); w_2(R); w_3(Q); w_2(Q);

10.9 What is a timestamp? How timestamp values can be generated? How are these values used in scheduling transactions?

10.10 What is timestamp ordering? Discuss the advantages and disadvantages of two-phase locking and timestamp ordering schemes of serializability.

10.11 How is strict timestamp ordering is different from basic timestamp ordering?

10.12 What is a deadlock? Explain how can you detect and prevent deadlocks with an example.

10.13 How can deadlocks be detected using wait-for-graph? What are the measures to recover from a deadlock?

10.14 Under what condition deadlock prevention may be considered better that deadlock detection are recovery?

10.15 Why deadlock cannot occur in a timestamp based protocol?

10.16 Consider the following transaction schedule (Table 10.15). Is it serializable?

Table 10.15 Transaction Table

Time	Transaction: T_1	Transaction: T_2
1	Read (A, *a*)	–
2	*a* = *a* – 10	–
3	Write (A, *a*)	–
4	–	Read (B, *b*)
5	–	Read (A, *a*)
6	Read (B, *b*)	–
7	*b* = *b* + 50	–
8	–	*c* = *a* + *b*
	–	Write (A, *c*)
	Write (B, *b*)	–

CHAPTER 11

Database Recovery

Various types of errors may occur in a database system which results in inconsistent data values in the database. Some important types of such errors are:

- **Logical error:** The program can no longer continue with its normal execution due to internal conditions, such as a bad input, data not found, overflow or resource limit exceeded etc.
- **System error:** The system has entered in an undesirable state (deadlock) as a result of some conflicting data request and the program cannot continue normally.
- **System crash:** The system may face hardware malfunctions, causing loss of content of volatile storage (main memory).
- **Disk failure:** A disk block loses its content as a result of either head crash or failure during a data transfer operation.

Since any of the above mentioned errors is a possible situation during a database operation, to keep the database unaffected, we need to maintain some automatic recovery strategy. A recovery scheme is one which brings the database to a consistent state when any of the failure causing events occurs.

The operations we perform over a database during running an application are called transactions. These transactions are program units whose execution preserves the consistency of the database. By definition, a transaction is atomic in nature, i.e. either a transaction will be executed completely or nothing will be executed. Whenever a transaction fails to be successfully completed it is termed *aborted*, and a transaction which successfully completes its execution is termed *committed.*

11.1 Transaction State Diagram

From the above description, we can draw a state diagram for a transaction using states in any of which a transaction may be in at an instance. There may be five states which are described here briefly and shown in Figure 11.1.

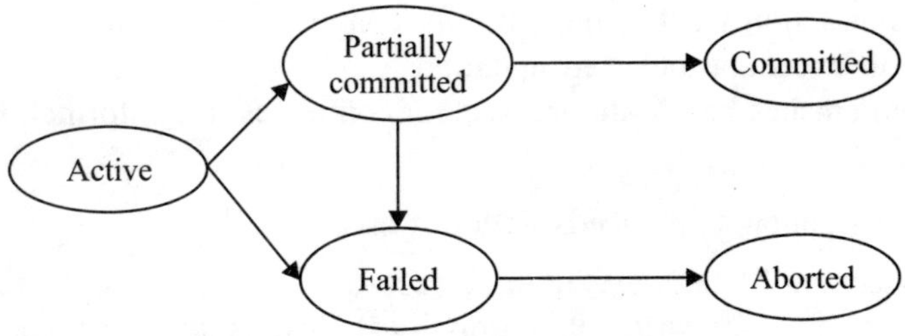

Figure 11.1 Transaction state diagram.

- **Active:** Initial state of a transaction.
- **Partially committed:** A transaction is about to complete its task. This state is arrived at only after the last executive statement in the program has been reached.
- **Failed:** After discovering that normal execution can no longer proceed.
- **Aborted:** After a transaction has been rolled back and the database is restored to a prior consistent state.
- **Committed:** After successful completion of a transaction.

From this diagram (Figure 11.1), it is seen that a transaction can enter the fail state from either active or partially committed states, i.e. at any instance during the running time of its execution. We shall now describe some strategies that may be considered as safeguards for maintaining system consistency even after any such unfortunate event.

11.2 Recovery Strategies

If a database is in an inconsistent state, it is necessary to restore it to an earlier consistent state. Such recovery of databases may be achieved either using log files or backup of the databases.

11.2.1 Write-Ahead-Logging

Write-Ahead-Logging (WAL) is a technique that may be used for database recovery. Here, a log file is maintained by the system that keeps records of all updations made by the transactions along with other necessary information. During the execution of a transaction, all the updations are written to the log file before actually writing them in the physical database. The physical database is updated only after successful completion of the transaction(s). The following subsections discuss commonly used log based recovery strategies.

Incremental log with deferred updation

During execution of a transaction T_i, all the write operations are deferred until the transaction partially commits. In other words, the effects of the transaction and associated information changes are not written in the physical database before the transaction reaches the partially committed state. The procedure can be described as the following sequence of steps.

- All updates are recorded in a system maintained log file.

- When the transaction reaches the partially committed state, the information on the log file is used in executing deferred updation.
- If the system crashes before the transaction completes, the information in the log file is simply ignored.

Execution of transaction T_i proceeds as follows:

- Before transaction T_i starts execution, a record $< T_i$, start $>$ is written in the log.
- During execution, any write operation by T_i results in writing a new record (like $< T_i, X, x_j >$) in the log. Each such record contains three necessary fields which are
  - Transaction name (here, T_i)
  - Data item name (here, X)
  - New value of the data item (here, x_j)
- Finally, when T_i partially commits, a record $< T_i$, commit $>$ is written in the log.

Using the log file, the system can handle any failure causing event which does any loss of information in non-volatile storage. The recovery proceeds as follows:

- After a failure has occurred, the recovery subsystem automatically consults the log file to determine whether the transaction is to be redone.
- A transaction T_i needs to be redone only if its log contains both the records
  - $< T_i$, start $>$
  - $< T_i$, commit $>$
- *Redo* (T_i): This sets values of all data items updated by transaction T_i to new values using the log file.

The *redo* operation involves redoing all the operations performed by a committed transaction, before system crash occurs, in the same order as they appear in the log. This operation must be idempotent in order to guarantee the correct behaviour even if a failure occurs during the recovery process itself.

Let us consider a banking system with three accounts A, B and C. The initial amounts in the three accounts are ₹ 1000, ₹ 2000 and ₹ 700 respectively. Let two transactions T_1 and T_2 are executed on the banking database serially in the same order. Transaction T_1 and T_2 are specified as given in Table 11.1.

Table 11.1 Specified Transaction

Time	Transaction: T_1	Transaction: T_2
1	Read (A, *a*);	
2	$a \leftarrow a - 50$;	
3	Write (A, *a*);	
4	Read (B, *b*);	
5	$b \leftarrow b + 50$;	
6	Write (B, *b*);	
7		Read (C, *c*);
8		$c \leftarrow c - 100$;
9		Write (C, *c*);

If both the transactions are successfully completed then the log file should contain the following as given in Table 11.2.

Table 11.2 Log File

T_1	Start	–
T_1	A	950
T_1	B	2050
T_1	Commit	–
T_2	Start	–
T_2	C	600
T_2	Commit	–

Now, let us suppose that the system crashes before completion of the transactions. Depending on the time of crash, three different situations are possible.

System crash before completion of the first transaction

- Let the crash occurs just after the log record for the step "write (B, *b*)" of transaction T_1 has been written to permanent storage. The log file at this time should look like as given in Table 11.3.

Table 11.3 Log File of Transaction T_1

T_1	Start	–
T_1	A	950
T_1	B	2050

- When the system comes back again, no recovery action needs to be taken since there is no commit record for transaction T_1 in the log. Values in accounts A and B will remain fixed at ₹ 1000 and ₹ 2000 respectively.

System crash before completion of the second transaction

- Let the crash occurs just after the log records for the step "write (C, *c*)" of transaction T_1 has been written to permanent storage. The log file at this time should look like as given in Table 11.4.

Table 11.4 Log File

T_1	Start	–
T_1	A	950
T_1	B	2050
T_1	Commit	–
T_2	Start	–
T_2	C	600

- When the system comes back, transaction T_1 is redone, i.e. the recovery subsystem performs *redo* (T_1) as the record $< T_1$, commit $>$ is present in the log. But no action is taken regarding transaction T_2. The values of accounts A, B and C will be ₹ 950, ₹ 2050 and ₹ 700 respectively.

System crash just after writing < T_2, commit > in the log

If the crash occurs just after the log record < T_2, commit > is written to the log in stable storage, then when the system comes back, we must perform both *redo* (T_1) and *redo* (T_2) as both < T_1, commit > and < T_2, commit > are now present in the log (Figure 11.2).

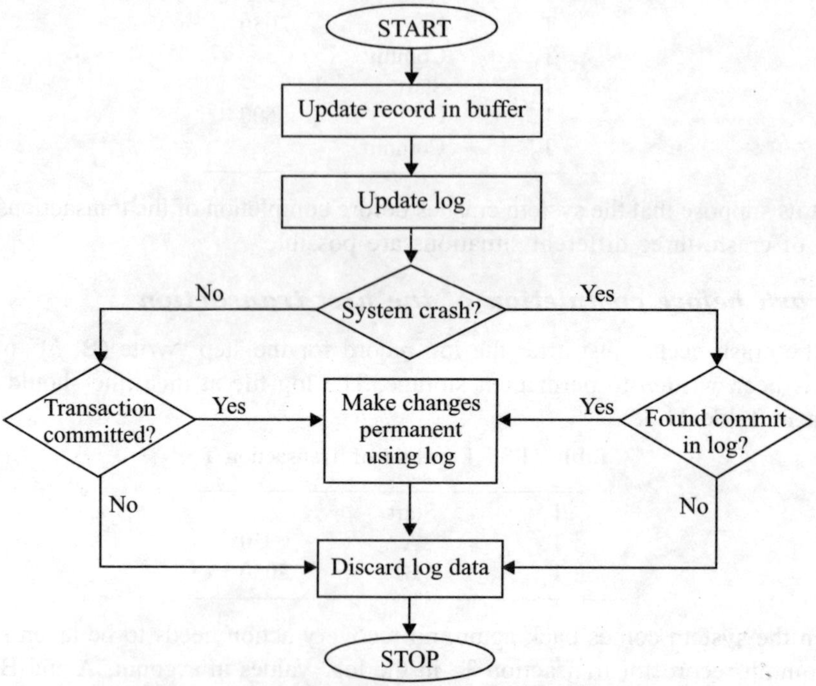

Figure 11.2 Incremental log with deferred updation.

Incremental log with immediate updation

Here all the updation operations are directly applied to the database immediately and the incremental log reflects the changes in the system states. If a crash occurs, the information in the log file is used in restoring the state of the system to a previous consistent state. Execution of a transaction, in this scheme, proceeds as follows.

- Before a transaction T_i starts its execution, a record < T_i, start > is written on the log file. During execution of T_i, any "write(X, x_i)" operation by T_i, is preceded by writing a new record to the log. Each such record has four fields:

  - Transaction name (here, T_i)
  - Data item name (here, X)
  - Old value of the data item (here, $x_{i\text{–old}}$)
  - New value of the data item (here, $x_{i\text{–new}}$)

- When T_i partially commits, a record < T_i, commit > is written to the log.

Using the log file the system can handle any failure causing event which does any loss of information in non-volatile storage. The recovery scheme utilizes two recovery procedures *undo* and *redo*.

- *Undo* (T_i): This restores the values of all data items updated by transaction T_i to their old values.
- *Redo* (T_i): This sets the values of all data items updated by the transaction T_i to new values using the log file.
- After a failure has occurred, the recovery subsystem consults the log to determine which of the transactions need to be redone and which to be undone.
- The transaction T_i for which both the log records < T_0, commit > and < T_1, commit > are present need to be redone and the remaining transactions to be undone.

The *undo* and *redo* operations must be idempotent in order to guarantee the correct behaviour even if a failure occurs during the recovery process itself.

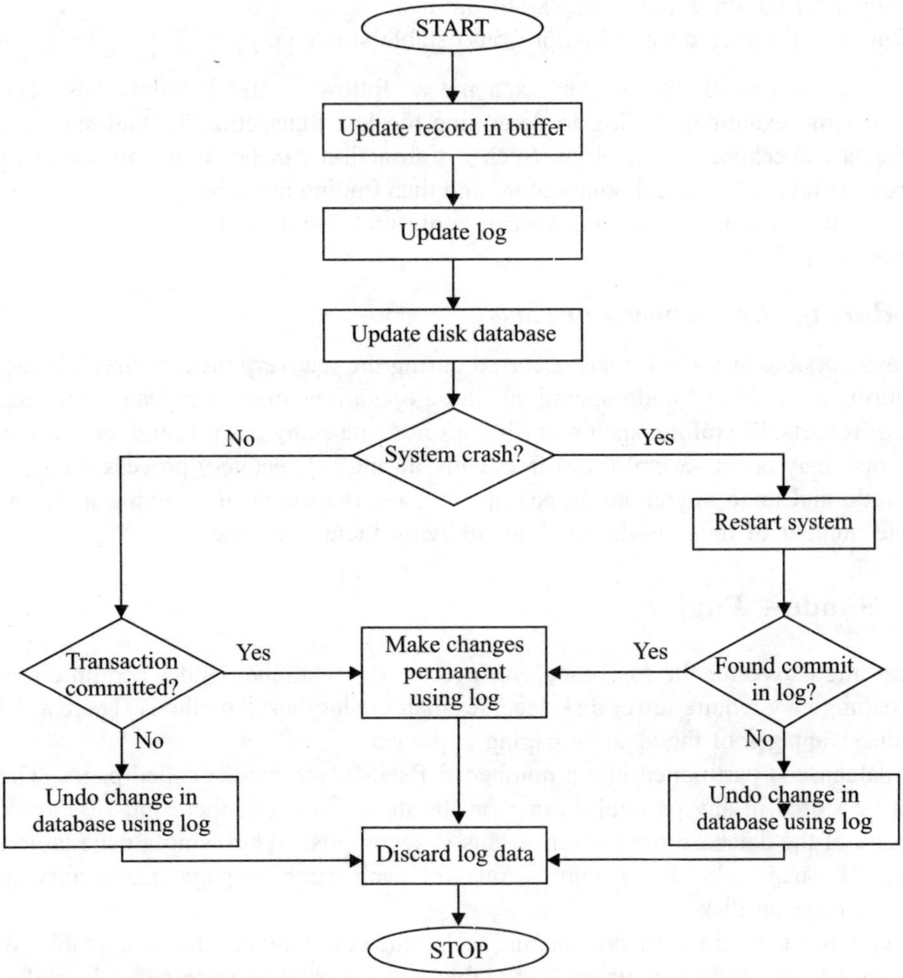

Figure 11.3 Incremental log with immediate updation.

Incremental log with checkpoints

When a system failure occurs, it is necessary to consult the log in order to determine which of the transactions need to be redone and which to be undone. That is the entire log file needs to be searched. Two major difficulties in this approach are:

- The search process is time consuming.
- Most of the transactions that need to be redone have already actually written their updates in the database, and do not actually need to be redone. Redoing will cause no harm, but will take longer time for recovery process to complete.

This overhead time can be reduced by the use of checkpoints. During execution, the system maintains the log, and in addition, the system periodically performs checkpointing which requires the following sequence of actions to take place.

- Output all the log records currently residing in the main memory onto stable storage.
- Output all modified buffer blocks to the disk.
- Output a log record <checkpoint> onto stable storage.

Now, we can modify the recovery scheme as follows. After a failure has occurred, the recovery scheme examines the log to determine the last transaction T_i, that started executing before the last checkpoint took place. Such a transaction can be found by searching the log backwards to find the first checkpoint record and then finding the subsequent $< T_i$, start $>$ record. Once such a transaction T_i is found, we can apply undo on T_i and all subsequent transactions that started after T_i.

Crash during the recovery process

It is always possible that a crash has occurred during the recovery process itself. If such a crash occurs during the redo and undo operations, these operations may be repeated once again when the system restarts. Therefore, such a crash does not cause any harm to the recovery processes. System crash may occur several times frequently during the recovery process. Thus, it requires that the redo and undo operations be idempotent, i.e. the effect of applying undo or redo for a multiple number of times is the same as applying them only once.

11.2.2 Shadow Paging

This is an alternative for the log based crash recovery technique. Under certain circumstances shadow paging may require fewer disk accesses than the log-based methods. There are, however, several disadvantages of the shadow paging approach.

The database is partitioned into a number of fixed length blocks called pages. These pages need not be stored in any particular order on the disk. However, there must be a way to find the *i*th page of the database for a given *i*. This is accomplished by using a page table as shown in Figure. The page table has *n* entries, one for each database page. Each entry contains a pointer to a page on disk.

The key idea behind the shadow paging technique is to maintain two page tables during the life time of a transaction, the current page table and the shadow page table. Initially, both the tables are identical. The shadow page table never changes during the execution of a transaction. The current page table may be changed when a transaction performs a write operation. All input or output operations use the current page table to locate the database pages on the disk.

Let the transaction performs a "write(X, x_j)" operation and that X resides on the *i*th page. The write operation is executed as follows:

- If the *i*th page is not already in main memory, then issue "input(X)".
- If this is the first time that the write operation is performed on the *i*th page by the transaction, then modify the current page table as:
  - Find an unused page on disk.
  - Delete the page found in the earlier step from the list of free page frames.
  - Modify the current page table so that the *i*th entry point to the page found in the first step.
- Assign the value of x_j to X in the buffer page.

Successful recovery requires that we find the shadow page table on disk after a crash. A simple way of this is to store the disk address of the shadow page table at a fixed location in the disk.

Now, if a crash occurs during execution of a transaction, we can get back to the state of the database prior to execution of the transaction, since the shadow page table is unaltered.

In order to commit a transaction, we must do the following:

- Ensure that all buffers in main memory that have been changed by the transaction are output to disk.
- Output the current page table to the disk (the shadow page table must not be overwritten).
- Output the disk address of the current page table to the fixed location in disk where the address of the shadow page table resides. So, current page table has become the shadow page table and the transaction is committed.

If a crash occurs prior to the completion of the final step in the above procedure, we can revert to the state prior to execution of the transaction. If the crash occurs after completion of the final step, the effects of the transaction will be preserved.

Advantages: Shadow paging offers several advantages over log-based techniques.

- The overhead of log-record output is eliminated.
- Recovery form crashes are significantly faster.

Disadvantages: There are some disadvantages also.

- Data fragmentation occurs.
- Garbage collection needed.
- Implementation is more difficult compared to log-based techniques, when several transactions run concurrently.

11.3 Recovery of Non-volatile Storage

The basic idea is to dump the entire content of the database to stable storage periodically. No transaction may be active during the dumping process. The disadvantages of this approach are:

- Interruption of database availability
- Degradation of update efficiency
- Storage of redundant data

In spite of these drawbacks, maintaining of periodical backup of all data is considered a safest approach toward security of a database.

11.4 Residual Dump Backup Strategy

Instead of dumping all the records periodically, only those records that have been changed may be dumped periodically.

Recovery process: The particular record that is changed is kept in duplication, and one can identify the last change by record identifier and the time factor attached to the record. Since the logging operation of a residual dump is spread out some book keeping is required so that the recovery process knows how far to go back to obtain a complete copy of the database.

The log file maintains a log record "<dump>" as well as before and after images of records logged as a result of update operations. The log records are stored first with the primary key as the unique record identifier, and the secondary sort key as the time the record was logged.

11.5 Other Backup Strategies

Besides the residual dump operation, four other dumping strategies are commonly used. These are:

- Dual recording
- Periodic dumping
- Logging input transactions
- Logging changes to the data

However, the residual dumping strategy yields some advantages compared to these other strategies. These are:

- Dumping can be done only when the machine is free without affecting updation operations.
- Dumping is faster than logging.
- In dumping, there is no performance degradation.

Actually, in the case of logging, we need to write only those records, in the log file, which are updated by the concerned transactions. And in the case of dumping, we have to write all the records in the database to a secondary copy. Residual dumping also keeps only those records which underwent modifications. However, the recovery time is relatively independent of the number of records in the database. Therefore, for large databases logging is a suitable recovery strategy.

Exercises

11.1 What is meant by system recovery? Why is it needed?

11.2 What is a system log? Write down the purpose of using a system log for system recovery.

11.3 Differentiate between a system crash and a disk crash.

11.4 Discuss various types of failures that may occur during running time of a system.

11.5 Write down the similarities and dissimilarities between immediate and deferred updation techniques using log files.

11.6 Why checkpointing is used in database recovery? What is effect on system performance?

11.7 How does the system handle occurrences of multiple system failures during log based recovery processes?

11.8 Write down the utility of checkpoint mechanism in log-based recovery.

11.9 Discuss shadow paging. How is it different from log based recovery schemes?

11.10 How databases can be recovered from disk failures and other fatal system errors?

11.11 What is the most significant difference between shadow paging and immediate update recovery schemes? Explain the issue.

CHAPTER 12

File Organization, Indexing and Hashing

Database is physically maintained as a number of files of records, stored in auxiliary storage devices like magnetic or optical disks. Files can be organized in a number of different ways, and their access methodologies are also different. Records may be maintained as sequences of unordered, ordered and hashed file structures. We shall briefly discuss these storage techniques and access methodologies for data in a database, in this chapter.

12.1 Storage Devices

Database files (or records) are stored in computer storage devices more or less permanently. They are organized in such a way so that the DBMS software can store and retrieve data from database very efficiently. For real-time applications access of data must also be performed in real-time. If all data could be maintained in the primary memory of the client computer during processing, then there would not be any problem in this regard. However, since data in a database is large in size, and security restrictions must always be applied over the database during parallel access of data by a number of concurrent applications, it is not possible. So, data can be accessed from a central repository only on demand basis. Generally, the server machine of the database system stores all data in its permanent storage, and supplies data to applications as per their requirements.

12.1.1 Storage of Database

Databases store large or huge amount of data that must persist over a long period of time. Hence data are maintained in permanent storage devices like magnetic disks (also called hard disks). During running time of an application, a part of the data may be retrieved and stored back repeatedly and frequently. Since magnetic storage devices can provide a low cost and relatively high speed technology, they are the most suitable for storing data records in a database.

Generally, database applications need a very small part of the database for processing at a time, they can be accessed and copied in the main memory during running time of the application, and then after the task is over, updated data are written back in the disk storage again. All data are stored as files of records. The organization of different files, however, may be different depending on the nature of their usage. There are several primary file organizations mentioned below.

- **Heap file:** Unordered file organization that places records on the disk storage without regard to any ordering among them. New records are simply appended at their trail (at the end of the existing file).
- **Sorted file:** Here all records are sorted according to some particular attribute values of records to be stored in the file. This particular attribute is called the ordering attribute or sort key.
- **Hashed file:** A hash function is applied over an attribute to generate a memory location within the file and the concerned record is stored there. Conflict with multiple records is resolved tactfully.
- **B-tree file:** This file structure is very commonly used for their efficient access capabilities. Here, a tree structure is maintained whose leaf nodes store physical data records, and the internal nodes help in the search processes.

12.1.2 Storage of Records

A record contains several fields or attributes. While creating a database table, we generally specify type and size of each attribute and thereby fix the total length of a record. For common and standard data items, data types may be Boolean, numeric, character etc. However, database records may have variable length strings as their data items. Also, in some cases, data may be very large unstructured objects like images, videos, audios, plain and hyper texts etc. These objects are commonly referred to as BLOBs (Binary Large Objects). Typically, BLOB data items are stored separately from the records, by maintaining a pointer in the record field only. Records may, therefore, be of two types: fixed length and variable length records. For fixed length records, all records are fixed in size (length), which is not the case for variable length records.

12.2 Heap File Structure

It is the simplest file structure. Here, records are stored in the file in the same order in which they are inserted in the file. Such an organization is called a heap or a pile. It is generally treated as a data collection and storage method where gathered data are stored for future use.

Here, records are arranged in disk blocks. Disk blocks are the units of storage that is read by a single access into the main memory. A block may contain several records. The total size of records in a block may be something lesser than or equal to the block size. The block may have some wasted space due to fragmentation effect (Fragmentation means wastage of space due to non-availability of sufficient space to store a single record).

Insertion of data records is very efficient in this structure and just append the new record at the end of the existing file within the final block. If the space remaining in the final block is smaller enough to keep the new record, the next block is used. Generally, a single record is seldom written in a block. During running time of some application, before insertion of records, they are gathered in a buffer whose size is equal to that of the block. When the buffer in the main memory becomes full, it is written completely in a block.

Searching is a little costly process here. Records are searched for in a block after block manner. If only a single record satisfies the search condition, then, on the average, an application program will search for and read into main memory about half of the file blocks before it finds the record. For file having b blocks, this process requires searching (b/2) blocks, on the average. In case of failure, search complexity equals to b, the maximum possible value.

To delete a record, we need to find the block at first, then to copy the block into a buffer, and then delete the record from the buffer. The block is finally rewritten into the concerned block in storage. This process causes wastage of memory (because of the gap created due to the deleted record). This wastage can be avoided by using a deletion marker along with each record. In this case, a record is deleted only by changing the marker value (generally binary). However, here we need a periodic reorganization of the heap to accumulate the deleted records and to free storage space. But the above process is a good idea for variable length records.

To read all records in a sorted fashion, we need to create a sorted version or copy of the original copy. If the file size is high, it becomes a very time costly process. Hence an external sorting method is applied for such reasons. For fixed length records, it is easier to access any record by using its starting location in the file. If the records are numbered 0, 1, 2, 3, . . . , r-1, and the records in each block are numbered 0, 1, 2, . . ., *bfr*1, where *bfr* is the blocking factor, then ith record of the file is found in block (i/*bfr*), and the record is (i mod *bfr*)th record in that block. Such files are called relative or direct files because records can be easily located and accessed by their relative positions.

12.3 Sorted File Structure

This type of files contains records which are sorted according ascending or descending order of some of the attribute values called ordering or sorting (key) attribute. This structure is also called an ordered sequential file.

Such ordered file structures have some access advantages. We can read records in an ordered fashion very easily. Searching any arbitrary record with a certain key value is very easy, because we can apply binary searching to locate the desired record. However, binary search is not generally applicable for disk storage. Hence, this search is applied over block numbers, and once the correct block is found, it is then searched sequentially for the desired record.

Let the blocks be numbered as 1, 2, . . ., b; and the records are ordered according to their ascending order of key values. We want to search for a record whose key field contains a value of v (say). Assuming that the disk addresses are available in the file header, the binary search method needs to access only ($\log_2 b$) blocks for the search, irrespective of whether it leads to a success or a failure. This is very small compared to the value (b/2) for a linear search. The binary search algorithm is given below.

Algorithm: Binary search for key-ordered disk files

```
begin
        l = 1; u = b;
        while (u < l) do
        begin
           i = (l + u) div 2;
           read block i from file into buffer;
           if (v > ordering key field value of the first record in block i)
           then u = u - 1;
           else if (v < ordering key field value of the first record in block i)
                then l = l + 1;
         else if the record with ordering key value = v is in the buffer
                then output success;
                else output failure;
        end;
end;
```

12.4 Indexed Files

The sorting of a large database file is a very time consuming operation. Also, since record searching is done in main memory, all the records, in the case of a sequential search, must be read in the main memory one by one. This process incurs huge I/O time. In general, data in a base file are ordered according to an ordering attribute. A file can have only one ordering attribute which is the primary key of the concerned table. But an application programmer may wish to sort the records according to any of the available attributes. In order to avoid huge sorting and searching times, *indexed sequential access method* (ISAM) has been developed. For indexed sequential search, an auxiliary file called an *index* file is created beforehand. A *file index* is a data structure that is used for speeding up the processes of record search and retrieval in a database. An index is generally created on a key attribute of a database file (index on other attributes are also possible).

In the simplest case, an index file contains only one field containing the set of values of the key attribute. During a record search operation, the index file is read in main memory and the search process is applied over it (for the required key value). Once the desired key value is found, the serial number of the record in physical database can be determined from the index location, and the desired record is read directly.

Index file structure and access mechanism can be of different types. In the simplest situation, as discussed above, an index file comes with a overflow area in order to provide the facility for insertion of new records. When an index entry is maintained for each record of complete base file, it is called *full indexing*. Sometimes, actual base records are divided logically into smaller groups (blocks), and the index file contains only one entry for each group, instead of an entry for each record separately. Here search is done for blocks of records only. Since disk I/O is generally performed on a block basis (i.e. one block of records are read in one access), if a block holds one group of records, both the searching effort and number of disk accesses will be reduced. However, in this case, after a disk access, the read block of records needs to be searched sequentially in the main memory. This method is called *partial indexing*.

An index can be primary or secondary. A *primary index* is automatically created by the system over the primary key of the base records. When the indexed attribute does not have unique values for all records then indexing may identify a group of records with the same value of the attribute. This type of index is called a *clustering index*. A secondary index, over a non-key attribute, may be created explicitly by the user.

12.4.1 Primary Index

A primary index over a base table is defined on an ordering key attribute. The primary index forms an ordered file with fixed length records having two fields. The first field contains the primary key attribute values of the base table, and the second field maintains a pointer to a disk block. A disk block may be considered to be a single record, or a group of records, in general. If we consider that there is one entry in the index for each record of the base table, then index size will be the same as that of the base table, in terms of number of records. If only blocks of records are identified by an index, this size is much smaller. This second strategy is generally accepted as a standard. If the base records are sorted in ascending (or descending) order of values of their key attribute, then each index entry contains the lowest (or highest) key value of the concerned disk block.

Let us consider an example of the STUDENTS table. Let records are sorted in ascending order of key attribute (registration number) values. Let, registration numbers are within the range of 0901002001 to 0901002100, and each block contains 10 records only. In such a situation, Tables 12.1 and 12.2 depict possible configurations of the index file, when tables are ordered according to the index key value in ascending and descending orders respectively.

Table 12.1 Index Entry with the Smallest Key Value in a Block

Index entry	Block number (pointer)
0901002001	Pointer to block 1
0901002011	Pointer to block 2
0901002021	Pointer to block 3
0901002031	Pointer to block 4
0901002041	Pointer to block 5
0901002051	Pointer to block 6
0901002061	Pointer to block 7
0901002071	Pointer to block 8
0901002081	Pointer to block 9
0901002091	Pointer to block 10

Table 12.2 Index Entry with the Highest Key Value in a Block

Index entry	Block number (pointer)
0901002100	Pointer to block 1
0901002090	Pointer to block 2
0901002080	Pointer to block 3
0901002070	Pointer to block 4
0901002060	Pointer to block 5
0901002050	Pointer to block 6
0901002040	Pointer to block 7
0901002030	Pointer to block 8
0901002020	Pointer to block 9
0901002010	Pointer to block 10

When we have one index entry for each record in the base table, it is called a *dense index*. If the block size is greater than one we have a *sparse* (*non-dense*) *index*. The record in a block which makes an index entry is called an *anchor record* or the *block anchor*.

The index file consumes significantly smaller storage area because of two reasons: it contains fewer number of records compared to the base file, and each index record is much smaller (only two fields) than a base record. Hence, it can be easily read into the main memory and search operations can be applied over it. In Figure 12.1, an example index file and the corresponding

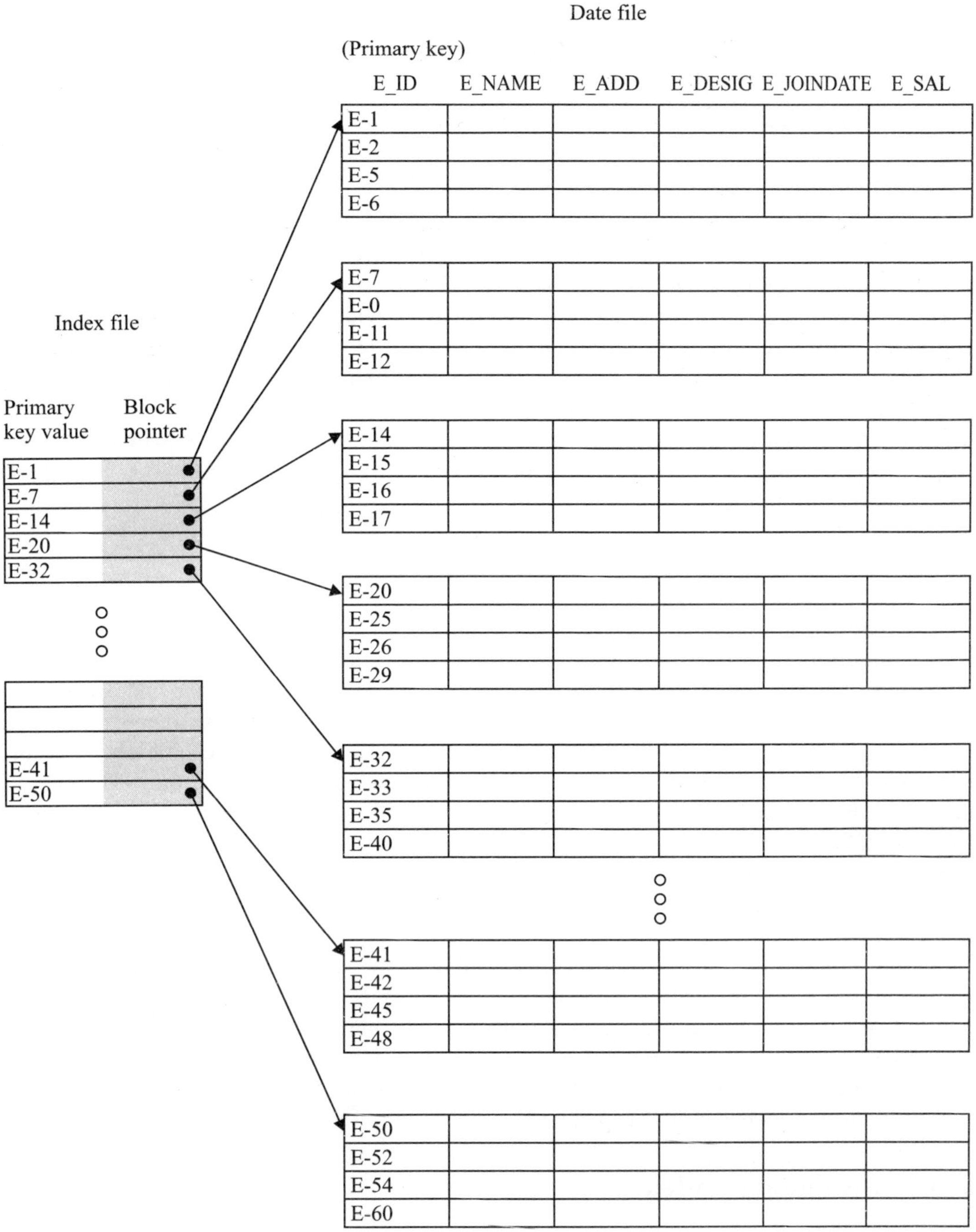

Figure 12.1 Primary indexing.

base file are shown. Here, the index is created over the primary key attribute E-Id (employee identification number) of the base table. Each block of the base file, arranged in ascending order of the key values, contains four records.

ILLUSTRATION 12.1 Let us consider a base file with r = 50,000 records having record length R = 100 bytes each, and let the block size is B = 1024 bytes. Compare the number of block accesses, using and without using indexing, to find a base record.

Solution The blocking factor will be bfr = floor$\lfloor B/R \rfloor$ = 10 records per block. Total number of blocks needed to store all records is b = ceiling $\lceil r/bfr \rceil$ = 5000. A binary search over the base file requires ceiling $\lceil \log_2 b \rceil$ = 12 block accesses.

Now, if we consider that the key field is 10 bytes wide and a pointer requires 6 bytes, each index entry size will be R_i = 10 + 6 = 16 bytes. The number of blocks needed to store the index file is bfr_i = floor $\lfloor B/R_i \rfloor$ = 64. Total number of index entries in the index file is r_i = 5000. Total number of index blocks required is thus b_i = ceiling $\lceil r_i/bfr_i \rceil$ = 79. A binary search over this index file requires ceiling $\lceil \log_2 b_i \rceil$ = 7 block accesses. To search the record using the index value, we need one additional block access of the base file, i.e. a total of 8 block accesses are needed.

12.4.2 Clustering Index

When records of a file are physically ordered on a non-key attribute which does not have a unique value for each record, the ordering attribute is called a clustering attribute. If values of indexing attribute for all records are not unique but ordered, a clustering index is used to facilitate the search operation. In this case, in a block, there may be multiple records having the same index entry. One entry in the clustering index contains a pointer to each block of records in the base file, and each block contains records with a distinct index value only. Therefore, in this case, variable number of records may be found in blocks. If the number of records with the same index value be large, they may be stored in two or more blocks. Insertion, deletion operations will be little complicated in this case. Therefore, this type of indexing is useful for searching and modification only. In Figure 12.2, a clustering index is shown over the attribute (E_DEPT) department of an employee.

In this figure, it is observed that records relating to the same department may spread over more than one block of records, and the same block may contain records relating to more than one department. We may, however, specify separate blocks for separate departments. One such situation is shown in Figure 12.3. Here, blocks of records are arranged in linked list fashion. More than one block may be assigned for a single department. The final block for each department contains a NULL pointer.

12.4.3 Secondary Index

In some cases, to assist the primary key index, a secondary index is created to improve search performance. This secondary index is generally on a non-key attribute and may have duplicate values. Since the secondary index may not have unique values, it requires one entry for each record, and hence it may be very large. Generally, a base table is associated with one primary index and several secondary indexes.

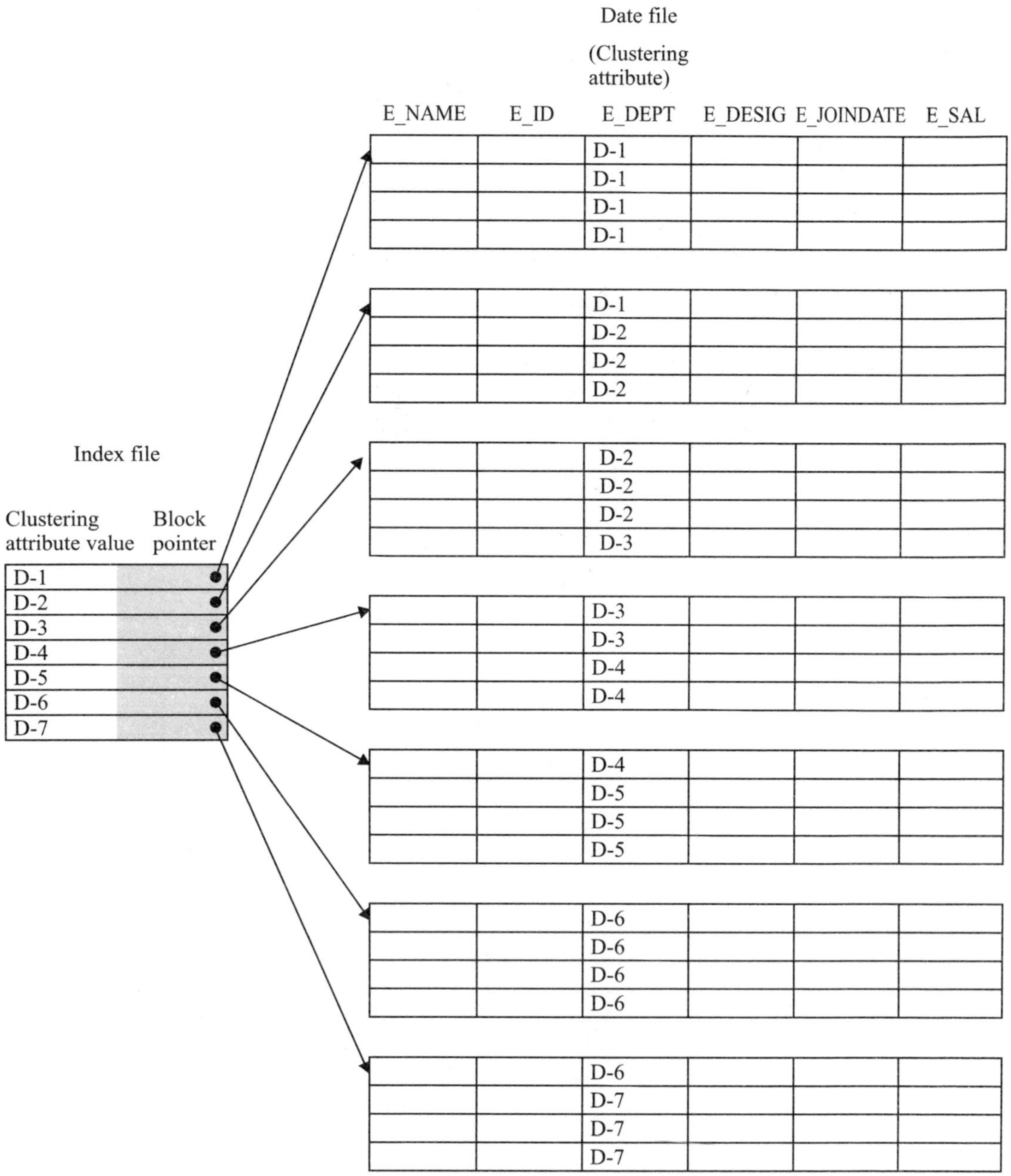

Figure 12.2 Clustering index.

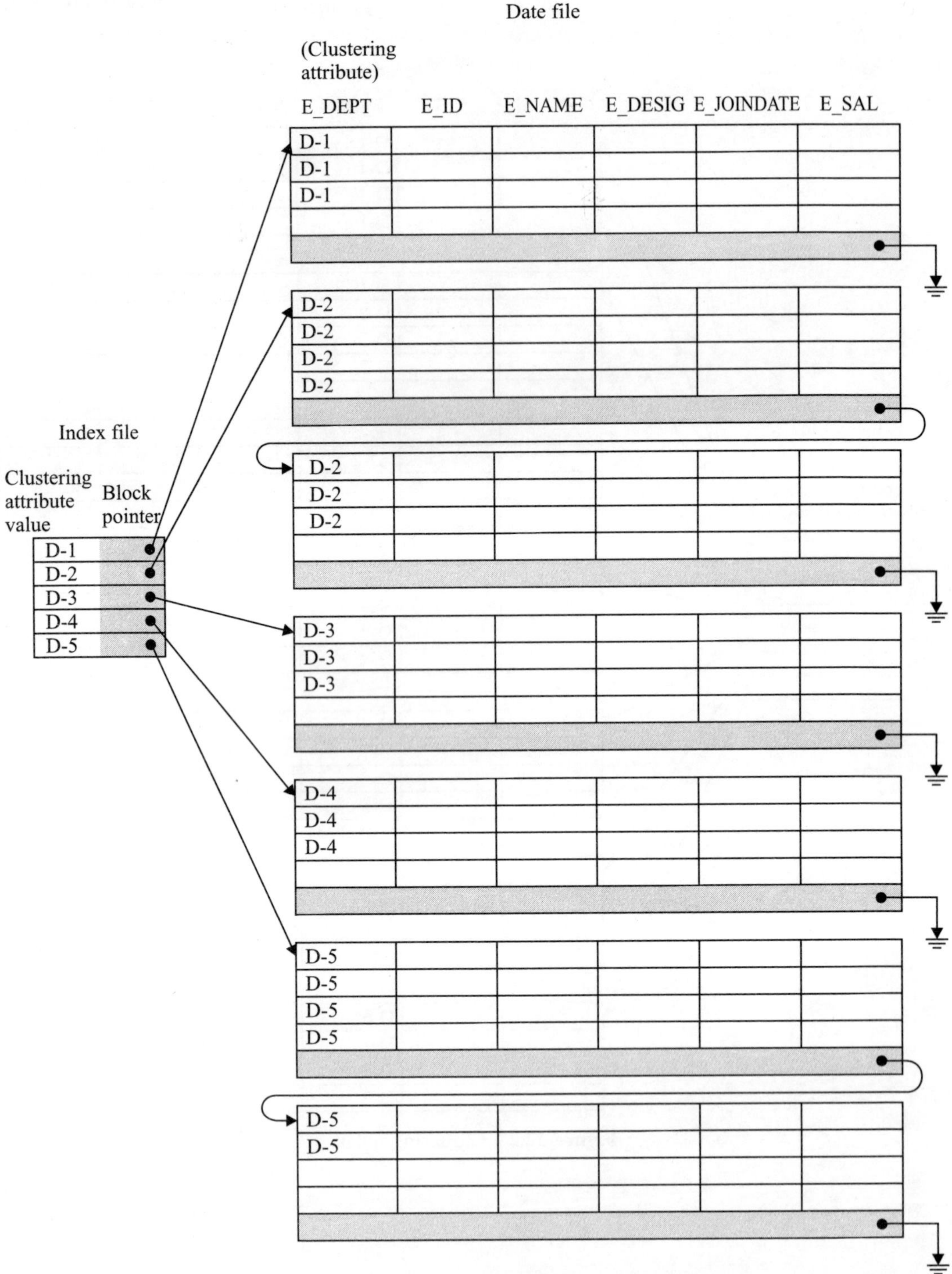

Figure 12.3 Clustering index with linked list of blocks.

If we use a key attribute (other than the primary key) to create a secondary index, there will be one index entry for each base record. In this case, the secondary index becomes a dense index. As base records are ordered according to the primary key index, each index entry, here, points to a single record block only. However, since the records are not ordered according to the secondary key, we cannot use block anchors.

A secondary index generally consumes more space and higher search time than a primary index. However, searching using the secondary is much faster compared to sequential search over the base file. For a primary index, we can use the binary search even if the index does not exist; but a secondary index must be created at first, before searching is done. A secondary indexing scheme is shown in Figure 12.4. Note that, multiple index entries point to the same block of records. In this example, the index itself has two blocks.

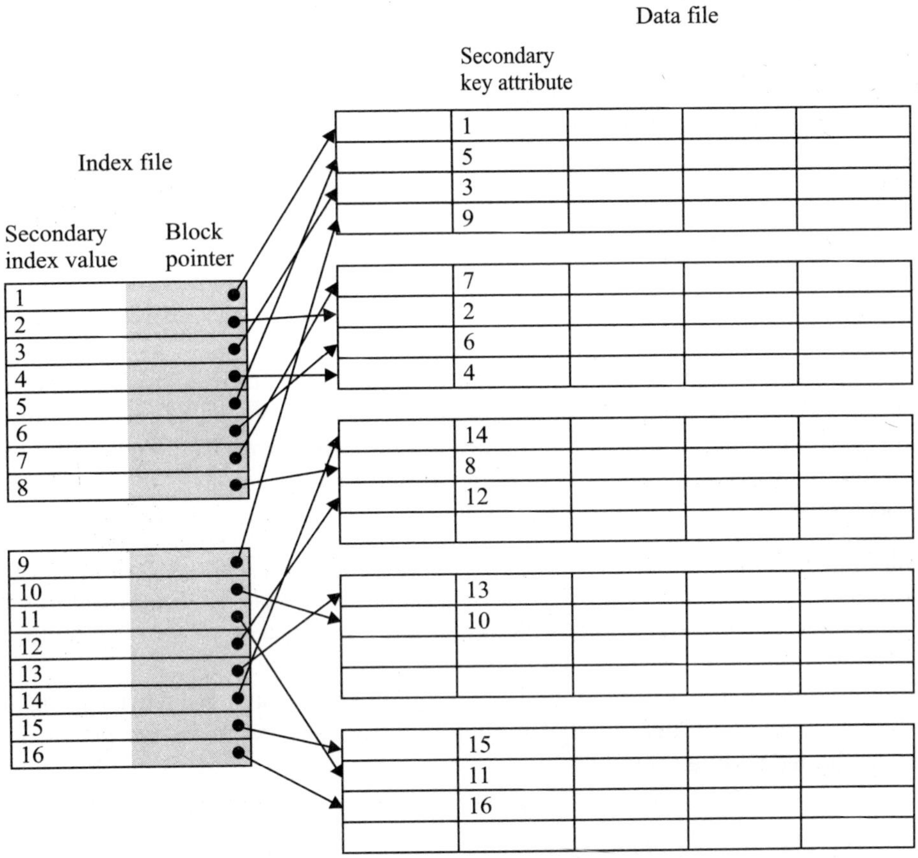

Figure 12.4 Secondary indexing.

ILLUSTRATION 12.2 Consider our earlier example base file with $r = 50{,}000$ records having record length R = 100 bytes each, and let the block size is B = 1024 bytes. Compare the number of block accesses, using a secondary index, to find a base record.

Solution For a linear search over the base file, the average number of block access will be $b/2 = 2500$.

We now construct a secondary index of record length 10 as in Example 12.1. Therefore, the key field is 10 bytes wide and a pointer requires 6 bytes, each index entry size will be

$$R_i = 10 + 6 = 16 \text{ bytes}$$

The number of blocks needed to store the index file is $bfr_i = \text{floor} \lfloor B/R_i \rfloor = 64$. Total number of index entries in the dense secondary index file is $r_i = 50{,}000$, i.e. equal to the number of records in the base file. Total number of index blocks required is thus

$$b_i = \text{ceiling} \lceil r_i/bfr_i \rceil = \text{ceiling} \lceil 50000/64 \rceil = 782.$$

A binary search over this index file requires ceiling $\lceil \log_2 b_i \rceil$ = ceiling $\lceil \log_2 782 \rceil = 10$ block accesses. To search the record using the index value, we need one additional block access of the base file, i.e. a total of $10 + 1 = 11$ block accesses are needed only.

In general, secondary indexes are defined over non-key attributes. Therefore, many records can have the same value for the indexing attribute. But, in the index file, we should maintain a single entry for a single attribute value. This can be implemented in various ways.

- In the simplest approach, we can maintain multiple index entries with the same attribute value, one entry per record. This is a dense index.
- We may use variable length index entries, where a list of pointers is associated with a single indexing attribute value. Each pointer points to a block of records that contains a record with the same attribute value.
- A second level of indirection can be used in the index itself. Here, the first level is a unique key-pointer pair, and the second level contains blocks of record pointers. This is a non-dense indexing scheme, where a key-pointer pair from the first level points a block of pointers at the second level, which, in turn, point to individual records or blocks of records.

The third scheme is very useful for insertion and deletion of records. Also, searching for a record with a certain indexing attribute value can be done efficiently by referring to the blocks of records pointed to by the concerned blocks of pointers (instead of searching the complete data file).

A secondary index provides a logical ordering on the records by the indexing attribute. If we access the records in the order of entries in the secondary index, we get them ordered according to the indexing attribute.

12.5 Multilevel Indexing

To avoid very large indexes, sometimes, multilevel indexing is used. In such cases, the indexes are also stored in permanent storage, and searching is done by first retrieving the highest level index, and then the lower level indexes in order. This reduces the searching overhead effectively. Multilevel indexing may be considered to indexing over indexes.

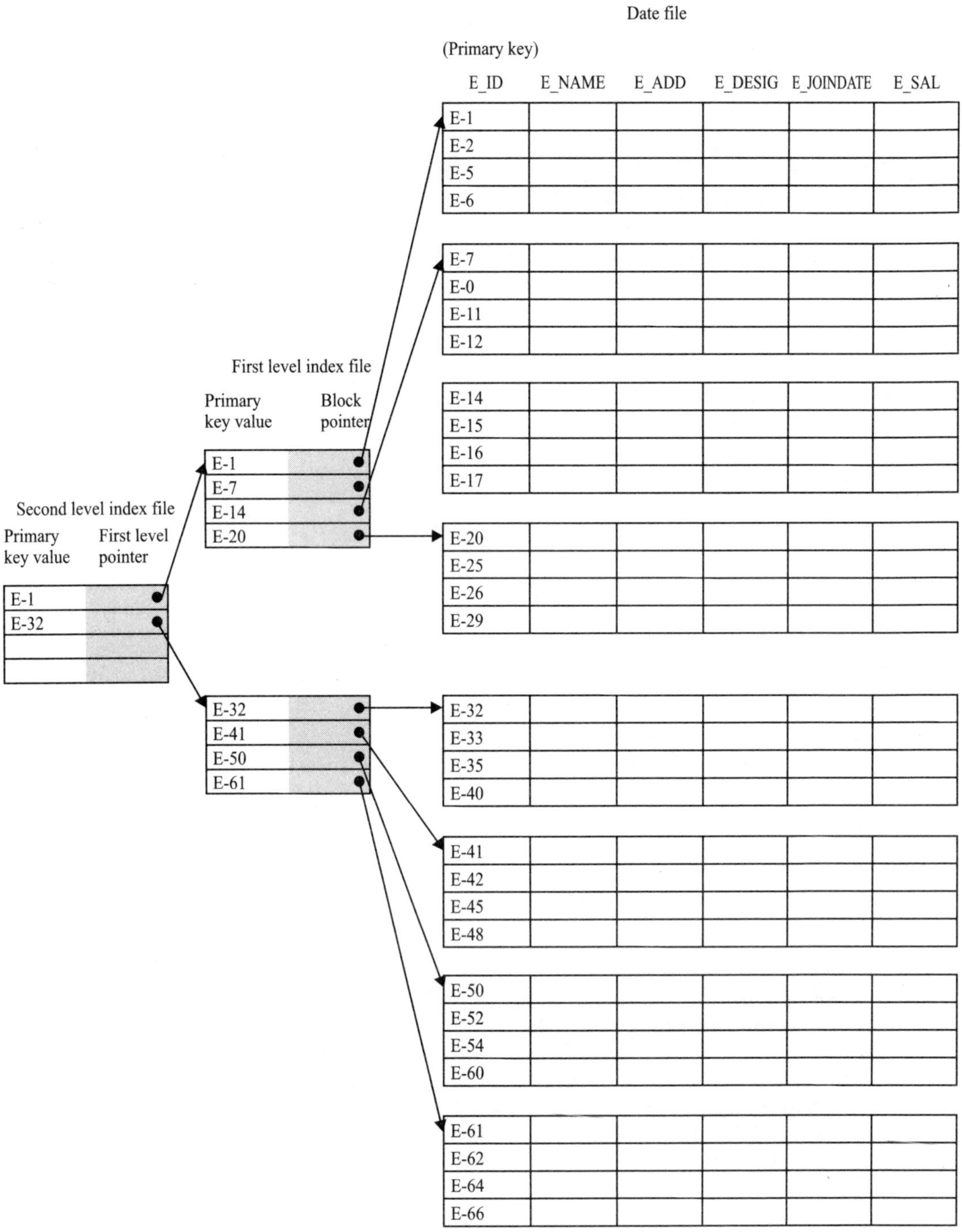

Figure 12.5 Multilevel indexing.

In the case of an ordered index file having b_i blocks, the number of disk accesses needed to find a record is approximately $\log_2 b_i$. Here, the index size is divided by a factor of 2 during every step of binary search, and hence the base 2 appears to the logarithm. In the case of multilevel indexing, the blocking factor bfr_i can be used as the base to the logarithm. Since bfr_i is much higher than 2, the search will be much faster.

In a multilevel index, the first level is an ordered index having a distinct index value for each record. Hence, we can create a primary key index for the first level index. This new index at the second level has one entry for each block of the first level index. There may be further subsequent levels also. The blocking factor, for all the levels, will be bfr_i. If the first level index has r_1 entries, it needs r_2 = ceiling $\lceil r_1 / bfr_i \rceil$ blocks; which is the number of entries at the second level of the index.

ILLUSTRATION 12.3 Consider a base file with r = 50,000 records having record length R = 100 bytes each, and let the block size is B = 1024 bytes. We have a dense secondary index over the base file. Convert it into a multilevel index and compare search efforts with the existing secondary index.

Solution Here the blocking factor is $bfr_i = 64$ entries per block.

The number of first level blocks will be b_1 = ceiling $\lceil r_i / bfr_i \rceil$ = ceiling $\lceil 50000/64 \rceil$ = 782. The number of second level blocks will be b_2 = ceiling $\lceil 782/64 \rceil$ = 13, and the number of third level blocks will be b_2 = ceiling $\lceil 13/64 \rceil$ = 1. Hence, the third level (L = 3) is the topmost level of the index. To access a record using this multilevel index, we need L + 1 = 3 + 1 = 4 block accesses. In the case of the secondary index, the number of block accesses was 11.

We shall present a search algorithm that can be used to search a record using a non-dense multilevel primary key. In this algorithm, we assume that the key value of the record to be searched is K, and an entry i at level j of the index is denoted by the pair $(K_j(i), P_j(i))$. Overflow of records is ignored, and in case the search is successful, there must be an entry at level 1 having $K_j(i) \le K < K_j(i + 1)$. The record will be found in the block of the data file at physical address $P_1(i)$.

Algorithm: Searching a non-dense multilevel primary index having L levels:

/* K is the primary key value of the desired record. An entry i at level j of the index is denoted by the pair $(K_j(i), P_j(i))$ */

```
begin
        p = address of the top level block of the index;
        for j < L to 1 in steps of -1 do
        begin
              read index block at level j whose address is p;
              search block p for entry i such that Kj (i) != K, and Kj (i + 1) != K;
              (if Kj (i) is the last entry then check only for it)
              P = Kj (i);
        end
        read the data block whose address is p;
        search block p for records with key value = K;
end;
```

12.6 B-Tree Indexing

A B-tree of order *m* is an *m*-way tree, i.e. a node in such a tree may have up to *n* children. A B-tree allows dynamic multilevel indexing. An index entry is nothing but a pair of a key value and a pointer. In a B-tree, each node represents a number of key-pointer pairs. Here, the lowest level nodes contain key-pointer pairs that directly point to disk blocks. The following are some properties of B-tree of order *m*.

- Every node has sufficient room to store $(m - 1)$ key-pointer pairs (K, P). Value of *m* should be odd.
- Each node has room for *m*-tree pointers (P_t) to other nodes at the next level. These pointers are different from those mentioned in the key-pointer pairs. The pointers in a key-pointer pair are called data pointers or block pointers (P_b), as they point to a data block in the base file.
- Every non-terminal node, except the root node, has at least *ceiling* $\lceil m/2 \rceil$ non-null pointers to other nodes in B-tree. The root node has at least two non-null pointers to other nodes in the B-tree. In other words, every non-terminal node, except the root node, has at least *ceiling* $\lceil m/2 \rceil$ children; and the root node has at least two children.
- All terminals or leaf nodes are at the same level (the lowest level) and the tree is balanced.
- If a node has $(m + 1)$ non-null pointers to other B-tree nodes, it must contain *m* key-pointer pairs for the index itself. Therefore, we can assume a B-tree node as the following list:

  $$P_{t_1}, (K_1, P_{b_1}); P_{t_2}, (K_2,P_{b_2}); P_{t_3}, (K_3,P_{b_3}); \ldots ; P_{t\,(m-1)}, (K_{(m-1)},P_{b\,(m-1)}); P_{tm}$$
- For each B-tree node, we have
  - The key value in key-pointer pair $K_{(i-1)},P_{b(i-1)}$ is less than the key value in the next key-pointer pair $K_i,P_{b\,i}$.
  - All key-pointer pairs in the node pointed to by $K_{(i-1)}P_{b(i-1)}$ contain key values that are less than the key value in $K_iP_{b_i}$.

Searching in a B-tree

Let us try to analyze how B-tree structure allows efficient searching. Search for any key value starts at the root node. At any node, we need to search sequentially through stored key values until

1. a match is found,
2. a key value greater than the target value is found, or
3. end of the node is reached without a match.

In case a match is not found (situations 2 and 3), we get a pointer to an appropriate follow-up node which will be searched next. We should remember that actually each B-tree node is a disk block, containing hundreds of keys, that is loaded in the main memory in one disk access. While processing data from a database, our main objective is to minimize the number of disk accesses, as I/O time is generally much higher than any search operation in main memory. Using a B-tree indexing technique, we can get efficiency in searching in terms of number of disk accesses. Actually, the number of disk accesses needed for any particular key is the number of levels in the tree. Therefore, the maximum number of levels needed to store r records will be the worst case efficiency.

Let, l = *ceiling* $\lceil m/2 \rceil$, where m is the order of the tree. Therefore,
Level 1 contains at least 1 node.
Level 2 contains at least 2 nodes.
Level 3 contains at least $2 \times l$ nodes.
Level 4 contains at least $2 \times l^2$ nodes.
And so on.

Thus, level h contains at least $2 \times l^{(h-2)}$ nodes.

The above expression indicates that the maximum number of levels (height of the tree) h_{max} for r number of records (i.e., key-pointer pairs) is

$$h_{max} = 1 + \log_m (r + 1)/2.$$

If we consider a file of 50,000 records, then a binary tree search may require 16 disk accesses to find a particular record, while the B-tree structure of order 250 needs only 3 disk accesses.

Insertion and deletion into and from a B-tree

Use of B-tree structure for insertion and deletion of records imposes a restriction that the space consumed and wasted by these operations should never be excessive. Otherwise, the process may be very time consuming. However, for many such operations, B-trees provide considerable efficiency. Whenever an attempt is made to insert in an already full node, or to delete a record that is already less than half full, situations may be complicated.

If we attempt to delete a record from a node which is only half full, the concerned node will be combined to its neighbouring nodes, and this process will be propagated up to the root node. Thus the process becomes very costly. However, on the average, it is observed that this kind of situations occur very infrequently. Similarly, during insertion of a new value, the node may be divided into its fragments and rearrangement of the tree structure may be needed.

Insertion into a B-tree: The following steps describe how to insert a new record into a B-tree. Insertions are made to existing leaf nodes. Initially, the root node itself may be considered a leaf node.

- If the insertion causes the leaf node to exceed its size, it is broken at its middle causing creation of two leaf nodes and promotion of the middle key value to the parent node.
- The above is done repeatedly for the parent nodes also (whenever needed).

Deletion from a B-tree: The following steps describe how to delete an existing record from a B-tree.

- Deletion of records can be done from any of the root, intermediate and leaf nodes.
- If the key is in a leaf node, and removal of the key does not leave the node with very few keys, it can be removed simply.

- If the key is not in a leaf node, then its predecessor or successor will be in a leaf node (by properties of a B-tree). Now, we can delete the key, and promote the predecessor or successor key to the position of the deleted key.
- In the above two situations, if the number of keys in a leaf node falls below the limit, we have to look for siblings immediately adjacent to it.
  - If one of the siblings has more than minimum number of keys, we can promote one of its keys to the parent and move the parent to the other sibling.
  - If neither of the siblings has more than minimum number of keys then the lacking leaf and one of its neighbours can be combined with their parent and the new leaf will have the correct number of keys. If after this step the parent is left with very few keys, then we repeat the process up to the root, if required.

ILLUSTRATION 12.4 Form a B-tree of order 5 with records having key values 1, 12, 8, 2, 6, 14, 25, 28, 17, 7, 52, 16, 48, 68, 3, 73 and 4.

Solution The root node may be constructed with the first four key values as shown in Figure 12.6. Values in a node should be ordered.

P_{t1}	K_1,P_{b1}	P_{t2}	K_2,P_{b2}	P_{t3}	... ...	$P_{t(m-1)}$	$K_{(m-1)},P_{b(m-1)}$	P_{tm}

Figure 12.6 A B-tree node.

The root node contains four records and reaches its maximum size. Hence, to add the fifth key value 6, we need to break the root node at its middle to create two child nodes as in Figure 12.7.

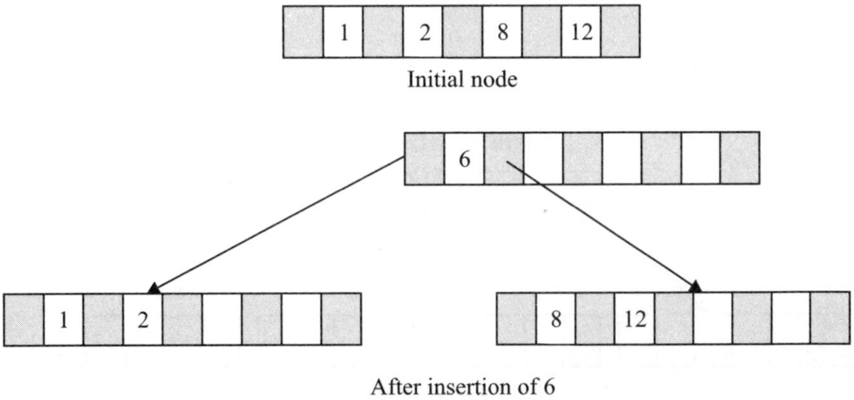

Figure 12.7 Creation of root node and insertion of value 6.

Next key value to be added is 14. It will fall in the right leaf node as its value is < 6 (the parent key value). Similarly, 25 can be added to the right leaf node only. The B-tree at this stage is shown in Figure 12.8.

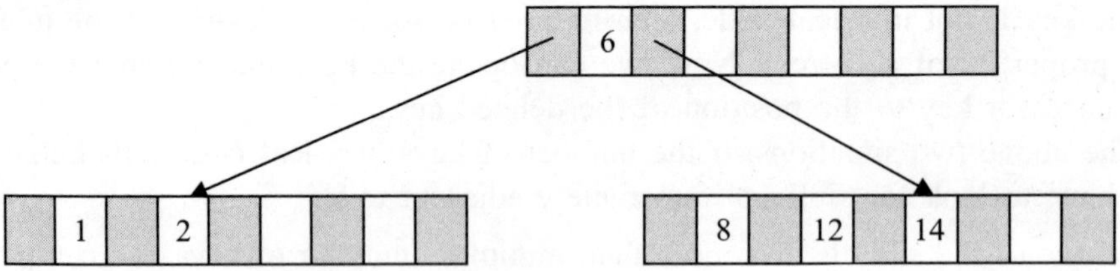

After insertion of 14

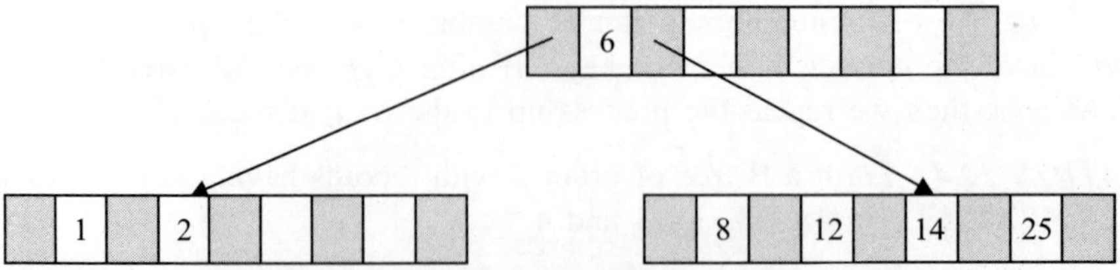

After insertion of 25

Figure 12.8 Insertion of values 14 followed by 25.

Next key value 28 should be added to the right side, but since its size exceeds the limit, this node is divided into two and 28 is placed in the right fragment by promoting the value 14 to the root node. 17 can then be inserted in the rightmost leaf node in a straightforward manner as shown in Figure 12.9.

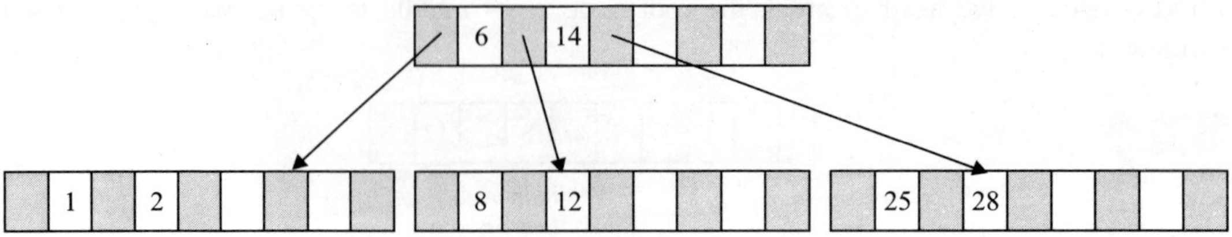

After insertion of 28

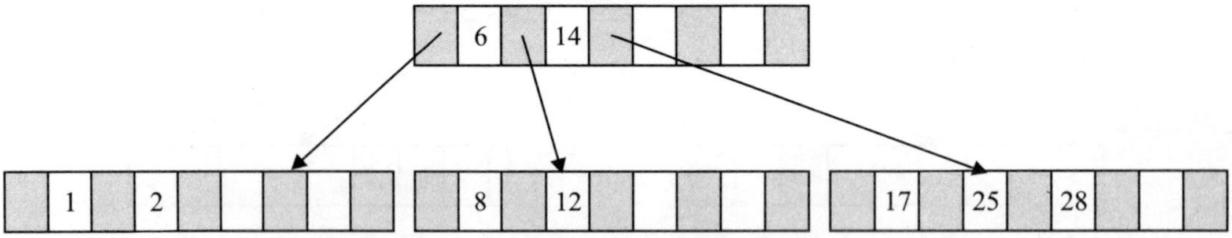

After insertion of 17

Figure 12.9 Insertion of values 28 followed by 17.

Values 7 is inserted in the second leaf node, 52 is inserted in the third leaf node, 16 is then inserted in the second leaf node normally as there are space available in these nodes. 48 can be inserted in the third leaf node only by promoting the key value 28 to the root and dividing the leaf into two fragments as shown in Figure 12.10.

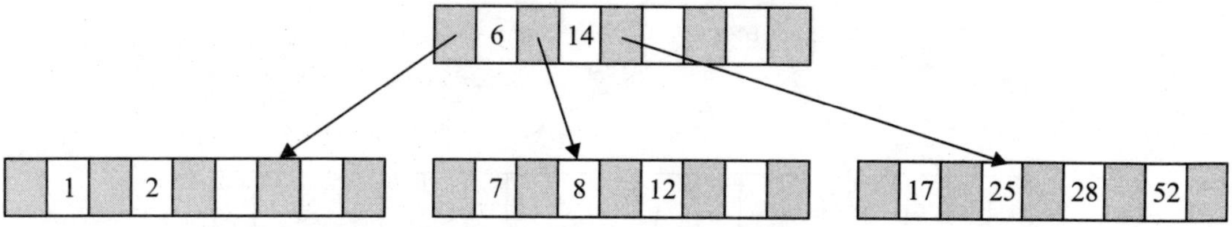

After insertion of 7 followed by 52

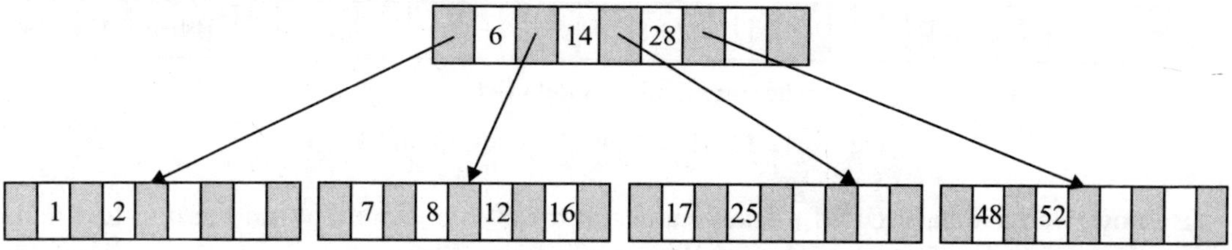

After insertion of 16 followed by 48

Figure 12.10 Insertion of values 7, 52, 16 and 48.

Values 68 and 3 can be inserted in a straightforward manner. In a similar manner, key values 56 and 5 can be inserted. The resulting structures are shown in Figure 12.11.

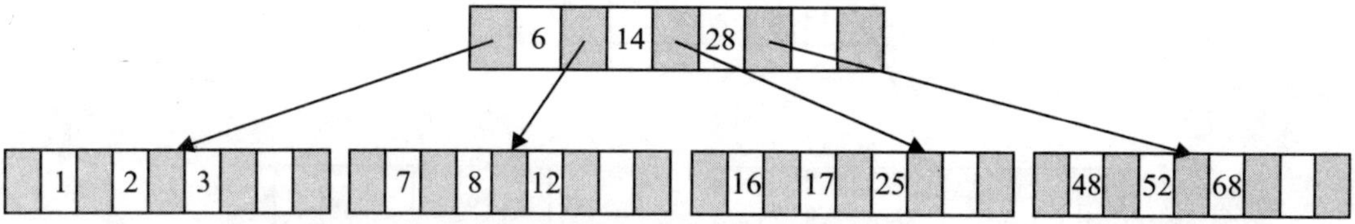

After insertion of 68 followed by 3

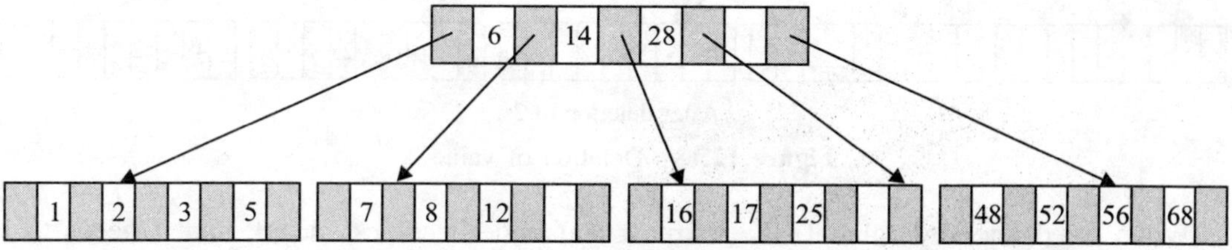

After insertion of 56 followed by 5

Figure 12.11 Insertion of values 68, 3, 56 and 5.

At this stage, the first and the fourth leaf nodes are full. Inserting values 73 and 4 need to promote the middle elements from these nodes to the root node. But since the root has not enough space to accommodate two promoted key values, it is again divided by creating two intermediate nodes and creating a new root node by promoting the key value 14. Now the B-tree becomes a three-level tree as shown in Figure 12.12.

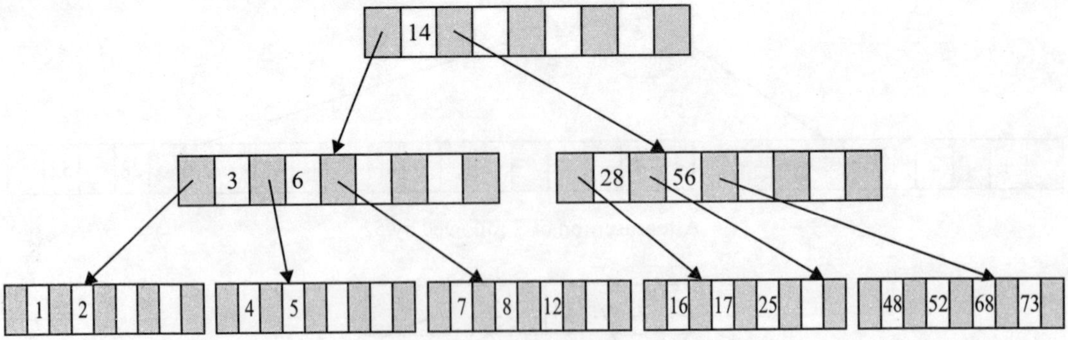

After insertion of 73 followed by 4

Figure 12.12 Insertion of values 73 and 4.

By now, we have inserted all the key values in the B-tree. Note that, all the non-leaf nodes, except the root node, are at least half full as desired in a B-tree.

ILLUSTRATION 12.5 Delete the key values 2 and 1, in that order, from the newly built B-tree.

Solution Deletion of key value 2 can be performed by simply removing it from the leftmost leaf node. The structure after this deletion is shown in Figure 12.13.

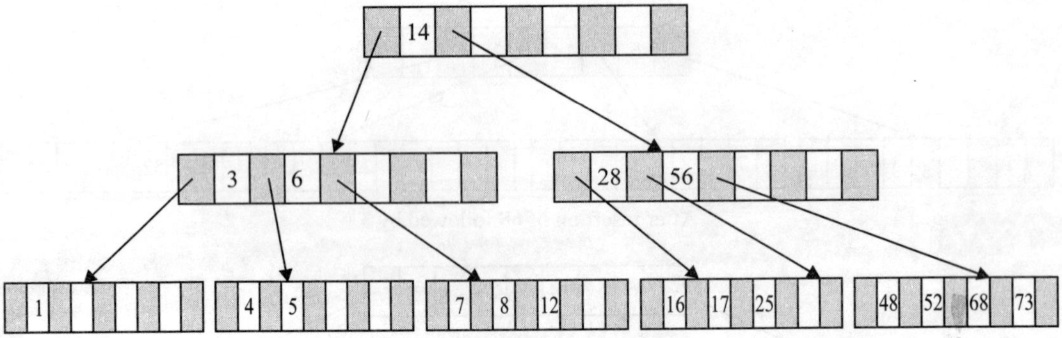

After deletion of 2

Figure 12.13 Deletion of value 2.

When we delete key value 1, the leftmost leaf node becomes vacant, and it needs to be removed from the tree. At the same time, we must move the key value 3 from the corresponding parent node to the next leaf node. At this stage, the parent node becomes less than half full and it is merged with its immediate sibling as shown in Figure 12.14.

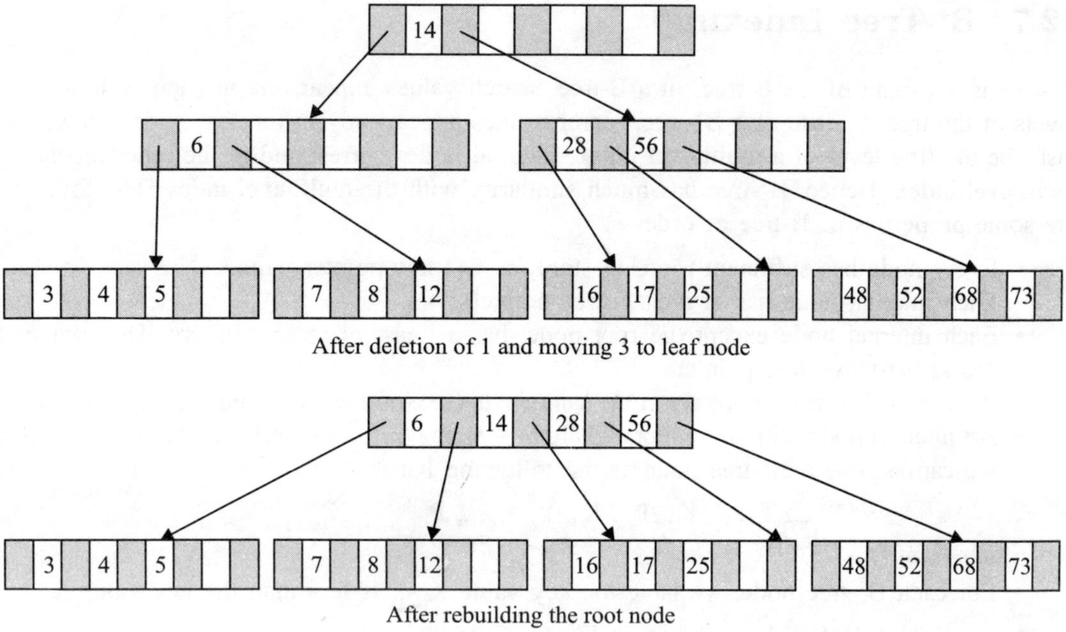

Figure 12.14 Deletion of value 1.

ILLUSTRATION 12.6 Find out the maximum number of records a B-tree of order n and height h can hold.

Solution

The root can hold $(n - 1)$ records.

Level 1 nodes contain a maximum of $n\ (n - 1)$ number of records.

Level 2 nodes contain a maximum of $n^2\ (n - 1)$ number of records.

And so on.

Level h holds a maximum of $n^h\ (n - 1)$ number of records.

Therefore, the total maximum number of $[1 + n + n^2 + n^3 + \cdots + n^h]\ (n - 1)$ records $= [(n^{(h+1)} - 1)/(n - 1)]\ (n - 1) = (n^{(h+1)} - 1)$ records.

ILLUSTRATION 12.7 Suppose that the key value is represented in 9 bytes, a disk block size is 512 bytes. If a data pointer is 7 bytes, and a tree pointer is 6 bytes, find out the order of the B-tree.

Solution Here, block size B = 512, key value size V = 9 bytes, data (block) pointer size P_b = 7 bytes, and tree pointer size P_t = 6 bytes.

Hence, if order of the B-tree be n, we have to satisfy the following relation:

$$n \times P_b + (n - 1) \times (P_t + V) \leq B$$

i.e. $n \times 6 + (n - 1) \times (7 + 9) \leq 512$

This inequality is satisfied by a value of $n = 24$ on the maximum. Hence, we can choose the order of B-tree to be 23.

12.7 B+-Tree Indexing

B$^+$-tree is a variant of the B-tree. In a B-tree, search values appear one in each node at every levels of the tree. In case of a B$^+$-tree, search values appear only in the leaf nodes of the tree, just like the first level of a multilevel index. Internal nodes correspond to the other levels of a multilevel index. Hence, B$^+$-tree has much similarity with the multilevel index. The following are some properties of B-tree of order n.

- Every node has sufficient room to store $(n - 1)$ key-pointer pairs.
- Each internal node has at most n tree pointers.
- Each internal node except the root node, has at least $n/2$ tree pointers. The root node has at least two tree pointers.
- All terminal or leaf nodes are at the same level (the lowest level) and the tree is balanced.
- An internal node with m pointers where $m \leq n$, has $(m - 1)$ search key values. Therefore, we can assume a B$^+$-tree node as the following list:

$$P_{t_1}, K_1, P_{t_2}, K_2, P_{t_3}, K_3, P_{t_4}, \ldots, P_{t\,(m-1)}, K_{(m-1)}, P_{tm}$$

  where $m \leq n$.
- For each B$^+$-tree node, we have the key value $K_{(i-1)}$ is less than the key value K_i .

A sample non-leaf node is shown in Figure 12.15.

P_{t1}	K_1	P_{t2}	K_2	P_{t3}	... ...	$P_{t(m-1)}$	$K_{(m-1)}$	P_{tm}

Figure 12.15 A non-leaf node in a B$^+$-tree of order m.

Leaf nodes in a B$^+$-tree has a different structure. Its features are as follows:

1. Each leaf node is of the following form:

$$(K_1, P_{b1}); (K_2,P_{b2}); (K_3,P_{b3}), \ldots , (K_{(m-1)},P_{b(m-1)}); P_{next}$$

   where $m \leq n$, and each P_{bi} is a data pointer, and P_{next} points to the next leaf node.
2. Within each leaf node, $K_1 < K_2 < K_3 < \ldots. < K_{(m-1)}$.
3. Each P_{bi} is a data pointer that points to the record whose search key value is K_i or to a block containing the record.
4. Each leaf node has at least $(n/2)$ key values.
5. All leaf nodes are at the same level.

A sample non-leaf node is shown in Figure 12.16.

K_1	P_{b1}	K_2	P_{b2}	... ...	$K_{(m-1)}$	$P_{b(m-1)}$	P_{next}

Figure 12.16 A leaf node in a B$^+$-tree of order m.

One interesting feature of the B$^+$-tree is that it has a next leaf node pointer P_{next}. So, starting at the leftmost leaf node, we can traverse all the leaf nodes as a linked list. Thus, ordered sequential access of data records is possible (over the ordering field). A $P_{previous}$ is also possible, to provide a backward traversal facility.

Note that, internal nodes in a B$^+$-tree does not contain any pointer to data blocks, hence the internal nodes of the tree consumes lesser storage compared to that of a B-tree. Therefore, for the same block size, order *n* of a B$^+$-tree will be higher than that of a B-tree.

Searching in a B$^+$-tree

We search for a key value K in a B$^+$-tree starting at the root node. In the root node, the smallest key value greater than K is searched at first. Let this smallest key value be K_s. Now, the following three situations may arise.

- $K_s = K_1$, i.e. $K < K_1$. We go to the node pointed to by pointer P_{t1}.
- $K_s = K_{m+1}$, i.e. $K_{m+1} < K$. We go to the node pointed to by pointer $P_{t(m-1)}$.
- $K_s < K < K_{s+1}$ where $1 < s < n$. We go to the node pointed to by pointer P_{s+1}.

For each of the above situations, we search for the smallest key value greater than K again, and repeat the same procedure.

At a particular node, the key value can be obtained if it is present in the tree.

Insertion into and deletion from a B$^+$-tree

Insertion: The sequence of steps needed to insert a record (key) in a B$^+$-tree is as follows:

- The search operation stated above is followed to find the leaf node in which the key value is to be inserted.
- If the key value is already present, no more insertion is needed.
- If the key value is not present, we insert it in the leaf node in an ordered fashion.

Deletion: The sequence of steps needed to delete a record (key) from a B$^+$-tree is as follows:

- Search the B$^+$-tree for the node with key value K.
- If the key value is present, remove it from the node.

ILLUSTRATION 12.8 Construct a B$^+$-tree of order 5 with records having keys 1, 12, 8, 2, 6,14, 25, 28, 17, 7, 52, 16, 48, 68 and 3 and then delete 2 and 1.

Solution The starting node and the construction processes are shown in Figures 12.17 to 12.23.

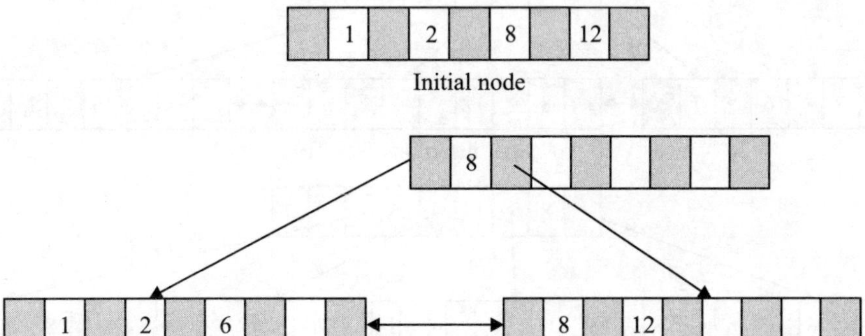

Figure 12.17 Creation of root node with first four values and insertion of the next value 6.

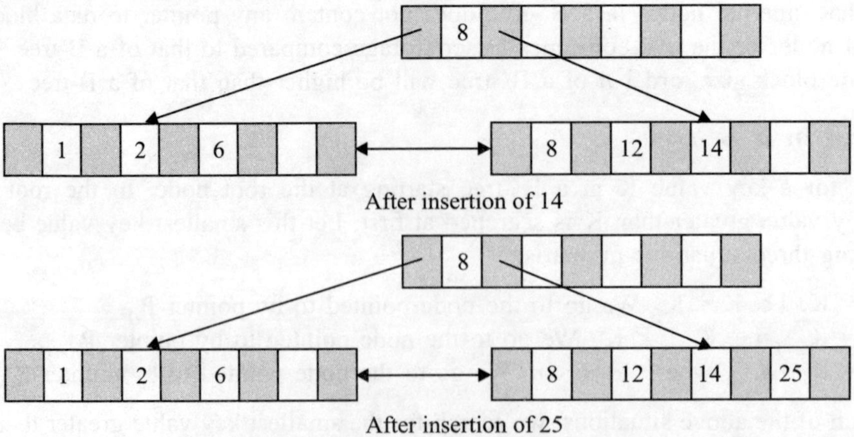

Figure 12.18 Insertion of values 14 and 25.

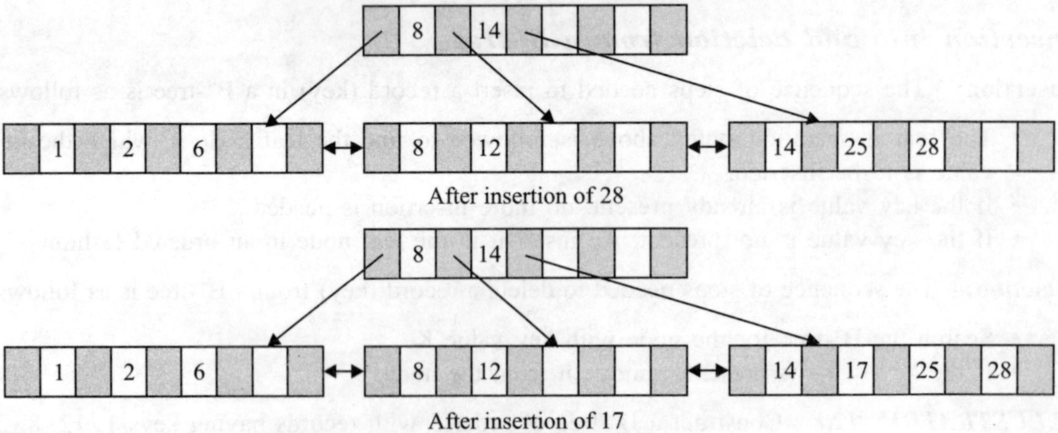

Figure 12.19 Insertion of values 28 and 17.

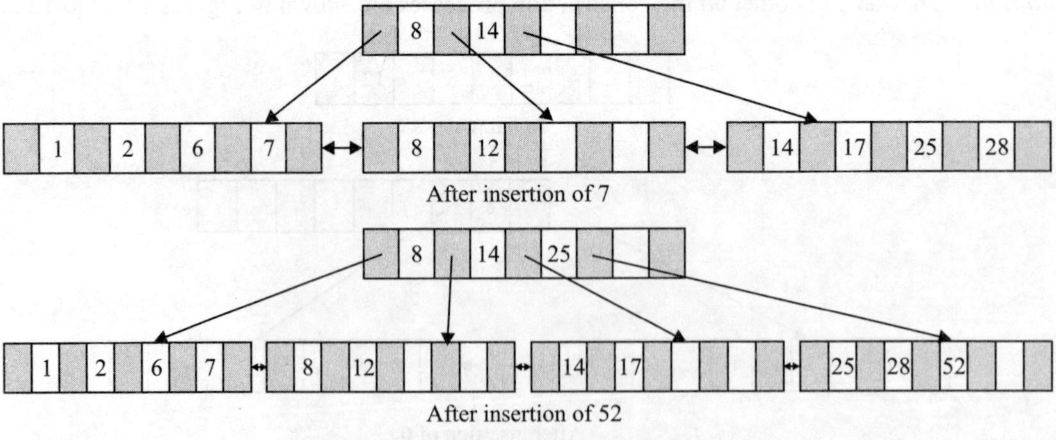

Figure 12.20 Insertion of values 7 and 52.

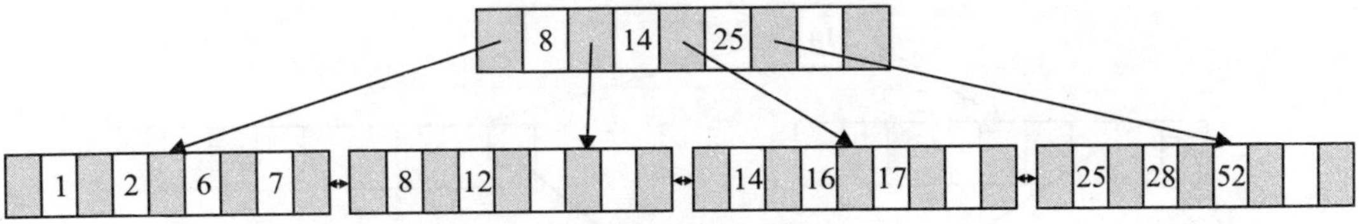

After insertion of 16

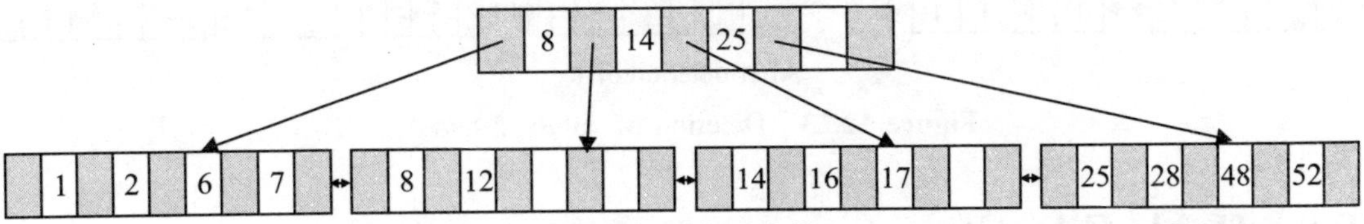

After insertion of 48

Figure 12.21 Insertion of values 16 and 48.

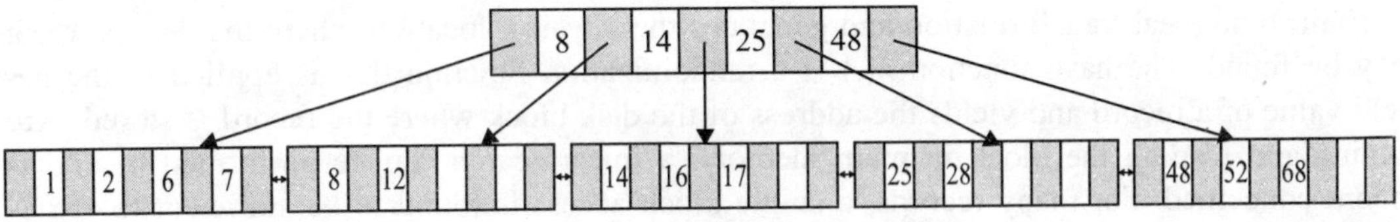

After insertion of 68

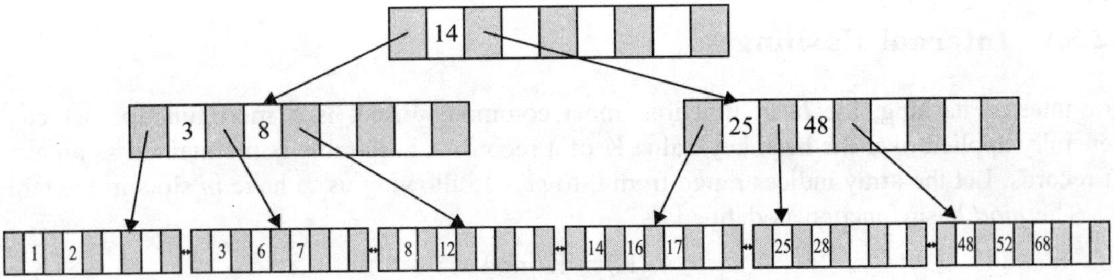

After insertion of 3

Figure 12.22 Insertion of values 68 and 3.

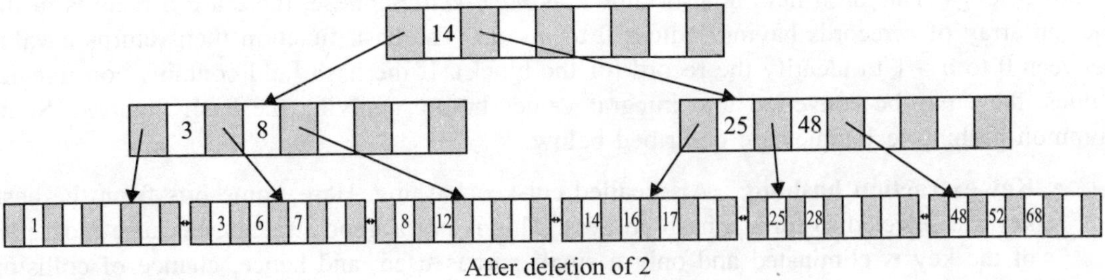

After deletion of 2

Figure 12.23 *Contd.*

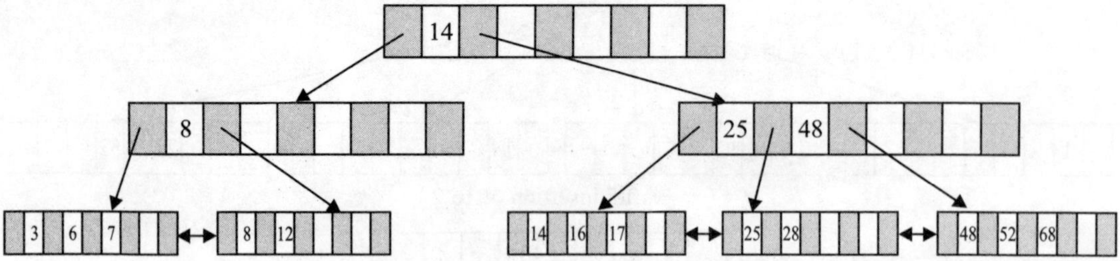

After deletion of 1

Figure 12.23 Deletion of values 2 and 1.

12.8 Hash File Structure

Hash file organization provides a very fast access to records at certain search conditions. In hashing, the search condition is specified by a hash field or hash key attribute which undergoes a certain functional transformation and generates the physical location where the desired record may be found. The hash function *h*(.) is a randomization function that is applied to the hash field value of a record and yields the address of the disk block where the record is stored. After finding and reading the block in main memory, a linear search can be performed to find the record concerned. For many records, a single block access is found to be sufficient to retrieve it. Hashing can be of two types: internal and external.

12.8.1 Internal Hashing

For internal hashing, the hash function, most commonly used, is a mod function which is generally applied over the hash key value K of a record. A hash table is maintained as an array of records. Let the array indices range from 0 to $m - 1$, allowing us to have *m* slots in the table.

The *mod* hash function is defined as:

$$h\ (\text{K}) = \text{K mod } m$$

and returns an integer between 0 and $m - 1$. This return value is used as address of the record. Hashing is implemented as a hash table in association with a file of records. A hash function *h* is applied on a field of the records, called the *hash field*, to determine the block to which the record belongs. This hash field is also known as *hash key*. Suppose, there are *n* records in the file (an array of *n* records having indices 0 to $n - 1$). The hash function then returns a value between 0 to $n - 1$ to identify the record (or the block). If the hash field contains non-integral values, they may be converted into integral values before applying the hash function. Some common hashing techniques are described below.

- **Key-extraction hashing:** Also called cut-key hashing. Here, some bits from the hash key are selected to form a hash address. This is not a good strategy, because most part of the key is eliminated and only a small part is used; and hence, chance of collision is high. For example, suppose, the hash field contains the string “IT”. By assigning numerical values to the characters (according to their position in the English alphabet), we get numerical values 9 (for 'I') and 20 (for 'T'). 8-bit binary codes for 9 and 20 are 00001001 and 00010100 respectively. Now, in binary form

IT = 0000100100010100

We can now select a number of bits from the above codeword (binary string) to form the hash function value. Let 3 bits; 0th, 2nd and 12th bits, are selected from the hash function value. Hence we get the string 010 in binary, i.e. 2 in decimal. This value 2 now represents the hash address.

- **Folded key hashing:** This hash function employs some kind of arithmetic and logical transformation of the hash field value. The result is used as the hash address. As the entire field is used, it is a better strategy than the cut-key strategy. For example, let, in decimal notation, a large hash field value becomes 928477924. We can fold this string into 3 parts (say). The parts are 928, 477 and 924 respectively. Now, we can add these three numbers and discard the carry generated. The result is taken as the hash address.
- **Division-remainder hashing:** This is nothing but the mod hash function as mentioned earlier. This function is found to perform better than all other techniques. For example, let the hash field has a numeric value of 234, and there are 17 locations in the memory to store records. Then the address of the concerned record is found as

$$h\ (234) = 234 \bmod 17 = 13$$

This mod function is simple but very useful in many cases.

A major problem with hashing is that it does not yield distinct addresses for distinct hash field values. That is, a many-to-one mapping is only available. Therefore, multiple records may compete for occupying a particular location. This phenomenon is called collision. When a collision occurs, we need to search for another available location where we can place the record. This kind of collision resolution is done in different ways, some of which are given below:

- **Open addressing:** Here, the program keeps checking the subsequent locations serially, starting with the location indicated by the hash function, until an empty location is found.
- **Multiple hashing:** Multiple hash functions may be used in a certain fixed order. When the first function encounters a collision, the second function is used, and so on.
- **Chained overflow:** Here, each location (to hold records) contains a pointer field. An overflow memory area is reserved a priori. Whenever a collision occurs, the new record is placed in the overflow area at a free location, and the pointer field of the hash address location is set accordingly.

All the above mentioned hashing functions have their own advantages and disadvantages, and all of them require their own insertion, deletion and searching strategies. *Chained addressing* is simple to implement but requires an extra memory of unknown size. *Open addressing*, on the other hand, has to face complications during deletion of records. Examples of open addressing and chained addressing are illustrated in Figures 12.24 and 12.25 respectively. The initial hash table contains records having key values 99, 67, 58, 72 and 109. The hash function used in h(K) = K mod 11. In the case of open addressing, to insert another key value 14, we face a collision at location 3. This is resolved by finding the next available location in sequence (this method is called *linear probing*). In the case of chained addressing, we have tried to insert three more records with key values 14, 77 and 36. Since 14 causes a collision at location 3, we added one node in a linked list fashion. This is repeated again during insertion of value 36. For 77, a collision at location 0 is encountered, and a new list is created there.

0	99
1	67
2	
3	58
4	
5	
6	72
7	
8	
9	
10	109

Initial configuration

0	99
1	67
2	
3	58
4	14
5	
6	72
7	
8	74
9	
10	109

After insertion of 74 and 14

Figure 12.24 Open addressing for hash file organization.

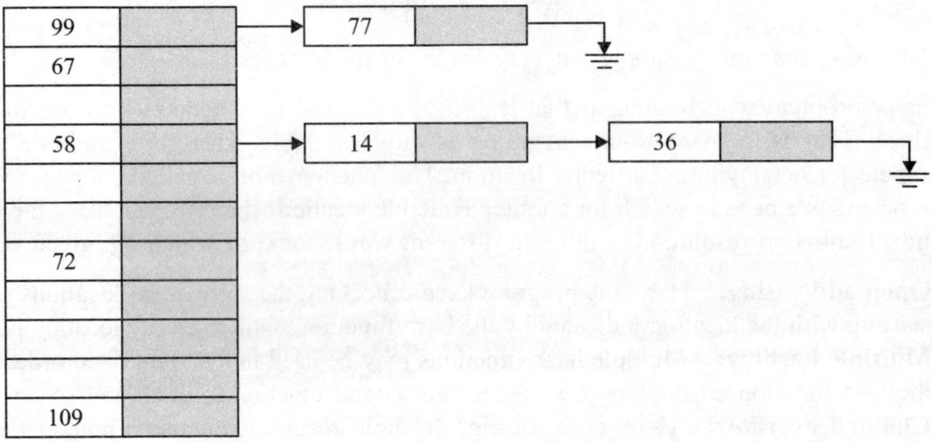

Figure 12.25 Chained addressing for hash file organization.

A good hash function should have the property of distributing records uniformly and sparsely over the available memory space. Also, it should be associated with efficient insertion, deletion and searching procedures, and collision resolution schemes. Generally, it is found that the *mod* function works very well when the total memory size N is a prime number. The collision problem can be significantly reduced when the concept of buckets of records instead of individual records is considered.

12.8.2 External Hashing

Internal hashing techniques can be applied when the hash table is present in the main memory completely. The concept can be applied to files in the secondary storage also. The underlying processes are called external hashing. Here, instead of records, we assume blocks of records as unit of information. A bucket may contain one or more records in contiguous locations. Depending on fixed and variable number of buckets allocated to a database file, hashing processes may be classified as *static* or *dynamic*.

Static hashing

In this hashing scheme, a fixed number of buckets are allocated to a file. Generally, one primary page and several overflow pages are allocated for each bucket.

To insert a record, the hash function identifies a bucket, and if a location is available there, the record is inserted. If the bucket is already full, the record is inserted in an overflow page and the page is connected to the bucket in a linked list fashion. When this overflow page becomes full, another page can be linked with it, forming an overflow chain.

To delete a record, the hash function determined bucket (primary page) is searched at first followed by searching in the overflow pages sequentially. If the record is found in the primary page, it is deleted. In case the concerned record is the only record present in an overflow page, the page is removed from the linked list.

Searching is done sequentially starting with the primary page followed by overflow pages. In order to speed up the search process, records are maintained in ordered fashion according to the hash field value.

Dynamic hashing

If the file size varies heavily and dynamically, it is undesirable to maintain a fixed number of buckets as in static hashing. In such situations, dynamic hashing technique is used. Here, the number of buckets can vary dynamically as per requirements, and hence, the hash function itself can be modified as needed. Dynamic memory allocation techniques are used in association with hash functions in order to cope with the growth and shrinkage of the database file. Dynamic hashing is again of two types as described below:

- **Extendable hashing:** This uses a directory of pointers to buckets. A directory is an array of 2^d elements where d is the number of bits of the hash value used to locate a directory element. d is also called the global depth of the directory. Elements of directory are pointers to buckets where records are stored. If the directory is not too large, it can reside in the main memory. Here, the hash function is applied over the hash field value, and the last d bits (high order) of the hash function value are used as an index to identify a directory entry. The pointer maintained in this directory location points to a bucket containing the record. It is, however, not necessary to have a distinct bucket for each of the directory entries. Several directory locations, having the same d' bits in their hash function values, may point to the same bucket if all the records that are hashed to these locations fit in a single bucket. d' is called local depth and its value (number of bits) is maintained in the bucket. A bucket with local depth d' can store only those records whose hash function values matches with the bit pattern specified by the local depth at the first d' positions.

  An extendable hash table with d = 3 is shown in Figure 12.26. Value of d can be increased or decreased by one at a time. The above cause the directory size to be doubled or halved respectively. Doubling is needed when a bucket, with local depth d′ = d, overflows. Halving is needed if d > d′, for all buckets, after some deletion. Most of the record retrieval operations need two block accesses—one for the directory and another for the bucket.

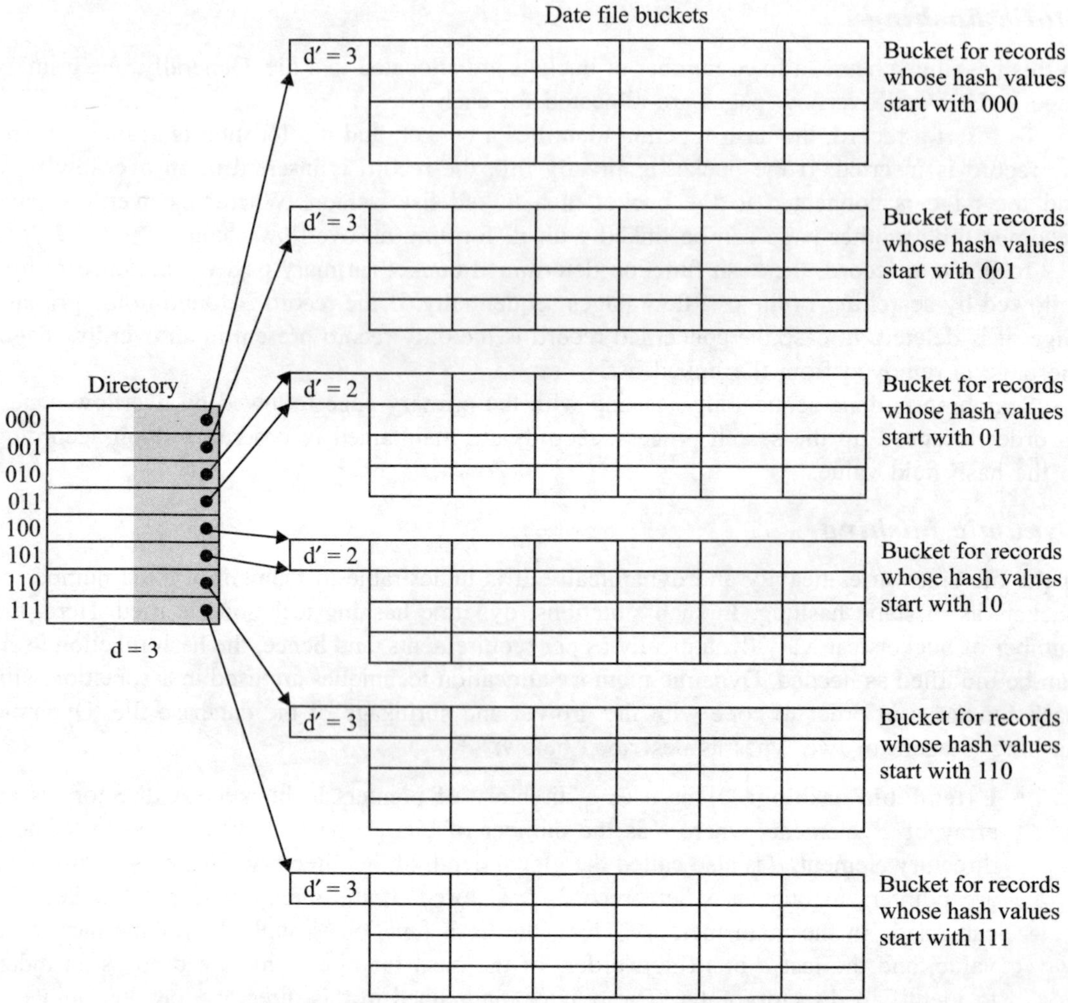

Figure 12.26 Extendable hashing scheme.

- **Linear hashing:** This allows a hash file to grow or shrink dynamically by allocating new buckets or removing existing buckets. There is no need to maintain a directory of pointers to buckets. Collisions can be handled by maintaining chained overflow pages as in the case of static hashing. In linear hashing, overflow of any bucket in the file leads to a bucket splitting. However, it is not necessary that the overflowed bucket need be split. Instead, buckets are split in linear order of bucket numbers 0, 1, 2, ...

Exercises

12.1 What is the importance of file organization? Describe structured and unstructured sequential files with suitable examples.

12.2 What are different index types? What types of index are created in SQL?

12.3 Compare between primary and secondary indexing. What are the advantages of an ordered file in this regard? What kind of index is specified on a non-ordering field of a file?

12.4 Why do we have only one primary or clustering index and several secondary indexes over a database file?

12.5 How does multi-level indexing improve efficiency of searching an indexed file?

12.6 What do you understand by dense index and non-dense index? Give examples.

12.7 Show that the height of an r-key B-tree with order n ($n > 2$) can be expressed as $h \leq \log_n (r + 1)/2$.

12.8 What is meant by order of a B-tree? Describe the structure of a B-tree.

12.9 Write down the similarities and dissimilarities between B-trees and B^+-trees.

12.10 Form a B-tree of order 5 with records having key values 1, 12, 8, 2, 6, 14, 25, 28, 17, 7, 52, 16, 48, 68, 3, 26, 29, 53, 55, 45.

12.11 From the B-tree you constructed in Exercise 12.5, delete the values 1 and 2 consecutively and show the resulting structures.

12.12 Form a B^+-tree of order 5 with records having key values 1, 12, 8, 2, 6, 14, 25, 28, 17, 7, 52, 16, 48, 68, 3, 26, 29, 53, 55, 45.

12.13 From the B^+-tree you constructed in Exercise 12.7, delete the values 1 and 2 consecutively and show the resulting structures.

12.14 What are the advantages of B^+-trees over B-trees?

12.15 Describe insertion, deletion and searching processes in a B-tree.

12.16 Describe insertion, deletion and searching processes in a B^+-tree.

12.17 What is hashing? Mention different hash functions along with their merits and demerits.

12.18 Differentiate between static and dynamic hashing techniques. Why are they needed?

12.19 Describe insertion and deletion operations in case of open addressing with linear probing.

12.20 Describe insertion and deletion operations in case of chained addressing with an example.

CHAPTER 13

Data Warehousing and Data Mining

Data Mining is a very recently developed subject area that deals with meaningful information extraction from large volumes of related or unrelated data gathered from various sources for the purpose of any possible future use. Present day information exploration forces us to maintain huge data or information arising out of numerous sources. Before the advent of data mining technologies, we were used to maintain databases that store data or information relevant to certain specific area of application(s). Such application areas include banking transaction, market analysis, reservation systems, criminology, process control, scientific study and many more. In data mining, we deal with data arising out of heterogeneous sources if they are, in some way, related to serve our perspective. In other words, while database technologies deal with data from some limited homogeneous data sources, data mining assumes heterogeneous sources of data. Thus, data mining technologies may be assumed as a superset of database technologies. Large heterogeneous data repository is termed *Data warehouse*. In general, data mining put stress on extraction of important patterns or information that are apparently hidden in data warehouse. There exist quite a number of information search and extraction tool in a data mining system. Scientists and researchers are continuing to develop more efficient and scalable tools almost every day.

13.1 Data Warehousing

Data warehouses can be defined as collection of subject-oriented, integrated, time varying, non-volatile data or information in order to support managerial decision making. While databases contain information and data related to daily business transactions of some organization, data warehouses maintain data or information from vary many sources which are related in some way to the business of the organization. The data source may be in-house business data records or the external business world. Business houses may be willing to collect and study business related data of other competitor companies from various permanent and on-line data sources. Corporate decision making requires this information from all possible sources.

It is notable that data collected in data warehouses are heterogeneous in nature. They are organized in different ways, and the most important is the fact that finding the essential information from a data warehouse is as difficult as finding a needle from a heap of straw. Therefore, collected raw data must pass through many data refinement processes. All such data collection and refinement processes constitute what is called data warehousing technology. After initial categorization, refinement and organization of data, they are fed to the Data Mining processes in order to generate decision.

13.1.1 Characteristic of Data Warehouse

Characteristic features of data or information gathered in a data warehouse can be summarized as:

- **Subject orientation:** Although data may be collected from various data sources, they should be able to answer specific business related queries for the concerned organization. Therefore, a data warehouse is organized around the major subjects (business area) and topics of the enterprise.
- **Integrity:** Data warehouse needs to be centralized, consolidated data repository, and an integrated source of information that can support the decision making system of the enterprise. Thus, initial inconsistent and heterogeneous data coming from many sources must be transformed and reorganized in order to maintain consistency among them. All the users of the system must be provided with a unified view of data for better understanding and smooth processing.
- **Time-variance:** Unlike data in a database (which are relatively fixed in nature), data in a data warehouse are time-varying. That is data sources may send data which varies in its contents from time to time. We may consider this as a time varying flow of data. Therefore, collected data needs to be updated from time to time, with newer information collected. Data warehouse must reflect the currently occurring events and convey corresponding updated information.
- **Non-volatility:** Data should be maintained in permanent storage for long term use. Although we want to update data or information on a periodic basis, newer data must be appended with the existing ones instead of replacement of earlier data.

13.1.2 Need of Data Warehouse

A suitable collection of data and information is the most important asset of an organization. Success of an organization in its day-to-day business activities depends on the ability of availability of relevant information and the capability to process it for decision generation by using sophisticated data analysis tools. Such kind of data processing facilities are supported by software tools like On Line Transaction Processing system (OLTP) and system (OLAP). While OLAP basically depends on historical data for future prediction, OLTP helps system users with higher level views of data, facilitate query processing and maintains system integrity. These software tools get their inputs from the data warehouse. The need of a data warehouse can be summarized as

- Data warehouse is the archive for organizational data.

- Millions of historical data records are needed for organizational decision making.
- Data warehouse can collect and store heterogeneous data from varying sources.
- Helps to generate quick and effective strategic decision.

13.1.3 Components of Data Warehousing System

Fundamental components of a data warehousing system are:

- **Data acquisition system:** This part is responsible for collection of data from various sources and converting them into suitable form for storage. Since data may be available in different formats, import and export features are considered to be integral components of a data acquisition system. Conversion programs, application software and interface software work together for acquisition.
- **Data repository:** It is the central part of a data warehouse. All collected, converted and filtered data are stored in a physical database for future processing. A very large database is assumed in this case. Data are organized in such a format so that searching of data for processing and periodic updation becomes faster and easier.
- **Data access software:** Data from a data warehouse are accessed by end-users for processing. Different sophisticated software tools are used for this purpose. These tools include different data mining applications that can perform statistical significance test and categorize data into suitable classes for filtering purposes. many statistical analysis programs, classification and clustering software, on-line analytical processing tools (OLAP), data discovery software, and pattern matching software are included as components of data mining software.

13.1.4 Functioning of a Data Warehouse

The function of a data warehouse can be described by the following operations:

- **Extraction of data:** Extracts relevant data coming from different sources.
- **Cleaning of data:** Identifies essential components of incoming data and filters out others.
- **Transformation of data:** Converts data in a unified format.
- **Loading of data:** Stores data in a suitable data structure within the data warehouse for future access.

Figure 13.1 shows a schematic for operations of a data warehouse.

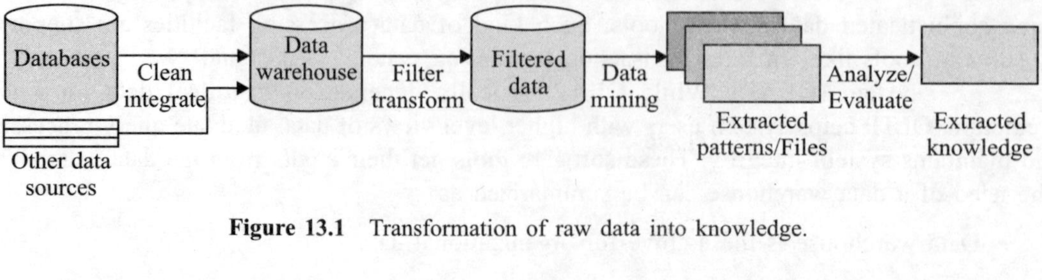

Figure 13.1 Transformation of raw data into knowledge.

13.1.5 Advantages of Data Warehouses

Following are potential advantages of a data warehouse:

- Significant returns on investments.
- Very cost-effective decision support.
- Improved enterprise intelligence.
- Improved productivity of decision makers.
- Enhanced customer services.
- Business and information re-engineering.

13.1.6 Limitations of Data Warehouses

Following are some of the limitations of a data warehouse:

- It is query intensive.
- Scalability problem appears.
- Hidden problems are evident.
- Increased end-user demands.
- High storage requirement.
- High demand of resources.
- High maintenance cost.
- Maintaining integrity is a complicated process.

13.2 Data Mining

Data mining primarily refers to the process of extraction of useful patterns or rules from a number of very large databases. Many of the artificial intelligence or machine learning based processes also attempt to discover knowledge from specific databases. The major difference between data mining and AI based techniques is that the former deals with many large databases simultaneously. By finding out useful rules hidden in the concerned databases, we are essentially empowered by some kind of knowledge. For example, by studying "income" database of salaried persons and "residential status" database of citizens, we may come to the conclusion that people within a certain income group have higher tendency for flats compared to own house. Many other complicated interrelationships among data from different databases may be found by applying suitable mechanisms.

Data Mining is the process of analyzing data from different perspectives and summarizing it into useful information that can be used to increase revenue, cut costs or both. Data mining tools allow users to analyze data from many different dimensions or angles, categorize them, and summarize the relationships identified. It is very useful for companies with a stronger consumer focus, such as retail, financial, communication, and marketing organizations.

The primary motivation behind data mining is the availability of huge data from various social, industrial, scientific, medical, commercial, and many other sources. Data mining tools enable us to extract important and useful data, information or pattern yielding knowledge bases.

Knowledge bases are essential for decision support systems. Database systems can support mainly transaction processing systems whose ranges are limited to an organization's daily operations. Decision support systems are able to generate higher level information from a collection of many databases. Such decision support systems, therefore, help their owners to predict appropriate future course of action related to their business, and hence rely on very large databases or data warehouses. We can summarize by saying that decision support systems help in knowledge discovery using logical, mathematical and statistical rules of artificial intelligence, and data mining attempts to develop tools for efficient knowledge extraction, from very large databases, by combining search processes derived from artificial intelligence along with the mathematical and statistical rules. Information flow in a data mining system is shown in Figure 13.2.

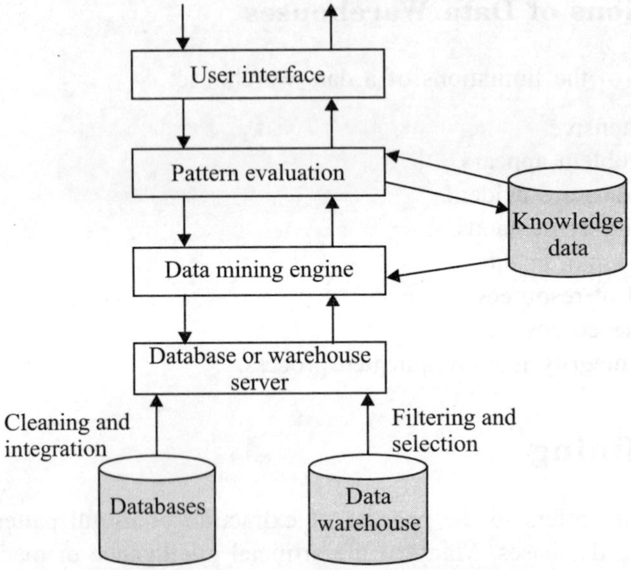

Figure 13.2 A data mining system.

Stated briefly, data mining is the process of extraction or mining of knowledge from tremendously vast amount of data. In real life, mining means extraction of essential elements from natural mines. Hence, the term data mining may be more appropriately termed as *knowledge mining from data* or simply *knowledge mining*. Actually, many other terms are used, that may carry a little different meaning, for data mining, such as *knowledge extraction*, *data dredging*, *data analysis* etc. One particular name *Knowledge Discovery in Databases* or KDD currently received a high reputation in literature.

13.2.1 Evolution of Data Mining

A major objective behind the development of database systems was to process data to extract information related to business applications. With the achievement of tremendous success in database technologies during the past several decades and with development of various types of database systems, the next target was naturally to develop a system that can extract more powerful information, i.e. knowledge. We, human being, generates decisions mainly based on our past experiences in the concerned field. While generating a decision, we rely on many different categories of information resulting from the related events or facts. Thus, if human being is able to generate good decisions, why machine should not be better one with its tremendous storage and processing capacity? Also, the huge amount of data stored in many databases exceeds the limit of human search and abstraction capacity without the help of powerful processing tools. Without data mining tools the decision might be generated by searching a limited amount of data and that mostly rely on decision maker's personal experience and intuition. Thus, knowledge bases created without using data mining were very poor and error prone. Data mining tools, on the other hand, effectively analyze vastly different types of data to generate the most appropriate data pattern or knowledge.

From the beginning of the autonomous computing technology, attempts were made to develop machines that can store more data and can retrieve stored data efficiently. A field of computing, named the so called artificial intelligence, had been developed. As more and more data are being available regarding certain business areas, the necessity for maintaining and manipulating them in a controlled fashion was felt. Although initially all data were being maintained in flat files, they soon became troublesome and backdated with the advent of centralized database systems. Data management and information extraction processes became more powerful and reliable. Different types of database technologies have been developed including network, hierarchical and relational databases. With its simple but robust data modelling capabilities, the relational database technologies soon became very popular. Many relevant database management systems and software packages have also been developed. Data manipulation languages, query processing, query optimization and transaction management processes enrich these packages to great extents. In parallel, the computer hardware technology has also been significantly improved over last few decades. Easy availability of different kinds of server and personal computers at low cost, development of data collection devices, different kinds of fixed and removable storage media, and of course advent of networking and internetworking technologies boosts the database technologies and information industries heavily. Users of different levels became very conversant with query generation, information retrieval and online transaction processing systems. Higher level decision generating processes are then developed that involve data analysis.

We can describe the development of data mining technology as follows:

- **File based systems:** Attempts to collect and store data for long term use started since 1950s. Very simple file processing system was in use at that time. A collection of flat files were generally used for storing different types of data.
- **Database management systems:** Attempts were made to develop centrally controlled databases. Within a period from 1970–1980, database technologies have been developed using network data model, hierarchical data model and relational data model. Entity-relationship model have been used as a data modelling tool for relational databases. Query generation and processing languages like SQL have been developed. Improved data structures like indexed file system, B-tree and B^+-tree structures have been used for physical data storage. Technologies have been developed for data management, security and recovery operations, query optimization, transaction processing etc.
- **Heterogeneous data models:** During 1980s, database systems have been developed using advanced technologies like advanced data models, extended relational data models,

object oriented data models. Data from various types like temporal data, multimedia data, scientific data etc. have been used to create databases.

- **Web data processing:** During 1990s, web-based databases and XML-based data bases have been developed. Processing of web based data are made possible with the development of multimedia processing and internet technologies.
- **Data warehousing:** In order to maintain and handle data from various sources (different categories), data warehousing and data mining techniques have been developed since middle of 1990s.
- **Statistical development:** During the last few decades, statistical and multivariate data processing technologies have been significantly improved. Many new technologies have been developed that are able to process huge amount of data in a very small time.

13.2.2 Data Mining Tools

Data mining methods are used to extract useful information or knowledge from a large database. A number of software packages have been developed for this purpose that work in association with some existing database under specific platforms. Majority of such software work under both UNIX and Windows operating systems. Most of the software includes data mining techniques like Decision Tree Algorithms, Statistical Reasoning, Neural Network Algorithms, Classification and Clustering Algorithms, Association Rule Mining Algorithms, Evolutionary Algorithms, etc.

Many of the existing DBMS packages, including Oracle, Sybase, DB2, Informix etc. provide data mining services through open database connectivity (ODBC) interface. This interface enables access to data in the above mentioned DBMS software.

13.2.3 Data Mining Algorithms

Common algorithms used in data mining are mentioned below:

Time series algorithms: Creates models that can be used to predict continuous variables over time from both OLAP and relational databases. For example, sales and profits can be predicted from historical data in a cube. Possible usage: sale forecast, inventory prediction, web hits prediction, stock value estimation, etc.

Decision tree algorithms: Supports both classification and regression and it works well for predictive modelling. This algorithm can be used to predict both discrete and continuous attributes. C4.5 and ID3 are two important decision tree algorithms. Their possible usage are: churn and risk analysis, predict profit and income.

Clustering algorithms: Uses iterative techniques to group records from a data set into clusters containing similar characteristics. Clusters can be used to explore the data, learning about data relationship (if exists) which may not be easy to derive logically through casual observation. The most well-known clustering algorithm is k-means algorithm. It is very easy to implement and can provide good results very quickly. Since it has a quadratic time complexity, it becomes slow for very large databases. Many derivatives and modifications of the original *k*-means algorithm have been developed to handle complicated situations. Possible usage are: customer grouping, mailing campaign, anomaly detection, etc.

Neural networks: Creates classification and regression mining models by constructing a multilayer perceptron (MLP), a network of neurons. A basic neuron is able to classify among two classes while MLPs can provide multicategory solutions. One specific category of neural network, called the self organizing map (SOM) can provide clustering solutions. Possible usage are: finding complicated relationship among attributes, representing patterns detected in the data, assessing the relationship quality between a customer and salesperson, etc.

Sequence clustering algorithm: Analyzes sequence oriented data that contains discrete-valued series. Usually, the sequence attribute in the series holds a set of events with a specific order. By analyzing the transition between states of the sequence, the algorithm can predict future states in related sequences. Possible usage are: customer behaviour, transaction patterns, customer segmentation, sequence prediction etc.

Naive bayes: Quickly builds mining models that can be used for classification and prediction. It produces a simple mining model that can be considered a starting point in the data mining process. This makes the model a good option for exploring the data and for discovering how various attributes are in the different states of the predicted attribute. Possible usage are: classification, association with multiple predictable attributes.

Association rule algorithms: Specifically designed for market basket analysis. The algorithm considers each attribute/value pair (for example product/ bicycle) as an item. An item set is a combination of items in a single transaction. The algorithm scans through the dataset trying to find item sets that tend to appear in many transactions. Possible usage are: market basket analysis, cross selling and recommendation, advanced data exploration, finds dependent item sets and rules etc.

13.2.4 Role of Data Mining and its Applications

Data mining processes help business organizations in operational monitoring and effective decision making. Efficient exploration of data, visualization of multidimensional data, categorization of data, and identification of interesting patterns in data are some of the common significant tasks performed by these mining tools.

Depending on the business of the organization concerned, data mining tools support a broad variety of business decision making processes. Important applications are found in market analysis, financial analysis, manufacturing, health care systems, web applications etc. Applications in specific fields are as follows:

- **Marketing analysis:** Analysis of customer behaviour on buying tendencies, identification of customer defection pattern and customer retention by preventing actions, determination of marketing strategies, classification of customers, products based on life-style patterns into different categories, delivering sales and customer services by proper aggregation and delivery of information to the front-end sales and service professionals, sale patterns of recently sold products, analyzing market growth etc. are some very common applications in the field of marketing.

- **Financial analysis:** Analysis of creditworthiness of customers, segmentation of account receivables, performance analysis of financial investments in stock market, mutual funds, bonds etc, risk assessment for investments etc. are important applications.
- **Manufacturing:** Optimization of resource usage for manpower, machines, materials energy and others, optimal scheduling of processes, optimal design techniques, identification of production problems and finding recovery processes, finding usage patterns for products and services etc.
- **Health care systems:** Analyzing infection tendency among people in a certain area, analyzing effects of drugs, predicting patient behavior after specific surgeries, analyzing success rate of medical therapies etc.
- **Web applications:** Categorization of web information, finding social development criteria from public opinion, predicting web usage patterns, etc.

Many other applications exist where data mining processes are successfully applied or can be applied. We have mentioned only a very few of them as examples. Some specific categories of data mining applications are briefly outlined in the following sections.

13.3 Association Rule Mining

Association rule mining is also known as *market basket analysis*. It is found that business data are related to each other, maintaining certain rules or conditions. Whenever, in a data set, majority of patterns are found to be related to others with some specific rules, these patterns become patterns of interest, and they are termed *frequent patterns*. Frequent pattern mining is an important technique in data mining. There exist many algorithms for finding frequent patterns and their associations. One such famous algorithm is the *Apriori algorithm*. Association rule mining can be described as finding frequent patterns to determine association rules. We can find two kinds of frequent patterns; frequent itemsets and frequent sequences. The former is an unordered collection of items, while the latter represents an ordered collection.

In frequent itemset mining, a set of records are input each of which contains a set of items. For example, in market data, we can find sales records having a category of customers purchasing a common set of items. The mining process tries to find out the subset of records that exhibit such correlation frequently. The outcome of such mining processes help running the business in a more guided way.

Frequent itemset mining algorithms first identify frequent itemsets, and then determines the useful and important association rules hidden within itemsets. Such mining methods have applications in market analysis, customer classification, medicine, e-commerce, bio-informatics, etc.

13.4 Text Data Mining

Finding important data from huge sources of textual messages, newspapers, magazines, web pages, blogs, etc., are included in text data mining. Since text data can be presented in various formats and structures, we need to process them to get a uniform structure, using some specific attributes or features, initially; then we have to extract important key words to identify the contents or subject matter. Term extraction and concept extraction processes are applied for this purpose.

Many techniques are applied for text mining including clustering, classification and association. Text mining processes are applied over a large collection of legal documents, financial documents, patents, medical articles, business documents, research documents etc. The common goal is to correlate such documents using associated (linked) contents.

13.5 Web Data Mining

It is the process of finding information from web data, hyperlink structures, and web log data (blog). Web content mining deals with discovering useful information from web page contents. Websites, nowadays, are the source of huge knowledge data related to different fields. The extraction of significant related data from web pages is, therefore, very useful in many applications. Web structure mining deals with exploring and modelling hyperlink structure of web directories. Web data search process can be made very efficient by such mining techniques. Web log mining deals with user behaviour in interacting with the websites. This helps in website reorganization for better suiting for the user. Web log data, i.e., web server log, proxy server log, and browser log, etc., are used for this purpose.

Exercises

13.1 Define Data Mining and describe its relationship with data warehousing. What are the objectives of data mining?

13.2 What are the motivations behind association rule mining? Give examples of its use.

13.3 Define supervised and unsupervised classification. Explain the role of training and testing phases in the later learning technique.

13.4 Describe the k-means clustering algorithm and its advantages and weaknesses.

13.5 Describe some commonly used distance metrics along with their significance.

13.6 What is web mining and what is its importance? What is its difference with conventional data mining?

13.7 Provide some guidelines for designing a data mining system.

13.8 List some major applications of data mining.

13.9 What are the motivations behind text mining? Describe the basic text mining technique and mention some of its applications.

13.10 Briefly, explain some of the classification technologies used in data mining.

Bibliography

Dasgupta, P.K., *Database Management System, Oracle and PL/SQL*, PHI Learning, New Delhi, 2009.

Date, C.J., *An Introduction to Database Systems*, Addison-Wesley, 2004.

Dunham, M.H., *Data Mining: Introductory and Advanced Topics*, Pearson Education, 2003.

Elmasri, R., S. Navathe, D. Somayajulu and S. Gupta, *Fundamentals of Database Systems*, Pearson Education, 2006.

Gupta, G.K., *Database Management Systems*, Tata McGraw-Hill, 2011.

Introduction to Database Systems, ITL Educations Solutions Limited, Pearson Education, 2010.

Jadav, P.K., *Database Management System*, Katson Books, 2010.

Kifer, M., A Bernstein, P. Lewis and P. Panigrahi, *Database Systems: An Application-Oriented Approach*, Pearson Education, 2008.

Majumder, A.K. and P. Bhattacharyya, *Database Management Systems*, Tata McGraw-Hill, 2004.

Miller, T.W., *Data and Text Mining: A Business Application Approach*, Pearson Education, 2008.

Panneerselvam, S., *Database Management System*, PHI Learning, New Delhi, 2009.

Silberschatz, A., H. Korth and S. Sudarshan, *Database System Concepts*, McGraw-Hill International, 2006.

Singh, S.K., *Database Systems: Concepts, Design and Applications*, Pearson Education, 2006.

Sunderraman, R., *Oracle 10g Programming*, Pearson Education, 2009.

Ullman, J.D., *Principles of Database Systems*, Galgotia Publication, 2008.

Index

Aborted, 204, 205
Abstract models, 15
Access anomaly, 5
Accessibility, 60
Algebraic languages, 48
All key relation, 86
Alternate keys, 25
Alter statement, 95
Anchor record, 218
Application developer, 11
Apriori algorithm, 252
Arithmetic functions, 103
Armstrong's inference rules, 66
Association rule
  algorithm, 251
  mining, 252
    algorithms, 250
Atomicity, 76, 186
Atoms, 54
Attribute preservation, 73
Augmentation, 66
Authentication, 6

Back-up/recovery, 10
Backward traversal, 234
Binary
  decomposition, 74
  relationship, 26
Block
  anchor, 218
  structure, 141
Blocking factor, 220
Boyce-Codd normal form, 83
Browser log, 253
B-tree
  file, 215
  indexing, 227
B^+-tree indexing, 234

Candidate keys, 25
Canonical
  cover, 67
  set, 63
Cardinality ratio, 27
Cartesian product, 42, 48
Centralized control, 1, 6
Central supervision, 4
Chained
  addressing, 239
  overflow, 239
Checkpoints, 210
Cleaning of data, 246
Closure, 63
Clustering algorithms, 250
Code generation, 171
Column constraint, 97
Committed, 204, 205
Composite index, 97
Composition, 66
Computational efficiency, 178
Conceptual
  level, 7
  schema, 8
Concurrent
  access, 1
  schedule, 187

Constraints, 97
Conversion algorithms, 84
Copy mechanism, 4

Data
- access software, 246
- acquisition, 246
- analysis, 248
- control language, 93
- definition language, 93
- description language, 11
- dictionary, 11, 106
- dredging, 248
- duplication, 5
- independence, 9
- isolation, 5
- manipulation, 2
  - language, 93
- mining, 244
- repository, 246
- sub languages, 93
- types, 143
- warehouse, 244

Database, 1
- administrator, 6, 11
- management system, 2
- manager, 11
- system, 2
- users, 106

Date functions, 103
Deadlock, 198
- detection, 199
- handling, 199
- prevention, 200

Decision
- support systems, 248
- tree algorithm, 250

Declaration section, 141
Decomposition, 66
Decryption, 11
Deferred updation, 205
Delete statement, 96
Deletion anomaly, 76
Dependency preservation, 73
Determinant, 83
Directory of pointers, 241
Disk
- block, 218
- failure, 204

Division-remainder hashing, 239
Domains, 42
Drop statement, 96
Durability, 186
Dynamic
- hashing, 241
- multilevel indexing, 227

Embedded SQL, 134
Encryption/decryption, 11
End-users, 11
Entities, 22
Entity integrity, 46
Entity-relationship model, 16
Equivalence of FDS, 66
Equivalent expression, 55
E-R
- diagram, 16
- model, 16

Evolutionary algorithms, 250
Exception
- handling, 159
- section, 142

Exclusive locks, 198
Execution section, 141
Existential quantifier, 55
Explicit reference, 83
Extendable hashing, 241
External level, 7
Extraction of data, 246

File index, 217
Financial analysis, 252
Flat files, 3
Folded key hashing, 239
Foreign key, 46
Formula, 54
Frequent patterns, 252
Full
- indexing, 217
- outer join, 128

Functional
- data models, 21
- dependency, 61, 76

General unification, 66
Group functions, 103

Hashed file, 215
Hash join, 180
Health care systems, 252
Heap file, 215
Heterogeneous, 5
Hierarchical data model, 17
Horizontal views, 134
Host variables, 135

Identifying
  entity, 25
  relationship, 25
Inconsistency, 5
Incremental log, 205
Index
  entry, 218
  statement, 96
Indexed files, 217
Indicator variables, 135
Inflexible, 5
Insertion anomaly, 76
Insert statement, 95
Integrity, 1, 245
  constraints, 46
  restrictions, 6
Internal
  hashing, 238
  levels, 7
Interrelated data, 1
Irreducibility, 60
Isolation, 186

Join, 49
  decomposition, 72
  dependency, 76

Key attribute, 24
Key-extraction hashing, 238
Key-pointer pairs, 227
Knowledge
  bases, 248
  discovery, 248
  extraction, 248
  mining, 248

Left outer join, 128
Linear
  hashing, 242
  probing, 239
Loading of data, 246
Lock, 189
  conversion, 197
Logical
  data independence, 45
  error, 204
  models, 15
  schema, 8
Lossless-join, 72

Manufacturing, 252
Many-to-many, 27
Many-to-one, 27
Market basket analysis, 252
Marketing analysis, 251
Multilevel indexing, 224
Multiple hashing, 239
Multi-valued dependency, 76, 86

Naive bayes, 251
Natural join, 49
Nested loop join, 179
Network data model, 17
Neural network, 251
  algorithms, 250
No-key entity, 25
Non-loss decomposition, 81
Non-procedural language, 140
Non-trivial dependencies, 63
Non-volatile storage, 212
Non-volatility, 245
Normal
  database, 76
  forms, 75
Normalization, 75

Object-based models, 16
Object-oriented data model, 21
One-to-many, 27
One-to-one, 27
On line
  analytical processing, 245
  transaction processing, 245

Open addressing, 239
Operating system, 6
Optimization, 171
Oracle server, 163
Outer join, 127
Output cost, 182

Parsing, 171
Partial
  dependency, 80, 88
  indexing, 217
Partially committed, 205
Physical
  data independence, 45
  model, 15
  schema, 8
PL/SQL
  package, 167
  records, 147
Predicate calculus languages, 48
Primary
  index, 218
  key, 25
Procedural
  language, 140
  query language, 92
Procedures, 157
Projection, 48
Propagation of updation, 5
Proxy server log, 253
Pseudo-transitivity, 66

Quantifier, 55
Query
  execution, 172
  graphs, 171
  handling, 110
  optimization, 175
  processing, 171, 172
  tree, 173
Quotient, 49

Record-based models, 16
Record keeping systems, 4
Recovery
  from deadlock, 199
  process, 210
  strategies, 205
Redo, 209
Redundancy, 5
Referential integrity, 46
Reflexivity, 66
Relational
  algebra, 48
  calculus, 54
  data model, 17
  decomposition, 72
  design, 60
  schema, 72
Relationships, 22
Residual dump, 212
Right outer join, 129
Rollback, 200
Row level trigger, 165

Scanning, 171
Schema, 8
  design, 60
Scope of variables, 146
Security, 1
  restrictions, 46
Selection, 48
  of victim, 199
Self determination, 66
Semantic data model, 21
Sequence clustering algorithm, 251
Set
  difference, 48
  division, 49
  intersection, 49
  valued attributes, 85
Shadow paging, 210
Shared lock, 198
Single
  loop join, 180
  row functions, 103
Sorted file, 215
Sort-merge join, 180, 182
Sparse (non-dense) index, 218
SQL
  cursor, 163
  trigger, 165
Starvation, 200
Statement level trigger, 165

Static hashing, 241
Statistical reasoning, 250
Storage devices, 214
Strict timestamp, 202
String/character functions, 103
Strong entity, 25
Structured query language, 92
Subject orientation, 245
Super key, 25
System
    crash, 204
    error, 204

Table constraint, 97
Tabular form, 46
Ternary relationship, 27
Text data mining, 252
Third generation languages, 140
Thomas' write rule, 202
Three-layer architecture, 7
Time series algorithms, 250
Timestamp, 200
    ordering, 201
Time-variance, 245
Transaction, 11, 185
Transformation of data, 246
Transitive dependency, 76, 82
Transitivity, 66
Trigger body, 165
Triggering event, 165
Trivial dependencies, 63
Tuple variable, 54
Two phase lock-unlock, 197
Two-phase protocol, 197

Unary relationship, 26
Undo, 209
Union, 48, 66
Universal relation, 72
Unlock, 189
Updation anomaly, 5, 76

Validation, 171
Vertical views, 134
Views of tables, 133

Weak entity, 25
Web
    applications, 252
    data mining, 253
    log data, 253
    server log, 253
    structure mining, 253
Write-ahead-logging, 205

XML data model, 21